I, You, and the Word "God"

Siphrut
Literature and Theology of the Hebrew Scriptures

Editorial Board
STEPHEN B. CHAPMAN   *Duke University*
TREMPER LONGMAN III   *Westmont College*
NATHAN MACDONALD   *University of Cambridge*

1. *A Severe Mercy: Sin and Its Remedy in the Old Testament*, by Mark J. Boda
2. *Chosen and Unchosen: Conceptions of Election in the Pentateuch and Jewish-Christian Interpretation*, by Joel N. Lohr
3. *Genesis and the Moses Story: Israel's Dual Origins in the Hebrew Bible*, by Konrad Schmid
4. *The Land of Canaan and the Destiny of Israel: Theologies of Territory in the Hebrew Bible*, by David Frankel
5. *Jacob and the Divine Trickster: A Theology of Deception and Y*HWH*'s Fidelity to the Ancestral Promise in the Jacob Cycle*, by John E. Anderson
6. *Esther: The Outer Narrative and the Hidden Reading*, by Jonathan Grossman
7. *From Fratricide to Forgiveness: The Language and Ethics of Anger in Genesis*, by Matthew R. Schlimm
8. *The Rhetoric of Remembrance: An Investigation of the "Fathers" in Deuteronomy*, by Jerry Hwang
9. *In the Beginning: Essays on Creation Motifs in the Bible and the Ancient Near East*, by Bernard F. Batto
10. *Run, David, Run! An Investigation of the Theological Speech Acts of David's Departure and Return (2 Samuel 14–20)*, by Steven T. Mann
11. *From the Depths of Despair to the Promise of Presence: A Rhetorical Reading of the Book of Joel*, by Joel Barker
12. *Forming God: Divine Anthropomorphism in the Pentateuch*, by Anne Katherine Knafl
13. *Standing in the Breach: An Old Testament Theology and Spirituality of Intercessory Prayer*, by Michael Widmer
14. *What Kind of God? Collected Essays of Terence E. Fretheim*, edited by Michael J. Chan and Brent A. Strawn
15. *The "Image of God" in the Garden of Eden: The Creation of Humankind in Genesis 2:5–3:24 in Light of the* mīs pî pīt pî *and* wpt-r *Rituals of Mesopotamia and Ancient Egypt*, by Catherine L. McDowell
16. *The Shape of the Writings*, edited by Julius Steinberg and Timothy J. Stone
17. *A Message from the Great King: Reading Malachi in Light of Ancient Persian Royal Messenger Texts from the Time of Xerxes*, by R. Michael Fox
18. *"See and Read All These Words": The Concept of the Written in the Book of Jeremiah*, by Chad L. Eggleston
19. *Identity in Conflict: The Struggle between Esau and Jacob, Edom and Israel*, by Elie Assis
20. *I, You, and the Word "God": Finding Meaning in the Song of Songs*, by Sarah Zhang

I, You, and the Word "God"
Finding Meaning in the Song of Songs

Sarah Zhang

Winona Lake, Indiana
EISENBRAUNS
2016

© 2016 by Sarah Zhang
All rights reserved.
Printed in the United States of America.

www.eisenbrauns.com

Library of Congress Cataloging-in-Publication Data

Names: Zhang, Sarah, author.
Title: I, you, and the word God : finding meaning in the Song of Songs / Sarah Zhang.
Description: Winona Lake, Indiana : Eisenbrauns, [2016] | Series: Siphrut : literature and theology of the Hebrew Scriptures ; volume 20 | Includes bibliographical references and indexes.
Identifiers: LCCN 2016027106 (print) | LCCN 2016027813 (ebook) | ISBN 9781575064758 (hardback : alk. paper) | ISBN 9781575064765 (pdf)
Subjects: LCSH: Bible. Song of Solomon—Criticism, interpretation, etc.
Classification: LCC BS1485.52 .Z43 2016 (print) | LCC BS1485.52 (ebook) | DDC 223/.906—dc23
LC record available at https://lccn.loc.gov/2016027106

The paper used in this publication meets the minimum requirements of the American National Standard for Information Sciences—Permanence of Paper for Printed Library Materials, ANSI Z39.48–1984. ♾™

Contents

Preface and Acknowledgments vii
Abbreviations ix
    General ix
    Reference Works ix

Introduction 1

1. Theory 10
    Subjectivity: The Rise of Lyrical Ethics 13
    Levinasian Lyrical Ethics 16
    Levinas and the Writing of Difference 19
    Writing as Encounter 23

2. Oneself as Awakened Sensibility (Song 4:1–7) 27
    A Snapshot of Song 4:1–7 28
    Delight 33
    Touch 44
    Approach 54
    Desire 63
    Ending Invitation 69

3. Restlessness and Responsibility for the Other 71
    Listening beside the Said 72
    De-Coring: Between Intrigue and Interruption 81
    Exposedness beyond Wounding 87
    Patience 99
    In Other Words, or Words of the Other 104
    Appendix 107

4. "The Human Form Divine" 108
    The Trace of God 111
    Detour on Human Finitude 128
    "The Question Mark in This Said" 141
    The Moment the Word "God" Is Heard 152

So to Speak 160
Bibliography 163
Indexes 173
    Index of Authors 173
    Index of Scripture 177

Preface and Acknowledgments

At this place where I am, I cannot be without infinite gratitude to the able mind and caring guidance of Chip Dobbs-Allsopp. It is due to his perceptiveness and patience in seeing something promising in my raw and rugged draft that this book could be carried from nascence to a provisional ending. The strength of his unfaltering support throughout the years is on a par with his unwavering demand for quality; both speak volumes to his dedication and responsibility.

To Dennis Olson, I am immensely thankful for his keen theological insight and pastoral sensibility. His affirming comments have critically recharged my passion and confidence in this project and as a biblical scholar. I am also greatly blessed in that Mark Taylor graciously provided insightful feedback on the philosophical and theological aspects of the book and enabled me to see what my own vision has obscured.

I cannot measure the influence of Choon-Leong Seow's exemplary scholarship on me or the compassionate support he provided throughout my years at Princeton Theological Seminary; to him, I will always be indebted. I give hearty thanks to Katharine Sakenfeld, for the opportunity to share a section of this book with her class, and for a precious friendship when I most needed it. Many thanks are also due to Prof. Jacqueline Lapsley, who was the first to challenge my uncritical assumptions and to introduce ethical criticism to me.

I am thankful for the numerous sparkles of intellectual exchanges with many colleagues whose names could not be enumerated here. I am especially thankful for Elaine James's proofreading and for the friendship, prayers, and support of Alice Yafeh-Deigh and Peter Altmann.

In the process of writing and rewriting, I have had the privilege of receiving constructive feedback on portions of this book from the members of the Old Testament Research Colloquium in Princeton Theological Seminary (ch. 3), from the friends of the Ethnic Chinese Biblical Colloquium (ch. 1, "Delight"), from the participants of the Mid-Atlantic Regional SBL (ch. 1, "Delight" and "Touch"), and the Society of Biblical Literature (two papers derived from the 3rd and 4th chapters).

I would also like to thank my friends who have helped me to balance life and work over the years: Sherry Regan, Haiyan Xu, Charles Leonard, Tom Bothe, Gwen Austin, Brian Bothe, and friends from GETS Theological Seminary. I especially thank God for the colleagues from Global Bible Initiative and GrapeCity, Inc., in whose lovingkindness I do indeed see the trace of God.

Finally, my utmost love and gratitude is reserved for my family—for my parents, Cuizhen Liu and Yubao Zhang, who support me with all their means; for my dearest son, Ari Z. Bothe, whose presence consoles me in my insomniac moments and whose love inspires me to be a more responsible person; and to my departed sister, Xiaoyan Zhang. Her untimely death at the hands of a jealous husband forever alters my reading of *qinʾâ* in Song 8:6.

Abbreviations

General

Akk.	Akkadian
Arm.	Aramaic
Arab.	Arabic
BH	Biblical Hebrew
ch(s).	chapter(s)
col(s).	column(s)
fig(s).	figure(s)
frg(s).	fragment(s)
ID	*Inanna's/Ishtar's Descent*
KJV	King James VErsion
LXX	Septuagint
MT	Masoretic Text
NRSV	New Revised Standard Version
OG	Old Greek
OL	Old Latin
Syh.	Syrohexapla
Syr.	Syriac
Ug.	Ugaritic
v(v).	verse(s)
Vulg.	Vulgate
α′	Aquila
θ′	Theodocian
σ′	Symmachus

Reference Works

ABD	Freedman, D. N. (editor). *The Anchor Bible Dictionary*. 6 vols. New York: Doubleday, 1992
AnOr	Analecta orientalia
AOAT	Alter Orient und Altes Testament
AOS	American Oriental Series
ATD	Das Alte Testament Deutsch
BibInt	*Biblical Interpretation*
BHS	*Biblia Hebraica Stuttgartensia*. Edited by K. Elliger and W. Rudolph. Stuttgart: Deutsche Bibelstiftung, 1983
BHQ	Schenker, A., et al. (editors). *Biblia Hebraica Quinta*. Stuttgart: Deutsche Bibelgesellschaft, 2004–
BKAT	Biblischer Kommentar Altes Testament
CAD	Gelb, Ignace J., et al., editors. *The Assyrian Dictionary of the Oriental Institute of the University of Chicago*. 21 vols. (A–Z). Chicago: Oriental Institute, 1956–2006

CBQ	*Catholic Biblical Quarterly*
COS	Hallo, William W., editor. *The Context of Scripture*. Leiden: Brill, 1997–2002
CTA	Herdner, A., editor. *Corpus des tablettes en cunéiformes alphabétiques*. 2 vols. Paris: Imprimerie Nationale, 1963
DCH	Clines, D. J. A., editor. *Dictionary of Classical Hebrew*. 8 vols. Sheffield: Sheffield Academic Press; Sheffield Phoenix Press, 1993–2010
DJD	*Discoveries in the Judaean Desert*
EAJT	*East Asia Journal of Theology*
EncJud	*Encyclopedia Judaica*. Jerusalem: Keter, 1971–72
GBH	Joüon, Paul, and T. Muraoka. *A Grammar of Biblical Hebrew*. 2 vols. Subsidia Biblica 14/1–2. Rome: Pontifical Biblical Institute, 2000
GKC	Kautzsch, E., editor. *Gesenius' Hebrew Grammar*. Translated by A. E. Cowley. 2nd ed. Oxford: Oxford University Press, 1910
HALOT	Koehler, L., W. Baumgartner, and J. J. Stamm. *The Hebrew and Aramaic Lexicon of the Old Testament*. Study Edition. Translated and edited under the supervision of M. E. J. Richardson. 4 vols. Leiden, 1994–99
HAR	*Hebrew Annual Review*
HSS	Harvard Semitic Studies
HThKAT	Herders theologischer Kommentar zum Alten Testament
HTR	*Harvard Theological Review*
HUCA	*Hebrew Union College Annual*
IB	Buttrick, George A., et al., editors. *Interpreter's Bible*. 12 vols. New York: Abingdon-Cokesbury, 1951–57
IBC	Interpretation: A Bible Commentary for Teaching and Preaching
IBHS	Waltke, B. K., and M. O'Connor. *An Introduction to Biblical Hebrew Syntax*. Winona Lake, IN, 1990
Int	*Interpretation*
JAAR	*Journal of the American Academy of Religion*
JBL	*Journal of Biblical Literature*
JHebS	*Journal of Hebrew Scriptures*
JNES	*Journal of Near Eastern Studies*
JQR	*Jewish Quarterly Review*
JSOT	*Journal for the Study of the Old Testament*
JSOTSup	Journal for the Study of the Old Testament: Supplement Series
JSS	Journal of Semitic Studies
JTS	*Journal of Theological Studies*
KAT	Kommentar zum Alten Testament
KBANT	Kommentare und Beiträge zum Alten und Neuen Testament
KHC	Kurzer Hand-Commentar zum Alten Testament
MLN	*Modern Language Notes*
MTZ	*Münchener theologische Zeitschrift*
NICOT	The New International Commentary on the Old Testament
NIDB	Sakenfeld, Katharine D., et al., editors. *The New Interpreter's Dictionary of the Bible*. Nashville: Abingdon, 2006
NLH	*New Literary History*
OLA	Orientalia Lovaniensia Analecta
OTL	Old Testament Library

ORA	Orientalische Religionen in der Antike
PEQ	*Palestine Exploration Quarterly*
PG	Patrologia Graeca
PMLA	*Publications of the Modern Language Association of America*
PTS	Patristische Texte und Studien
RTR	*Reformed Theological Review*
SSN	Studia semitica neerlandica
TBT	*The Bible Today*
TBC	Torch Bible Commentaries
TDOT	Botterweck, G. J., and H. Ringgren. *Theological Dictionary of the Old Testament*. Grand Rapids, MI: Eerdmans, 1974–2006
TSAJ	Texte und Studien zum antiken Judentum
TUAT	Texte aus der Umwelt des Alten Testaments
UBL	Ugaritisch-biblische Literatur
UT	Gordon, C. H. *Ugaritic Textbook*. Rome: Pontifical Biblical Institute, 1965
VT	*Vetus Testamentum*
VTSup	Vetus Testamentum Supplements
WBC	Word Biblical Commentary
ZA	*Zeitschrift für Assyriologie*
ZAW	*Zeitschrift fur die alttestamentliche Wissenschaft*
ZDPV	*Zeitschrift des Deutschen Palästina-Vereins*

Introduction

Can prose, being "secular, rational explanation,"[1] apprehend how it differs from poetry? Derived from the linear reasoning, narratival configuration, and thematic summary of everyday life, can prose capture poetry, which breaks away from this continuity even in its discontinuous form of going to the line-end and starting over again?[2] "*Poetry, not prose*"[3]— thus Robert von Hallberg begins his book *Lyrical Powers*. In the context of contemporary critical discourse, however, commentators on poetry not infrequently repress the radical difference between poetry and prose. The repression is not due to a lack of reasoning but to too much reliance on it, to the assumption that reason can adequately transmute poetry into prose. However, in practice the light of reason does not shine far enough to illuminate the deep reaches of poetry.

This is not to say that prosaic writings about poetry cannot be of any use but that, no matter how excellent such prose is, it always suffers an original inadequacy. Even an admirable book such as Robert Pinsky's *The Sounds of Poetry* confesses the inadequacy of prose measured against poetry: "[D]escription lags, in its cumbersome way, far behind what it gestures toward. Much is always left-out, even as the sentences of description pile up."[4]

What can be described and domiciled completely in rational discourse is much like a plastic image or a breathless idol. By rational discourse, I refer to the kind of writing that upholds the sovereignty of reason in the dichotomous backdrop of reason versus emotion or objectivity versus subjectivity. My distrust of reason in reading poetry neither goes so far as to discredit reason and objectivity all together—especially in writing my own prosaic response to poetry—nor to uphold instead the other pole of the dichotomy—that is, emotion. Rather, this delimitation of reason is only polemic to and seeks to disabuse the assumed *adequacy* of thinking when applied in poetic reading.[5]

---

1. Robert von Hallberg, *Lyric Powers* (Chicago: University of Chicago Press, 2008), 1.
2. Jonathan Culler, "Approaching the Lyric," in *Lyric Poetry: Beyond New Criticism*, ed. Chaviva Hošek and Patricia Parker (Ithaca, NY: Cornell University Press, 1985), 31.
3. Von Hallberg, *Lyric Powers*, 1.
4. Robert Pinsky, *The Sounds of Poetry* (New York: Farrar, Straus and Giroux, 1998), 83. Though this present book does not concern itself with narrative and its goal is not to argue that poetry contains truth claims, Martha C. Nussbaum's argument that "[s]tyle itself makes its claims, expresses its own sense of what matters" (*Love's Knowledge: Essays on Philosophy and Literature* [New York: Oxford University Press, 1990], 3) corroborates my observation; namely, poetic body contains meaningfulness that prose summary and description leave out.
5. Emmanuel Levinas, "Notes on Meaning," in *Of God Who Comes to Mind*, trans. Bettina Bergo (Stanford, CA: Stanford University Press, 1998), 154.

The dominant mode of approaching poetry in biblical studies has been to study poetry as linguistic, stylistic, cultural, and thematic data. It is conducted under an uncritical assumption that separates the reader from the poem with an indifference, which is interested in objectively discovering and applying rules and regulations of Hebrew poetry or in extracting thematic claims befitting historical, cultural, or theological panorama.[6] Style or theme, form or content, this mode of research is generated as the work of thinking and judged by its level of coherence (within the writing itself and in relation to the poetic data). Such rational predisposition, however, is fundamentally at odds with poetry: it lacks the wakefulness of the self in writing, avoids touching the poet's hand given in the form of the poem, bypasses the poetic space wherein significance is released, and thus takes only parts of the poem and leaves its meaningfulness still calling.

The unbridgeable gap between rational analysis and poetry's touch appears in how one assumes subjectivity. For a rational critic, subjectivity is something to be temporarily suspended while objectivity is at work; the search for meaning begins with the intention of the consciousness as a free act and returns at the end to answer to it. For poetically inclined individuals, the root of subjectivity reaches beyond the confines of consciousness, and its last trace perceivable to consciousness is passivity—the passivity

---

6. Think, for instance, of some classic works on biblical Hebrew poetry: Robert Lowth, *Lectures on the Sacred Poetry of the Hebrews* (1787), trans. G. Gregory (Boston: Buckingham, 1815); George Buchanan Gray, *The Forms of Hebrew Poetry; Considered with Special Reference to the Criticism and Interpretation of the Old Testament* (London: Hodder & Stoughton, 1915); Terence Collins, *Line-Forms in Hebrew Poetry: A Grammatical Approach to the Stylistic Study of the Hebrew Prophets*, Studia Pohl: Series Maior 7 (Rome: Pontifical Biblical Institute, 1978); Stephen A. Geller, *Parallelism in Early Biblical Poetry* (Missoula, MT: Scholars Press, 1979); Michael Patrick O'Connor, *Hebrew Verse Structure* (Winona Lake, IN: Eisenbrauns, 1980); James L. Kugel, *The Idea of Biblical Poetry* (New Haven, CT: Yale University Press, 1981); Wilfred G. E. Watson, *Classical Hebrew Poetry: A Guide to Its Techniques* (Sheffield: JSOT Press, 1984); Adele Berlin, *The Dynamics of Biblical Parallelism* (Bloomington: Indiana University Press, 1985). The directions in *Directions in Biblical Hebrew Poetry* (ed. Elaine R. Follis, JSOTSup 40 [Sheffield: JSOT Press, 1987]) remain hinged to the same self-distancing academic approach. The beautiful readings in Robert Alter's work *The Art of Biblical Poetry* (New York: Basic Books, 1985) require but a well-trained, impersonal reader to apply and appreciate poetic stylistics. Adele Berlin's concise "Introduction to Hebrew Poetry" (*New Interpreter's Bible* [Nashville: Abingdon, 1996], 4.301–15) and T. David Anderson's survey "Problems in Analysing Hebrew Poetry" (*EAJT* 4/2 [1986]: 68–94) stop at representing Hebrew poetry and its research through an epistemic lens. Fondness for the analytical treatment of syntax, semantics, structure, and parallelism continues to yield essays of theory and practice, of which there are too many to list here. The ideological approach does introduce the suppressed dimension of the reader's participation in the making of sense and significance; e.g., David J. A. Clines, "Why Is There a Song of Songs, and What Does It Do to You if You Read It?" *Jian Dao: A Journal of Bible and Theology* 1 (1994): 3–27. However, its difference in goal does not alter the same analytical method; it just adds the rhetoric of power struggle to the language game.

F. W. Dobbs-Allsopp's new book, *On Biblical Poetry* (Oxford: Oxford University Press, 2015), came out after this survey. It offers fresh insight into this question.

and obligation to alterity that had roused them into intentional thinking and action.

Concerned by the fissure between poetry and critical prose, I propose a new approach to biblical poetry in this book—Levinasian lyric ethics. As one who grew up immersed in ancient Chinese poetry and later studied Chinese and Western esthetic theories extensively, I had long been hungry for a way of writing that bridged my poetic experience and critical discourse, until I came across Emmanuel Levinas's writings. In my view, Levinas's ethical approach offers essayists the much-needed "optics"[7] to see and write about poetry poetically.

The significance of Levinas's philosophy lies not in how he positively extends the lineage of Western philosophy but in giving hope by prying open its totalitarian grip on truth. While agreeing with postmodern thoughts about dismissing a *universal statement* of truth, Levinas does not stop at deconstructive negativity or ideological plurality. His writings bring human thinking and writing to the edge of consciousness, expose an anterior passivity that underlies intentionality, and embody an ethical approach to the outside through an encounter with the other. The life force of his writings originates outside reason yet "not beyond reason into the facility of the irrational or towards a mystical effusion, but rather towards another reason, towards the other as reason or demand."[8] His phenomenological-ethical philosophy continues Western philosophy at the point where it seems most impossible to continue, through "a new and paradoxical *patience*."[9] The importance of Levinas's contribution to Western philosophical and theoretical development is increasingly being recognized and appreciated.[10]

Levinasian lyrical ethics, as I propose, agrees with the model of Levinasian literary criticism,[11] which, in David-Antoine Williams's words, features

---

7. "[E]thics is an optics" (Emmanuel Levinas, *Totality and Infinity: An Essay on Exteriority*, trans. Alphonso Lingis [Pittsburgh: Duquesne University Press, 1969], xii).

8. Maurice Blanchot, "Our Clandestine Companion," in *Face to Face with Levinas,* ed. Richard A. Cohen (Albany: State University of New York Press, 1986), 42. This essay was originally published in French as "Notre compagne clandestine," in *Textes pour Emmanuel Levinas*, ed. F. Laruelle (Paris: Jean-Michel Place, 1980), 79–87.

9. Paul Davies, "A Fine Risk: Reading Blanchot Reading Levinas," in *Re-Reading Levinas*, ed. Robert Bernasconi and Simon Critchley (Bloomington: Indiana University Press, 1991), 202.

10. Salomon Malka, *Emmanuel Levinas: His Life and Legacy* (Pittsburgh: Duquesne University Press, 2006), 274–77.

11. The impact of Emmanuel Levinas's ethics is already evident in literary criticism in the last decade of the twentieth century. See Jill Robins, *Altered Reading: Levinas and Literature* (Chicago: University of Chicago Press, 1999); Robert Eaglestone, *Ethical Criticism: Reading after Levinas* (Edinburgh: Edinburgh University Press, 1997); Steve McCaffery, "The Scandal of Sincerity: Toward a Levinasian Poetics," *Pretexts* 6 (1997): 167–90; Adam Zachary Newton, *Narrative Ethics* (Cambridge: Harvard University Press, 1995). Poetic studies also began to see the application of Levinasian ethics in the same period, but more

"an importation of categories and concerns from the language of philosophy to the language of poetic commentary, with the aims and methodologies of the latter taking priority over those of the former."[12] Hence, my philosophical "categories and concerns" will come from Levinas's writings and be welded to the lyrical concrete, letting theory play in "a field different than that wherein the concepts of a pure abstraction move."[13] Briefly and abstractly stated, they are woven through the following three strands: challenging the hegemony of knowledge; defending ethics ethically; and being anchored in sensibility. Since my account of a Levinasian lyrical ethics will be elaborated in ch. 1, "Theory," I will only introduce a few key points here.

Poetry embodies the poet's vision, whether the content leans toward feelings, thoughts, or judgments. "The poet's vision," says Levinas, "is an original experience in both senses of the adjective: a fundamental experience, and an experience of the origin."[14] Essayists follow outlines, but poets respond to intrigues. An intrigue breaks the closed, continuous flow of cause-and-consequence. As a caress on the skin that cannot be distilled in abstraction, an intrigue exposes the poet's provoked initiatives[15] in response to the touch of alterity. In writing, the poet tests the forms, ideas, and sounds of words against the traces of intrigue that linger on the poet's sensibility. In William B. Yeats's practice, for instance, writing poetry is

---

thorough interactions have appeared in recent years. For example, see Paul Kane, *Australian Poetry: Romanticism and Negativity* (Cambridge: Cambridge University Press, 1996), 170–84; G. Matthew Jenkins, "Saying Obligation: George Oppen's Poetry and Levinasian Ethics," *Journal of American Studies* 37 (2003): 407–33; Leslie Hill, "Distrust of Poetry: Levinas, Blanchot, Celan," *MLN* 120 (2005): 986–1008; G. Matthew Jenkins, *Poetic Obligation: Ethics in Experimental Poetry after 1945* (Iowa City: University of Iowa Press, 2008); David-Antoine Williams, "Tête-à-tête, Face-à-face: Brodsky, Levinas, and the Ethics of Poetry," *Poetics Today* 30 (2009): 207–35; Ian Cooper, "'Equanimity': Les Murray, Lévinas and the Breath of God," *Literature and Theology* 23 (2009): 192–206. Most recently, a new strand of modern poetry criticism called "New Ethics" is being observed. Influenced by Emmanuel Levinas, New Ethics has emerged in the last decade, showcasing "a burgeoning critical concern at the nexus of ideas between modernist poetry through the twentieth century and ethics" (see the program description of the "Roundtable Session: Modernist Poetry Criticism and the New Ethics" *MSA* 15, http://johnwrighton.com/portfolio/msa15-roundtable-modernist-poetry-criticism-and-the-new-ethics/ [accessed February 6, 2014]).

12. Williams, "Tête-à-tête," 228.

13. Emmanuel Levinas, "The Will of God and the Power of Humanity," in *New Talmudic Readings*, trans. Richard A. Cohen (Pittsburgh: Duquesne University Press, 1990), 56.

14. Idem, "The Poet's Vision," *Proper Names*, trans. Michael B. Smith (London: Athlone, 1996), 130. He also describes Paul Celan's poetry in similar terms: "[T]he poem is situated precisely at that pre-syntactic and . . . pre-logical level, but a level also pre-disclosing: at the moment of pure touching, pure contact, grasping, squeezing—which is, perhaps, a way of giving, right up to and including the hand that gives. A language of proximity for proximity's sake, older than that of 'the truth of being'" (Levinas, "Paul Celan," ibid., 41).

15. Alphonso Lingis, "Introduction to *Otherwise than Being*," in Emmanuel Levinas, *Otherwise than Being: Or, Beyond Essence*, trans. Alphonso Lingis (Pittsburgh: Duquesne University Press, 1998), xxi.

sculpturing an "appropriate body" to fully convey the aura of his mind.[16] When a poem satisfyingly resuscitates the originary intrigue in its poetic body, it can in turn provoke echoing traces in the reader's sensibility, on which the poet's original experience is resurrected.[17]

In other words, poetry's significance resides in the materiality of its media, which is manifested in the contact between language and sensibility. Materiality here does not refer to "the matter opposed to thought and mind, which fed classical materialism" but to the unreflected somatic impression that resists assimilation into rational reflection.[18] With the materiality of poetic language, poetry resurrects the traces of intrigue in the reader's provoked sensibility before, and in spite of, the grip of rational configuration.

Of course, this does not mean that poetry is irrational or that poetry yields no epistemic value. On the contrary, thoughts and thinking patterns constantly appear in poetry.[19] Yet I find that even in the case of poems that austerely address intellectual issues, they are regarded as poetry because they rely on and evoke more than intelligence.[20] Poetry can invite reason to partake in its dance and it will still be reason, but reason cannot reduce poetry to analytical prose and still let it be poetry. The issue at stake is that poetry overflows reason, as an other overflows what one can categorize.

Originating in sensibility, poetic meaning differs from that which comes into language from totality and logos. Poetry exceeds the limits of what is

---

16. Helen Vendler, *Our Secret Discipline: Yeats and Lyric Form* (Cambridge: Belknap, 2007), 3.

17. Poetic resurrection is not a modified form of mimesis. The poet's original experience and the reader's lyrical experience indeed bear a family resemblance. But given readers' varying cultural milieu, what one reader generates genuinely differs from another's response. The accent of the poetic resurrection is not on the (dis)similarity of the content but on the anterior donation of oneself *as-for-the-other*, which is the ethical imperative embedded in lyrical experience.

18. Emmanuel Levinas, *Existence and Existents*, trans. Alphonso Lingis (Boston: Kluwer, 1988), 57. Here Levinas bases the idea of materiality on his esthetic experience of modernist avant-garde art (see Peter Schmiedgen, "Art and Idolatry: Aesthetics and Alterity in Levinas," *Contretemps* 3 [2002]: 150–51). He writes, "[M]ateriality is thickness, coarseness, massivity, wretchedness. It is what has consistency, weight, is absurd, is brute but impassive presence; it is also what is humble, bare, ugly" (*Existence and Existents*, 57). Yet materiality is not to be exhausted in this concrete reference. The excess of the aforementioned material impressions over coherent description reveals a different medium of art critique than pure reason.

19. See von Hallberg, *Lyric Powers*, 105–42; Helen Vendler, *Poets Thinking: Pope, Whitman, Dickinson, Yeats* (Cambridge: Harvard University Press, 2004); Charles Altieri, "Taking Lyrics Literally: Teaching Poetry in a Prose Culture," *New Literary History* 32 (2001): 259–81.

20. See von Hallberg's readings of William Bronk, "Poem for the Nineteenth of March, St. Joseph's Day" (*Life Supports: New and Collected Poems* [San Francisco: North Point, 1981], 216) and John Koethe's poem "The Secret Amplitude" (*Falling Water: Poems* [New York: HarperCollins, 1997], 21ff.); see von Hallberg, *Lyric Powers*, 108–9, 115–26.

said by letting the saying be understood without making it understandable.[21] Even though it cannot be caught alive in consciousness, the saying leaves tangible traces in poetic space. The latter absorbs the material impressions of poetic body, which releases the turn of breath (*Atemwende*) in the reader.[22] For instance, one word may roll into or leap toward or elide from another, depending on the sounds of adjacent syllables, the length of words, the syntax of thoughts, or how the lines slice a reader's sounding of the sentence against or along the syntactic energy (to speed or slow its flow). As the poetic rhythm tightens or relaxes, the reader's breathing alters. One may even say with Les A. Murray, "The poem is dancing us to its rhythm, even as we sit apparently still, reading it. It is, discreetly, borrowing our body to embody itself."[23] In voicing poetic words to the poem's rhythm, the reader is taken between words to where words emerge, to the erotic proximity of the reader to the poem. Freed and estranged from the self in this encounter, the reader's here-and-now, or the Hebraic *hinĕnî*, is exposed to its preoriginal as-for-the-other, from which authentic responses to the poem originate.

Overflowing the totality of rational coherence, poetic saying forces us to find a different ground for the prose commentary on poetry.[24] This ground precedes and subtends reason, emotion, and will. Consciousness can only see its back; to reason, it is the untouchable pluperfect. It is sensibility, a prior receptivity, susceptibility, and vulnerability to the touch of alterity. In lyrical experience, poetry's touch cannot be synchronized in rational

---

21. Emulating how Levinas uses the saying and the said (*le dire et le dit*), I differentiate this pair as follows: the said is the manifestation of the saying in language, while the saying precedes and subtends the said. The saying is the proximity of the subject to the other that gives meaning to the said. However, subject to the inherent linguistic and cultural structures in language, the said absorbs and betrays the saying while expressing it. An interpretation of a text, therefore, is first a phenomenological reduction that unsays the said in order to resurrect the saying. See Levinas, *Otherwise than Being*, 45–46, 119–20, 143; Richard A. Cohen, "Levinas, Spinozism, Nietzsche, and the Body," in *Nietzsche and Levinas: "After the Death of a Certain God,"* ed. Jill Stauffer and Bettina Bergo (New York: Columbia University Press, 2009), 171–72; Simon Critchley, "Introduction," in *The Cambridge Companion to Levinas*, ed. Simon Critchley and Robert Bernasconi (Cambridge: Cambridge University Press, 2002), 17–19; Jeffrey L. Kosky, *Levinas and the Philosophy of Religion* (Bloomington: Indiana University Press, 2001), 54–56.

22. See Paul Celan, "The Meridian," in *Paul Celan: Selections*, ed. Pierre Joris, trans. Rosmarie Waldrop (Berkeley: University of California Press, 2005), 162.

23. Les A. Murray, "Embodiment and Incarnation," in *The Paperbark Tree: Selected Prose* (Manchester: Carcanet, 1992), 259.

24. See Murray's distinction between "Wholespeak" and "Narrowspeak":

> I call properly integrated poetic discourse Wholespeak, while discourses based on the supposed primacy or indeed exclusive sovereignty of daylight reason I call Narrowspeak. The former embraces all good poetry, including that of religion, the latter embraces most of the administrative discourse by which the world is ruled from day to day. (Murray, "Embodiment and Incarnation," 263)

representation; but it can be appeased through the subject's response from sensibility, where lyrical impressions linger.[25]

Approaching poetry through sensibility rejuvenates the reader's senses, for such poetic experience reaches the root of esthetics (*aisthesthai*, "to perceive"). It synaesthetically evokes the reader's bodily memories (of seeing, hearing, smelling, tasting, touching, and feeling) and their accompanying emotions. Memories, which form the unique texture of each individual, are indexed not by facts but by the feelings that they evoke.[26] Feelings, in turn, are enabled by sensibility. When a person's sensibility is repressed as if it were anesthetized,[27] there is no longer an ethically different "I" or "you" but, rather, replaceable agents. Then indifference instead of ethics reigns, at the price of the humanness of the human.[28] However, sensibility is like the hope and root of a dying tree, which will revive the tree at the first smell of water (Job 14:7-9). In this modality, lyrical experience is a small wakeup call that spurs the reader's lapsed sensibility to its acute state[29] and so awakens the reader's humanness.

To introduce Levinasian lyrical ethics better, I will engage them—instead of meditating on theoretical concerns in a hypothetical sphere—through a close reading of poems from the Song of Songs, in a writing that constantly seeks a contact at the heart of the chiasmus. For the same reason that the Song of Songs is sidelined in historical-political research on the Hebrew Bible, it readily lends itself to the approach of lyrical ethics—through its sensuality, its foregrounding of language, its interest in the relation between one and the other, and God's presence that is felt in the trace of the other. Its unsophisticated theme, the erotic love between man and woman, both disarms readers' epistemological apprehension and evokes their rich sensual experiences. In a "purposelessly purposive"[30] way, the poetic intrigue is diffused into the extremely subtle weaving of words, to the caressing of the lyrical texture over the reader's sensibility. Hence, vivified by the sensual lyrical experience, the reader is brought back "without knowing" (Song 6:12) to the very beginning of ethical responsibility, the primordial site of sensibility.

---

25. Gabriel Riera, *Intrigues: From Being to the Other* (New York: Fordham University Press, 2006), 144.

26. Antonio R. Damasio, *Looking for Spinoza: Joy, Sorrow, and the Feeling Brain* (Orlando, FL: Harcourt, 2003), 71, 100, 200, and 204.

27. "The immediacy on the surface of the skin characteristic of sensibility, its vulnerability, is found as it were anaesthetized in the process of knowing. But also, no doubt, repressed or suspended" (Levinas, *Otherwise than Being*, 64).

28. For an artistic imagination of such a state, see *Equilibrium*, dir. Kurt Wimmer, produced Jan de Bont et al. (Dimension Films and Blue Tulip Productions, 2002, DVD).

29. Elaine Scarry, *On Beauty and Being Just* (Princeton, NJ: Princeton University Press, 1999), 81.

30. Immanuel Kant, *Critique of Judgement* (New York: Hafner, 1951), 45.

Henceforth, the convergence of the Song and Levinasian writings in the present monograph is not achieved through a teasing-out of the similarities of the said in the two resources, or an incarnation of one in the other, both of which are based on a re-presentation of these two works. With writing as an effort to encounter the trace of an other, as a response to alterity, I seek to write in reverberation with what has caressed my sensibility, which is the significance of the words beyond the linguistic game of the signified and the signifier, which has never appeared in the present tense of consciousness. Of course, in this trilogy of interaction, when the third[31] comes, ethical responsibility alone would not suffice, and justice is very much a living question at every turn. In the service of justice, knowledge and intelligibility join the play, not understood as the repositioning of being but as assisting in determining how I justify my attention given to the two interlocutors in every concrete, living situation.

Through a close reading of selected lyrics from the Song, I will explore three topics after the chapter on "Theory": the Self, the Other, and God (who is always coming but never arriving on the scene). In ch. 2, "Sensibility and the Awakening of Oneself," I draw from the originary moment when beauty awakens sensibility, to pen a portrait of subjectivity, which becomes the assumed canvas of the beloved's portraiture in Song 4:1–7. Chapter 3 ("Restlessness and Responsibility") addresses the fine line of responsiveness at which "my" speaking from restlessness (Song 5:2–8) exposes that the soul of my soul is already *for-the-other*. Derived from a close reading of Song 8:6 in its immediate context (8:1–7), ch. 4, "The Human Form Divine," proposes an ethical turn of love from erotic to non-erotic within eros's movement, while drawing attention to the ineffable poetic saying as the site of proximity, as a human response to God's trace in the face of the other. In this process, these three chapters also argue against common tendencies toward description, narrative, and thematization, respectively, in defining poetic meaning. The concluding thought, "So to Speak," will linger on the underlying knot of how to emulate poetic saying in prose, to make necessary allowance for the other in my words. It should be acknowledged that this project does not cover all the important topics that a sufficient account of Levinasian ethics (such as the topics of the third interaction: justice, sociality, and politics) or of the Song (e.g., authorship, composition, gendered reading) should contain, because it stresses only what I see as the most important points of contact between the two.

In the end, I find in Levinas's question—"[i]s the meaningful always correlative to a thematization and a representation?"[32]—sufficient provoca-

---

31. In this case, the question which is the second and which the third has no definite answer. Fluidity exists as I turn to one as the primary and the other as correlative, as the streams of rudimentary ideas grow and merge.

32. Emmanuel Levinas, *Entre Nous: On Thinking-of-the-Other*, trans. Michael B. Smith and Barbara Harshave (London: Continuum, 2006), 108.

tion for my writing of the Song with Levinas uppermost in mind. And yet there are also more direct correlations between Levinas and the Song. In fact, he appears to have been quite fascinated with this biblical book of love songs. While commenting on Song 7:3 in his talmudic readings, he called out for the audience to enjoy the paradox that the Song affords—that is, an erotic text bearing austere meaning.[33] He also referenced the Song in his philosophical writings, such as in the cases of the self's wakefulness to the other (5:2),[34] the subject's belatedness (5:6),[35] the "dread of the night" (3:8),[36] and above all, of "love, strong as death" (8:6).[37] Among the unpublished manuscripts that he left behind, one even finds a handwritten translation and reading of the Song.[38] Thus my own aspiration to read the Song lyrically and ethically through a Levinasian lens may not seem so farfetched after all, because it finds and roots its originary inspiration in Levinas's own preoccupation with and affection for this particular biblical text.

---

33. Emmanuel Levinas, *Nine Talmudic Readings*, trans. with an introduction by Annette Aronowicz (Bloomington: Indiana University Press, 1990), 76, 76–83. Other verses from the Song that are discussed in his talmudic readings are 2:3 and 4:3 (pp. 45–46, 83).

34. Idem, "From Conciousness to Wakefulness: Starting from Husserl," *Of God Who Comes to Mind*, 15.

35. Idem, *Otherwise than Being*, 88.

36. Idem, "Exercise on 'The Madness of the Day,'" *Proper Names*, 158.

37. Idem, *God, Death, and Time*, trans. Bettina Bergo (Stanford, CA: Stanford University Press, 2000), 104.

38. Malka, *Emmanuel Levinas*, 284.

Chapter 1

Theory

> Wring about writing would be poetry itself.[1]

"From poetry to prose":[2] without an established code or a metalanguage that enables the translation of poetry into prose, can a prosaic writing pass this initial fissure with integrity?[3] Poetry's excellence is not tied to its ability to represent reality correctly. Instead of being a *mimesis* of reality, more properly speaking, poetry is a *poesis* of words (compare *ma'aseh* in Ps 45:2). The linearly streamed reality is but a skeleton, or even a shadow[4] on which the poet imparts lyrical forms as flesh and blood to generate a vivifying body. The lyrical forms, though acquired with epistemological effort, are not applied purely according to stylistic, linguistic, and cultural rules. Poetic language excels over legal, business, or academic language in that it retains the poet's original feelings while refracting the reality that had provoked them. A lyrical body so made expresses emotional textures that objective languages cannot contain, and evokes subtle feelings that those languages cannot touch. Poetry is, therefore, not "a purely esthetic event"[5] that exhausts its power within egoistic complacency. By making felt the materiality of words, it embodies the rupture of the closure "to which language is condemned."[6]

In contrast, critical essays about poetry are interested in and capable of answering the technical question "What about . . . ?"[7] One frequently encounters such phrases: "This poem is about . . ." or "the message of this

---

1. Emmanuel Levinas, *Otherwise than Being: Or, Beyond Essence*, trans. Alphonso Lingis (Pittsburgh: Duquesne University Press, 1998), 41.
2. Emmanuel Levinas, "Exercise on 'The Madness of the Day,'" *Proper Names*, trans. Michael B. Smith (London: Athlone, 1996), 156–58.
3. Maurice Blanchot, *The Writing of the Disaster* (Lincoln: University of Nebraska Press, 1986), 63.
4. William. B. Yeats states in his 1910 essay "The Tragic Theatre": "If [in poetry] the real world is not altogether rejected, it is but touched here and there, and into the places we have left empty we summon rhythm, balance, pattern, images that remind us of vast passions" (*Memoirs*, transcribed and edited by Denis Donoghue [New York: Macmillan, 1972], 211).
5. Levinas, "The Servant and Her Master," *Proper Names*, 185 n. 4.
6. Ibid.
7. Idem, *Otherwise than Being*, 155.

poem is. . . ." With the assumption that the interpretation of poetry is a cognitive process, these comments typically do not arise from the contact with the poetic body but descend from an interpreter's rational framework and hypothesis. If the goal of reading poetry is to pursue truth, poetry is necessarily decomposed into an extravagant expression of truth. Its interpretation then becomes a process of unpicking the embellishments and employing a more efficient language—logical, objective, and universal—to describe the transferable content. Thus, interpreters would rely on rationality to analyze and deduce a poem's setting, content, and purpose, based on the data of historical background, a poet's personal style, and shared lyrical techniques. Poetic language would be regarded as linguistic symbols that can be exhausted in the overlapping structures of grammar, culture, and psychology, and simplified as the transparent wrapping paper for truth claims.

This rational premise is the result of a universal application of natural sciences' methodologies and assumptions in all disciplines of social sciences, fueled by a worship of the universal reason that accompanied the rise of natural sciences.[8] The most common manifestation is the objective and rational attitude assumed in academic writing. Objective and logical language, derived from reason, corresponds to epistemology. Indeed, when scholars study particular issues in poetry such as dating, philology, grammar, lineation, and so on, analytical language is a sharp tool. Pedagogically, it is also a heuristic means to distill poetic themes and stylistics in introductory textbooks. However, these benefits do not support reason's totalitarian control of poetic studies and interpretations, especially when it comes to questions such as poetic meaningfulness[9]—for objectivity's other name is indifference. The theoretical subject overseeing immobile poems participates in the power of universal reason by miming "the dissolution of all positions,"[10] including one's own materiality. Sensibility, the very flesh and soul of poetry, is suppressed in the name of reason's representation. Is

---

8. Robert Eaglestone observes that contemporary literary criticism is commonly built on a deep rational structure: "We rely at a deep level on methodologies and presuppositions taken from the natural sciences, and this includes the natural sciences' way of understanding truth: the correspondence of a proposition with a state of affairs" ("One and the Same? Ethics, Aesthetics, and Truth," *Poetics Today* 25 [2004]: 606). One should be reminded, however, that the scientific approach is no longer equated with a rational and objective approach. Reflecting on the philosophy of science, for instance, some scientists have pointed out that scientific research is conditioned by subjective and sociopolitical factors (Thomas S. Kuhn, *The Structure of Scientific Revolutions* [Chicago: University of Chicago Press, 1962]; Michael Polanyi, *Personal Knowledge: Towards a Post-Critical Philosophy* [Chicago: University of Chicago Press, 1958]).

9. See also Steve McCaffery, "Insufficiency of Theory to Poetical Economy," in *Prior to Meaning: The Protosemantic and Poetics* (Evanston, IL: Northwestern University Press, 2001), 3.

10. Julia Kristeva, *Revolution in Poetic Language*, trans. Margret Waller (New York: Columbia University Press, 1984), 97.

not the assumption of objective meaning, which the thought invests on the reality, "already a restriction of meaning?"[11]

Rational thinking relies on the *I* of *I think*, the consciousness that comes into being after sensibility responds to the intrigue of alterity. Therefore, the *I* enwrapped in thinking is always already lagging behind poetry. To consciousness that always stays in the present, poetry is always a pluperfect happening. "In me the tiger sniffs the rose":[12] this is a good line. But when the question "What makes it good?" arises, my mind only sees the back of that goodness passing. The interpretations resulting from rational analysis unavoidably come after the intervention of consciousness, which is already too late for lyrical experience. In other words, between lyrical intrigue and consciousness lies a diachronic gap that the *I* cannot cross, that trips commentaries on poetry. As Levinas quotes from the Song of Songs, "I opened . . . he had disappeared."[13]

A rational premise exchanges the humanness of human for the impersonal logos, or the sociocultural symbols that the latter undergirds. Such assumption is necessary under certain circumstances, such as a surgeon during an operation, but it suffers a prior deficiency when it comes to reading poetry. It cannot feel. With an automatic suppression of the lyrical touch, a rational interpreter has already lost a connection with the poetic vision before research begins.[14] The grasping mind, wrapped in intention at its birth, has always already forgotten alterity. Originating from reason and epistemology, therefore, critical writings cannot respond to the pre-original fissure between poetry and prose.

It should also be noted that, in recent years, the sufficiency of rational expositions has already been undermined by the thriving practice of cultural hermeneutics in the field of biblical studies. The latter emphasizes the concrete sociocultural settings of the readers, which bear on the formation of meaning as much as that of the text. With this alternative, it is fair to ask whether humanness and poetic touch can be conveyed fully through cultural hermeneutics. Can the subject be identified with one's sociopolitical location? If so, then writing remains a power struggle in which different "I"s compete for the right to speak about what *I think* of the text. In Levinas's words, "Communication would be impossible if it should have to begin in the ego, a free subject, to whom every other would be only a limi-

---

11. Emmanuel Levinas, "God and Philosophy," *Of God Who Comes to Mind*, trans. Bettina Bergo [Stanford, CA: Stanford University Press, 1998]), 57.
12. Siegfried Sassoon, "The Direction of Human Potential," *Collected Poems* (London: Faber & Faber, 1947), 178.
13. Song 5:6; quoted in Levinas, *Otherwise than Being*, 88.
14. "The immediacy on the surface of the skin characteristic of sensibility, its vulnerability, is found as it were anaesthetized in the process of knowing. But also, no doubt, repressed or suspended" (ibid., 64).

tation that invites war, domination, precaution and information."[15] Following Levinas, I would say that the irreducible core of subjectivity lies not in different cultural locations but in a subject's non-indifference and responsibility to alterity. What enables commentaries that rise from different social groups—Asian American, African American, Latin American, feminist, gay and lesbian, people with disabilities, and so on—to engage each other is a prior susceptibility and exposure to alterity. When encouraged, this anterior responsiveness/responsibility would mobilize each commentator to write differently about the same caress from the text, which would then become a shared ground for dialogues or roundtable discussions.

In short, the subject of lyrical experience—poet or reader—is not confined to the *I* of *I think*, whether due to universal reason or to having a certain sort of social membership. With the subject's beginning being humbly acknowledged in the pluperfect intrigue, with the writing on poetry being understood as the subject's response to alterity, prose commentaries—rational or culturally relative—can be grounded in the foundation of authenticity, responding to poetry's otherness through the singularity of their respective literary bodies.

Subjectivity: The Rise of Lyrical Ethics

In an effort to assist interpreters of biblical poetry to keep their subjectivity wakeful, I propose a new approach—*lyrical ethics*. Even though this is a new attempt in the field of biblical poetry, the marriage of lyrics and ethics is nothing drastically new. In the great explosion of ethical critical studies throughout the humanities in the last decade of the twentieth century, poets, philosophers, and literary critics have sought to give poetry moral credit.[16] Most relevant to the present study is Charles Altieri's essay "Lyrical Ethics and Literary Experience."[17] In this essay, Altieri expresses his disappointment with contemporary ethical criticism that operates under a philosophical superstructure and proposes *lyrical ethics* as an alternative that pays attention to the suppressed literary experience.

To go back even further, Joseph Brodsky declared decades ago in his Nobel address: "Aesthetics is the mother of ethics."[18] If *esthetics* and *ethics* are defined as in traditional Western philosophy, Brodsky's statement

---

15. Ibid., 119.
16. Martha C. Nussbaum, *Poetic Justice: The Literary Imagination and Public Life* (Boston: Beacon, 1995), 79–121; Alan Shapiro, *In Praise of the Impure: Poetry and the Ethical Imagination—Essays, 1980–1991* (Evanston, IL: Northwestern University Press, 1993); Seamus Heaney, *Crediting Poetry: The Nobel Lecture* (New York: Farrar, Straus & Giroux, 1996); idem, *The Redress of Poetry: Oxford Lectures* (London: Faber & Faber, 1995).
17. Charles F. Altieri, "Lyrical Ethics and Literary Experience," *Style* 32 (1998): 272–97.
18. Joseph Brodsky, "Nobel Lecture," http://www.nobelprize.org/nobel_prizes/literature/laureates/1987/brodsky-lecture.html (accessed October 3, 2013).

would appear at best a casual musing. For as Marcia Muelder Eaton has contended, the "history of philosophy does not offer many theories in which aesthetics is prior to ethics."[19] However, if one takes into consideration Brodsky's political and personal experiences, it is clear that he is not arguing for the ontological precedence of esthetics but, rather, that poetic language is capable of making an ethical impact before communicating its content.[20] The key is that esthetic experience (lyrical experiences included) is squarely anchored by the irreplaceable individuality of the reader. Brodsky believes that, through esthetic experiences, individuals assert their singularity beyond the thematic control of the state, for such an experience concerns poetic language that touches the reader, not the content that it carries.

> In other words, into the little zeros with which the champions of the common good and the rulers of the masses tend to operate, art introduces a "period, period, comma, and a minus", transforming each zero into a tiny human, albeit not always pretty, face.[21]

Brodsky's statement reveals that, before being abstracted into esthetic judgment, esthetic experience is attention and feeling. I can be trained to repeat the esthetic judgments of paintings or symphonies. But no one can duplicate my experience of an artwork as it caresses my senses and urges my response. The transparent light of intelligence cannot pass through human corporality, which casts different shadows in individual esthetic tastes. In the wake of the provoked feelings, the singularity and humanness of a person is revived, otherwise than the plastic identity subsumed under power and totality. Thus, David-Antoine Williams rephrases Brodsky's idea, saying, "Ultimately, the ethical value of poetry comes from this irreducibility, from its grounding in that which cannot be shared or counterfeited."[22]

The irreducible contact between poetry and reader protects poetic language from being assimilated into the tautology of reason. It awakens (instead of neutralizing) the reader's subjectivity, as sensibility that touches and is being touched by the poem:

---

19. Marcia Muelder Eaton, "Aesthetics: The Mother of Ethics?" *Journal of Aesthetics and Art Criticism* 55 (1997): 355; quoted from Williams, "Tête-à-tête," 209 n. 4.

20. Brodsky, who is considered by his fellow-poet Yunna Moritz to be "apolitical," was sent into exile because, in Lev Loseff's words, the state "sensed something subversive in the very linguistic matter of his verse" (Williams, "Tête-à-tête," 209). Indeed, Brodsky maintains that ethics "is a linguistically managed notion, which leads the poet and state into direct conflict over the rights to the same medium" (David Macfadyen, "Politics, Aesthetics, and Ethics in Joseph Brodsky's Poem *On the Death of Zhukov*," in *Between Ethics and Aesthetics: Crossing the Boundaries*, ed. Dorota Glowacka and Stephen Boos, SUNY series in Aesthetics and the Philosophy of Art [Albany: State University of New York Press, 2002], 240).

21. Brodsky, "Nobel Lecture."

22. Williams, "Tête-à-tête," 212.

> In starting with sensibility interpreted not as a knowing but as proximity, in seeking in language contact and sensibility, behind the circulation of information it becomes, we have endeavored to describe subjectivity as irreducible to consciousness and thematization.[23]

Subjectivity cannot be reduced to the *I* of *I think* that designates entities, substantives, and relations in a coherent prose. In writing poems, the poet breaks down the substance of his or her identity into modes of temporization that is etched on sensibility, like the aging skin instead of the constant ego. That is to say, subjectivity is revealed as passivity before the active recuperation of consciousness. Though poetry carves a niche for itself by resonating with the essence, and though it is always "on the verge of being identified as entities,"[24] it does not identify but, rather, tears the essence that it modulates. Instead of being a reflection, poetry refracts through the materiality of the "vocables."

> In painting, red reddens and green greens. . . . In music sounds resound; in poems vocables, material of the said, no longer yield before what they evoke, but sing with their evocative powers and their diverse ways to evoke.[25]

Can the form be more important than the theme? Yes, but not in terms of technicalities and skills that are confined to epistemology. Harmonized vowels and consonants are important to the sound of poetry. But if one works them to death throughout the whole poem, it will not be read.[26] Only when the technique "becomes as much material as material itself,"[27] when the forms—colors, sounds, and vocables—awaken the recipients' sensibility, can one say that esthetic experience activates ethical significance.

In the "vocables" of poetry, therefore, ethical significance is evoked by the "irreducible" depth of subjectivity, the proximity beneath and before knowledge, the excess of sensibility over rationality. However, unfortunately, this unique aspect of poetic experience is often bypassed in biblical poetic studies, mostly due to a lack of felicitous theoretical language. When retextured in Levinas's writings of sensibility, Brodsky's simple axiom gains philosophical substance and offers an entrance to a Levinasian lyrical ethics. The rise of the Levinasian lyrical ethics, therefore, helps to extend the theoretical root of the long-loved idea of a "close reading" and reaches beyond intellectual musings in soliciting ethical significance from where it happens.

---

23. Levinas, *Otherwise than Being*, 100.
24. Ibid., 40.
25. Ibid.
26. Robert Frost, *Robert Frost on Writing*, ed. Elaine Barry (New Brunswick, NJ: Rutgers University Press, 1973), 59.
27. Ibid., 68.

Levinasian Lyrical Ethics

What is "Levinasian" in the ethical approach to lyrics is shown in a set of convictions that Lyrical Ethics shares with Levinasian ethics: challenging the hegemony of knowledge; defending ethics ethically; and being anchored in sensibility. First, knowledge starts from consciousness, which cannot be defined with the concepts of knowledge.[28] Unable to illuminate its own origin, knowledge knows by reducing meaning to what it can comprehend.

> Knowledge, by itself—as has become nearly transparent today—is incapable of determining worth, value, or purpose. It knows, to be sure, but it cannot rank importance. Its object is "difference," not excellence. No knowledge is more or less urgent than any other. In truth, then, contrary to its own paeans, knowledge cannot defend even its own priority. Instead, as a sort of displacement, a masking of its indifference, it reduces everything else to knowledge, until there is nothing else but itself or ignorance. Knowledge, by itself, thus remains indifferent to the very humanity of the human. This latter, the humanity of the human, Levinas finds not in knowledge but in ethics. More important than epistemology is ethics: the demands of morality and justice.[29]

Abiding by the cardinal rule of indifference, knowledge cannot make decisions of value or importance. It cannot do justice to consciousness, not to speak of ethics, which "operates otherwise than epistemology."[30] Not even an ethical criticism that expands epistemology to include emotion can comprehend ethics, for it too succumbs under the paradigm of knowing. To meet ethical demands, the most important thing is not to delineate and advocate certain sets of moral proscriptions but to awaken and maintain one's sense of ethical responsiveness to alterity, which invests meaningfulness into moral laws.

Ethics happens at the level of sensibility, which resides only in contact, as in "the nakedness of a skin presented to contact, to the caress."[31] Sensibility is here seen as "the living human corporeality."[32] It characterizes the self that does not coincide with itself in identity but is already for-the-other: "In its skin it is stuck in its skin, not having its skin to itself, a vulnerability."[33] It is most readily felt in one's susceptibility to wound.

Admittedly, sensibility has been known as the faculty that feeds cognitive function by providing the content of perception. Yet, more impor-

---

28. Levinas, "God and Philosophy," 58.
29. Richard A. Cohen, *Ethics, Exegesis and Philosophy: Interpretation after Levinas* (Cambridge: Cambridge University Press, 2001), 5.
30. Ibid., 6.
31. Emmanuel Levinas, "No Identity," *Collected Philosophical Papers*, trans. Alphonso Lingis (Dordrecht: Nijhoff, 1987), 146.
32. Idem, *Otherwise than Being*, 51.
33. Ibid.

tantly, it signifies the proximity that subtends perception in the form of a donation of attention.[34] Before I configure the "perceptive equilibrium,"[35] the felt touch on my skin already assumes a prior responsiveness to alterity. The subject is inseparable from the appeal of alterity, which can be forgotten but cannot be declined (Deut 8:12; Judg 2:11, 3:7).

As far as the current topic is concerned, intelligibility requires the writer, the book, and the reader. Applying human reason as a mini-me version of the universal logos, as the sole ground and tool of intelligibility, is inherently an un-universal assumption. It was born in Greek culture and usurped the throne of intelligibility during the Englightenment era. When the saying that gives meaning, the attention that welcomes the other, are bracketed out as insubstantial, the "substantial" risks losing its footing in genuiness and humanness. When the said thus becomes petrified in rationally coherent discourse, the death of philosophy as Western ontology knows it happens naturally.[36]

For rationally coherent writing is, in essence, being that is weaving its closure. In such writing, the "I" of *I think* is busy feathering "my" nest with threads of culture, history, and world. The "I" is writing about alterity; and yet through the medium of "coherent discourse," alterity is bleached in the sameness of *I think* and loses its very strangeness. Simply put, coherent discourse is the tautology of reason.

Reflection brings up the old foundation stones and mixes them with current things. That simultaneity of conditioning and the conditioned is known as coherent discourse. But, in looking back to examine their condition, words are immobilized, become pillars of salt.[37]

---

34. Idem, "Two Texts on *Merleau-Ponty* by Emmanuel Levinas: Sensibility," *Ontology and Alterity in Merleau-Ponty*, trans. Michael B. Smith; ed. Galen A. Johnson and Michael B. Smith (Evanston, IL: Northwestern University Press, 1991), 64–65; idem, *Totality and Infinity: An Essay on Exteriority*, trans. Alphonso Lingis [Pittsburgh: Duquesne University Press, 1969], 118; idem, *Otherwise than Being*, 14; Alphonso Lingis, "Introduction to *Otherwise than Being*," in *Otherwise than Being*, xxx.

35. Borrowing the model of John Rawls's "reflective equilibrium," Martha Nussbaum advocates one of "perceptive equilibrium" (*Love's Knowledge: Essays on Philosophy and Literature* [New York: Oxford University Press, 1990], 183). She accepts Rawls's idea of negotiating conflicting views for the purpose of arriving at a harmonious, tension-free overall picture (p. 174; John Rawls, "The Independence of Moral Theory," in *Proceedings and Addresses of the American Philosophical Association* 47 [1974]: 5–22; see also his book *Justice as Fairness: A Restatement* [Cambridge: Harvard University Press, 2001]). But Nussbaum finds that Rawls's model includes only rational thinking and leaves no space for other faculties. Through her model of perceptive equilibrium, she envisions that, through the process of exposing and negotiating different feelings and perceptions, all perceptions will "hang beautifully together," both to one another and to the general principles. This perceptive equilibrium is also ready to reconstitute itself when facing new situations (*Love's Knowledge*, 183).

36. Emmanuel Levinas, "Foreword," *Proper Names*, 4–5.

37. Idem, "The Servant and Her Master," 146.

Even the unlikely prodigals—postmodern relativism that refuses thematic closure or the deconstructive play of polysemy that defers definition—begin with a "committed consciousness"[38] that does not respond to proximity but generates variables within a situation. Their writings are "the result of a reverting of susceptiveness into a project,"[39] in which alterity that inspires subjectivity is forgotten. The "I" of *I think*, which in its bright illumination has lost sight of its origin, parades its power in writing. "Despite all refusal, somewhere in the brain, 'it keeps on knitting'"[40]—knitting up the closure of being.

Genuine intelligibility requires one to go back to the proximity of one to the other, of one facing the other in non-in-difference, not demanding "What's it in for me?" but offering "Après vous, Monsieur."[41] Unless the reader first gives ear to the voice that commands "Listen! . . ." (Deut 6:4, Prov 1:8), the book exists in vain. Conversely, an intelligent reading of the book can only arise from one's giving attention in the form of *hinĕnî*—from one's responsibility to the other who has reached out through the words. Hence Levinas claims, "Non-indifference, humanity, the-one-for-the-other is the very signi-fyingness of signification, the intelligibility of the intelligible, and thus reason."[42] Reason here refers to that which is found in the expression "the reason of/for . . ." instead of the faceless Reason that dominates critical discourses. Intelligibility ultimately appeals not to the impersonal logos but to a renewing empathetic engagement with the other, with the reader's hand that is reaching out to warm up the poet's cold, outstretched hand in the poem.

Responsibility to alterity is an integral extension of subjectivity as sensibility. It is carried out in the provoked initiatives with which the subject seeks to restore peace after the intrigue of alterity. It is best preserved in the writing and reading of poetry, because the materiality of poetry embraces both the trace of intrigue embodied in the poem and the receptiveness of the reader at encountering the poem.

Henceforth, unlike traditional esthetic judgment or thematic abstraction, a Levinasian lyrical ethics advocates a hermeneutic that rests on the reader's "pre-originary *susceptiveness*"[43] to the materiality of lyrical language. From the reader's responsiveness to the otherness of the poem, prose commentaries on poetry may arise with ethical integrity. The approach that does not automatically follow the track of thinking does not

---

38. Idem, *Otherwise than Being*, 137.
39. Ibid., 136.
40. Idem, "Exercises on 'The Madness of the Day,'" 146.
41. Simon Critchley reports that Levinas was fond of summarizing the entirety of his philosophy with this phrase (Simon Critchley, "Appendix 3: Emmanuel Levinas," in *The Ethics of Deconstruction: Derrida and Levinas*, 3rd ed. (Edinburgh: Edinburgh University Press, 2014], 287).
42. Levinas, *Otherwise than Being*, 166.
43. Ibid., 122.

necessarily interrupt thinking, but invites it into the weaving of a lyrical response. To retain responsibility in words, this prosaic response does not seek to wrap up knowledge for purchase and consumption but draws attention to the lyrical space in which the poem gives itself. Writing in response to a poem is not consumed in writing *about* it (that is, circumscribing it), in creating another warring voice of *I think*.... Instead, this different way of writing is inspired by one's responsibility, which has been awakened in proximity to alterity. Such ethical writing distinguishes itself by the materiality of its own language in modulating poetic language.

Levinas and the Writing of Difference

Levinas's writings not only give philosophical substance to Brodsky's perceptive and sentimental maxim but also exemplify in the materiality of its language how prose can respond to poetry ethically. His writing does not claim to preserve the otherness of the other in writing but insists on being answerable to the trace of the other "according to a modality of awakening and sobering up."[44] Oftentimes his written words patiently resist and fragmentize comprehension, not to show off some suave deconstructive moves, but to release their meaningfulness only in the prescribed space that is not a mere exchange of information.

Until now, I have refrained from addressing the strong impression that Levinas himself discredits esthetics and art, thinking them to be of little ethical significance.[45] This assessment is mainly based on his early writings, such as his 1948 essay "Reality and Its Shadow" and *Totality and Infinity*.[46] However, it does not take into full consideration the context of these writings. For one thing, they are situated in the context of a surviving Jewish philosopher writing against Martin Heidegger—who had been an inspiring master but turned out to be an unrelenting Nazi member—and under such weight, against Heidegger's ontological poetics of dwelling.[47] Poetry

---

44. Idem, "Exercises on 'The Madness of the Day,'" 158.

45. See Jill Robins, *Altered Reading:Levinas and Literature* (Chicago: University of Chicago Press, 1999), 75–90; Sean Hand, "Shadowing Ethics: Levinas's View or Arts and Aesthetics," in *Facing the Other: The Ethics of Emmanuel Levinas*, ed. Sean Hand (Richmond, Surrey: Curzon, 1996), 63–90.

46. Levinas, "Reality and Its Shadow," *Collected Philosophical Papers*, 1–14; idem, *Totality and Infinity*, 202.

47. However great Heidegger's philosophy may be in other terms, Levinas holds fast to its fundamental flaw. Applying Franz Rosenzweig's critique of impersonal reason, he writes that "Heideggerian ontology, which subordinates the relationship with the Other to the relationship with Being in general, remains under obedience to the anonymous, and leads inevitably to another power, to imperialist domination, to tyranny" (*Totality and Infinity*, 47). For further discussions on the relationship between Levinas and Heidegger with respect to poetry and art, see Gabriel Riera, *Intrigues: From Being to the Other* (New York: Fordham University Press, 2006), 55–134. For more balanced surveys of Levinas's writings on art and poetry, see Richard Kearney, "Levinas and the Ethics of Imagining,"

in this context is more precisely poetry such as Heidegger praises in *Being and Time*,[48] which falls in the Kantian and Romantic esthetic tradition. Moreover, aside from the Heideggerian lens, Levinas's understanding of art at this stage was influenced by the writings of Jean-Paul Sartre and Maurice Blanchot.[49] Under these constraints, Levinas's criticism of poetry is subsumed under his view that representational art could become the cold illusion for egoistic consumption.

Stacked against his negative view of art in this period are the facts that in real life Levinas was brought up by a mother who instilled in him a love for Russian literature, that he was married to a wife who loved reading and music, and that, for years, he sat with his son during his piano practice. Besides the fact that Levinas could recite Pushkin by heart, even in the realm of music (for which he himself confessed not to have an ear), his son testified that he had a comprehensive view:

> Having done his studies with Maurice Blanchot, he shared with him this superficial sensibility that made him so circumspect in the realm of aesthetics. He had extreme restraint when it came to an art to which he did not have technical access. But all the same, to deny any musicality whatsoever to someone who was, during my entire childhood, until the age of twelve or thirteen years, in the same room where I prepared for my exams—*Totality and Infinity* was written approximately one meter away from my piano—is equally difficult.[50]

It comes as no surprise, then, that Levinas comfortably uses artwork of all kinds to finesse the texture of, to double up with, or to make accessible his philosophical arguments. One can easily glean examples from *Otherwise Than Being*: Macbeth's death wish on the first page and Yehuda Halevi's "eternal word" on the penultimate page; Levinas's impressions of Raoul Dufy's paintings and Xenakis's "Nomos Alpha for Unaccompanied Cello"; and even direct quotations from Paul Claudel's play *Satin Slipper*, Fyodor Dostoyevsky's novel *Brothers Karamazov*, and the Song of Songs.[51] Furthermore, Levinas has written extensively on poetic works, such as those

---

in *Between Ethics and Aesthetics*, 86–87; William Edelglass, "Levinas's Language," in *The Enigma of Good and Evil: The Moral Sentiment in Literature*, ed. Anna-Teresa Tymieniecka; Analecta Husserliana 85 (Dordrecht: Springer, 2005), 53–54; M. Sevcik, "Lévinas' Conception of Art and Poetry" *Estetika: The Central European Journal of Aesthetics* 42 (2006): 80–148 [in Czech].

48. Levinas's projection of art during this time is surprisingly close to Heidegger's later writing, "The Origin of the Work of Art" (in Heidegger, *Poetry, Language, Thought* [New York: Harper & Row, 1975], 15–86), which was not yet published (Martin Heidegger, *Der Ursprung des Kunstwekes* [Stuttgart: Reclam, 1988]).

49. Hent de Vries, *Minimal Theologies: Critiques of Secular Reason in Adorno and Levinas*, trans. Geoffrey Hale (Baltimore: Johns Hopkins University Press, 2005), 415–16, 419.

50. Salomon Malka, *Emmanuel Levinas: His Life and Legacy* (Pittsburgh: Duquesne University Press, 2006), 257.

51. Levinas, *Otherwise than Being*, 3, 30, 40, 147, 146, 88.

of Shmuel Yosef Agnon, Paul Celan, Edmond Jabès, Marcel Proust, Maurice Blanchot, and Michel Leiris.[52] These essays show that, in spite of his criticism of art in his early writings, Levinas is sympathetic to poetry. But this is not to say that in practice Levinas "justifies art despite himself."[53] Rather, Levinas's later commentaries on poetic writings reveal that he takes a radically different position on poetry compared with the Kantian and Romantic esthetic tradition, which he criticizes in "Reality and Its Shadow."[54]

More essentially, a sweeping conclusion about Levinas's negative evaluation of esthetics does not do justice to the evolution of Levinas's philosophy, which is palpable in the difference between *Totality and Infinity* and *Otherwise than Being*.[55] Salomon Malka, the biographer of Levinas, even asserts: "There were two Levinases: the one who wrote *Totality and Infinity* in 1961, and the other who wrote *Otherwise Than Being* in 1973."[56] In *Totality and Infinity*, Levinas ascribes sensibility to the sphere of enjoyment, in which "the ego pursues its own closure and contentment."[57] Esthetic pleasure, therefore, is of egoistic enjoyment that can be brutally indifferent to human suffering. In contrast, *Otherwise than Being* reaches beyond esthetic judgment and locates sensibility as vulnerability, susceptibility, and exposedness to alterity. As the overall paradigm shifts, Levinas realigns poetry with sensual experiences that expose sensibility. For instance, rhythm, an alienating force in "Reality and Its Shadow" and in *Totality and Infinity*, enjoys the ethical significance of "emphatic mutation" in *Otherwise than Being*.[58]

Lastly and most relevantly, like Marcel Proust who engages the trace of the other through poetic language in *À la recherche du temps perdu*, or Derrida who through a pure literary effect generates "nothing for thought to dwell in,"[59] Levinas fuses poetry and prose in the integrity of sensibility and uses poetic language to write the other in his philosophical writings. Employing poetry as "an unheard-of modality of the *otherwise than being*,"[60] Levinas is able to write in response to alterity without enclosing it in the said. His words are not used to designate reality, transparently or with the color and weight of history, but to bear witness to the other in the

---

52. In addition to the relevant essays collected in *Proper Names*, see also Emmanuel Levinas, "The Transcendence of Words: On Michel Leiris's *Biffures*," *Outside the Subject*, trans. Michael B. Smith (Stanford, CA: Stanford University Press, 1993), 144–50.

53. Travis Anderson, "Drawing upon Levinas to Sketch out a Heterotopic Poetics of Art and Tragedy," *Research in Phenomenology* 24 (1994): 92.

54. Edelglass, "Levinas's Language," 53.

55. Lingis, "Introduction," xxi.

56. Malka, *Emmanuel Levinas*, 184.

57. Lingis, "Introduction," xxii.

58. Riera, *Intrigue*, 135.

59. Levinas thus exclaims about "the poetry of Derrida" ("Wholly Otherwise," in *Re-Reading Levinas*, trans. Simon Critchley [Bloomington: Indiana University Press, 1991], 4).

60. Levinas, "Paul Celan," *Proper Names*, 46.

amphibology of the said and the saying.[61] In fact, the unique modality of Levinasian language has become a topic of study for its own sake.[62]

To a mind trained in Anglo-American academics, Levinas's writings are convoluted beyond reconfiguration and yet hauntingly straightforward. They do not conform to the rules and assumptions of a coherent discourse like perspicuous definitions and linear argumentation. Hence, they do not capture, pin down, or demobilize an object in a universal language; and conversely, a universal language will fail to contain his writings. For instance, Levinas's descriptions of his key concepts are ever evolving, gaining different textures by blending in new references. His discourse moves by means of substitution and repetition—"of the same wave against the same shore, every return also a perpetual renewal and enrichment."[63] The same that keeps returning in his writings, however, is not reducible to any of the said. The diverse said in Levinas's writing expresses the same saying, the caress of alterity on sensibility, which is embedded in the different textures of words. Among Levinas's last words in *Otherwise Than Being*, one reads:

> The caress of love, always the same, in the last accounting (for him that thinks in counting) is always different and overflows with exorbitance the songs, poems and admissions in which it is said in so many different ways and through so many themes.[64]

The perpetual recurrence of the same caress in Levinas's writing modulates, not only the ethical "contraction of ipseity and its breakup,"[65] of a vigilance that summons continuous restaging, but also the infinite recommencements of being in the diversity of artwork,[66] of incessantly opening up the self to the touch of alterity. In his daughter Simone's testimony, Levinas's writing was not merely a bottling up of his thoughts in words but an intense process of alterations toward the good and, therefore, "It

---

61. Levinas, *Totality and Infinity*, 205; idem, *Otherwise than Being*, 34–43, 151–52. Compare with "[a] word may give me its meaning, but first it suppresses it. For me to be able to say, 'This woman,' I must somehow take her flesh and blood reality away from her, cause her to be absent, annihilate her. The word gives me the being, but it gives it to me deprived of being" (Maurice Blanchot, *The Gaze of Orpheus, and Other Literary Essays* [Barrytown, NY: Station Hill, 1981], 42).

62. Cf. Edelglass, "Levinas's Language"; Ewa Rychter, *(Un)Saying the Other: Allegory and Irony in Emmanuel Levinas's Ethical Language* (Frankfurt am Main: Peter Lang, 2004); Kathryn Bevis, "'Better than Metaphors'? Dwelling and the Maternal Body in Emmanuel Levinas," in *Literature and Theology* 2007 (3): 317–29; John Llewelyn, "Levinas and Language," in *The Cambridge Companion to Levinas*, ed. Simon Critchley and Robert Bernasconi (Cambridge: Cambridge University Press, 2002), 119–38.

63. Riera, *Intrigues*, 139; Jacques Derrida, "Violence and Metaphysics," in *Emmanuel Levinas, Phenomenology and His Critics*, ed. Claire Katz with Lara Trout (London: Routledge, 2005), 1.116.

64. Levinas, *Otherwise than Being*, 184.

65. Ibid., 109.

66. Ibid., 40.

was forever 'not ready.'"[67] I, for one, am tempted to apply the following description to Levinas's writing: it "takes its position at the edge of itself; in order to be able to exist, it without interruption calls and fetches itself from its now-no-longer back to its as-always."[68] Is it surprising that, in Paul Celan's original sentence, the subject of this statement is "the poem?"

If a reader approaches Levinas's writings as being written in poetic language, then much of the pain in reading them can be altered into an experience of contact. If read like Blanchot's *L'attente l'oubli*, like Celan's poems toward the end of his life,[69] Levinasian language—aside from looking rather approachable now by comparison—will not be a problem but a solution to an ethical writing of alterity. That is to say, instead of grasping and extracting knowledge from his text, the reader bears the agitation of its fabric in accord with an attentive passivity and sobers up through this exercise. For, the fabric of Levinas's writings—sentient materiality embodying "the human or interhuman intrigue"[70]—prescribes the space of reading as the proximity to the other instead of a platform of exchange. The obscurity of his text releases its significance in the reader's encounter with his text.

Writing as Encounter

Now it is appropriate to introduce the last question: how can Lyrical Ethics embody Levinasian ethics? Should one tease out from poems Levinasian ideas (such as "the face" or "the other") or advocate certain sets of perceived Levinasian ethical rules and gauge poetic writings by them? These practices would be little different from other branches of ethical criticism that fall under ontology, for they betray the very spirit of Levinasian writings.

---

67. Simone recalls the time when Levinas prepared the paper for the annual conference at Jean Wahl's Collège:

> He worked on his paper nonstop, erasing, tearing up and revising right up to the last minute. It was forever "not ready." And I have this horrible memory of him being in such despair one time—he had finished his essay but felt that it was no good—that he rushed outside, flying onto rue Erlanger. Mom ran after him, and I ran behind her. She was afraid of I don't know what, that he would do something stupid or that he would fall under a car, all simply because of dissatisfaction in writing! (Malka, *Emmanuel Levinas*, 238)

68. Paul Celan, "The Meridian," in *Paul Celan: Selections*, ed. Pierre Joris, trans. Rosmarie Waldrop (Berkeley: University of California Press, 2005), 164.

69. Edmond Jabès comments on Celan's language: "The love-hate relationship with the German language led him toward the end of his life to write poems of which one can only read the tearing.... Hence the reader's difficulty to approach them straight on" (Edmond Jabès, "The Memory of Words," in ibid., 221).

70. Levinas regards the "search for the human or interhuman intrigue as the fabric of ultimate intelligibility" ("Transcendence and Intelligibility," *Emmanuel Levinas: Basic Philosophical Writings*, ed. Ariaan T. Peperzak, Simon Critchley, and Robert Bernasconi [Bloomington: Indiana University Press, 1996], 158). Cf. Chris Thompson, "The Look of Ethics: Emmanuel Levinas, Léo Bronstein, and the Interhuman Intrigue," in *Textual Ethos Studies, or Locating Ethics*, ed. Anna Fahraeus and AnnKatrin Jonsson (Amsterdam: Rodopi, 2005), 317–23.

Levinas affirms that "[t]he mode of revelation of what remains *other*, despite its revelation, is not the thought, but the language, of the poem."[71] Poetic language does not go through the elevation of rational assimilation but remains on the skin as pure touching. The "inherent obscurity of poetry," which the daylight of reason cannot penetrate, releases its meaningfulness only in "an encounter."[72] In this sense, he praises Celan's poetic language as "[a] language of proximity for proximity's sake, older than that of 'the truth of being.'"[73]

This encounter appears as the contact between sensibility and poetic body. In life, one never feels or responds to the other directly but always through the mediation of one's body.[74] In writing, one encounters the other through the mediation of the literary body. This body "is not only an image or figure here; it is the distinctive in-oneself of the contraction of ipseity and its breakup."[75] A contact with this literary body interrupts my sameness and thus awakens my subjectivity as a reader. From John Keats's perspective as a poet, the desire to touch is vividly portrayed as an awaited handshake in his poem, "This Living Hand, Now Warm and Capable":

> This living hand, now warm and capable
> Of earnest grasping, would, if it were cold
> And in the icy silence of the tomb,
> So haunt thy days and chill thy dreaming nights
> That thou would wish thine own heart dry of blood,
> So in my veins red life might stream again,
> And thou be conscience-calm'd. See, here it is—
> I hold it towards you.[76]

As the reader places his or her hand in the poet's, the poem receives the warmth to revive its "red life" in the vein of its lines. The poet relies on the poetic body to embody his or her original experience; the commentator relies on another literary body to extend his or her response to the poem. In the modality of incarnation, the latter's responsive writing instantiates the recurrence of inspiring the inertia of things for the other. The two writings are like the hands of the poet and the commentator touching in a handshake. Such is "the first of the languages, response preceding the ques-

---

71. Levinas, "The Poet's Vision," *Proper Names*, 130.
72. See Celan, "The Meridian," 162.
73. Levinas, "Paul Celan," 41.
74. "A feeling in essence is an idea—an idea of the body and, even more particularly, an idea of a certain aspect of the body, its interior, in certain circumstances" (Antonio R. Damasio, *Looking for Spinoza: Joy, Sorrow, and the Feeling Brain* [Orlando, FL: Harcourt, 2003], 88). For more discussion on the mechanism of the feeling brain, see pp. 83–136.
75. Levinas, *Otherwise than Being*, 109.
76. John Keats, "This Living Hand, Now Warm and Capable," *Complete Poems*, ed. Jack Stillinger (Cambridge: Harvard University Press), 384.

tion, responsibility for the neighbor, by its *for the other*, the whole marvel of giving."[77]

The trace of a poem provokes each audience differently, as do the writings that express the provocations. It should be noted that this difference does not lie exclusively in the cultural bearings of the commentators but can be traced to the exotic origin of poetry. In fact, the "irresistible temptation of commentary"[78] attests to poetry's inspired origin, which exceeds "the simultaneity of systems or the logical definition of concepts."[79] The unicity and necessity of each commentary lies in the commentator's irreplaceable responsibility to warm up the poet's hand.

Infinite commentaries find their common breathing room in this nonindifferent contact. The erotic contact, the silent attention, the saying without the said, the donation of the self without holding back, the substitution of my sensibility for the other antecede a responsible reading of poetry. It is physically carried in the whiteness of the poetic space, in "the voice of silence" to which the song or poetry of language attends,[80] and in the altered breath of the reader.

As a way of writing, Lyrical Ethics responds to poems as traces of the commentator's sensibility. The commentator writes not as the source of illumination but as the origin of vulnerability, having already subjected herself/himself to the unassumable obligation to catch up with the provocation of the poetic body. Hence, writing does not begin as discovery and immobilization but as a testimony and confession to the pre-original touch in the proximity of prayer and prophecy. It is baring my innermost in order to reveal the other, who is already the soul of my soul. Its saliency is tasted in "the verbal body of its singularity"[81] that opens onto sensibility.

In my view, compared with other hermeneutic theories, a Levinasian lyrical ethics is concerned less about theory than "the foundation of theory," that is, "the-one-for-the-other." This ethical imperative implicates the commentator before any form of commitment, intention, or assumption.[82] It alerts us to the reality that, beneath a reader's sensuous experience of poetry is "the exposure to alterity."[83] The detour from poetry to prose

---

77. Levinas, "Paul Celan," 41.
78. Idem, "Exercises on 'The Madness of the Day,'" 158; idem, *Otherwise than Being*, 169–70.
79. Ibid.
80. David Patterson, *Hebrew Language and Jewish Thought* (London: Routledge, 2005), 181. See Levinas, *Otherwise than Being*, 135.
81. Jacques Derrida, "Poetics and Politics of Witnessing," *Sovereignties in Question: The Poetics of Paul Celan*, ed. Thomas Dutoit and Outi Pasanen (New York: Fordham University Press, 2005), 66.
82. Levinas, *Otherwise than Being*, 136.
83. Lingis states, "Levinas wants to locate, beneath the sensuous exposure to material and as its basis, the exposure to alterity" ("Introduction," xxxiii).

goes back to the origin of poetry and ethics, the pre-original sensibility as subjectivity.

To conclude, by Lyrical Ethics, I emphasize a donation of oneself as *for the other* prior to reading and writing. The said of the commentaries justly differs from one respondent to another; still I am looking for the same saying, the same caress that testifies to the non-indifference of the commentator, which makes "one" a responsible "you."

Henceforth, when it comes to writing on the Song of Songs, I liken my taste to the taste of wine. Crushed and mixed with fresh air, the juice of ancient grapes seeps through the reader's senses, infusing the provoked vibrancy therein ever deeper into the soul. A long while will have passed before, out of the soul, the wine pours forth. It is delightfully aged, dry and hearty. No corny romance, no rowdy pornography, no occluded allegory. The good wines are the juice of the poems, fermented through the reader's attention and caress.

They do taste differently, given the infinite variations of the air and barrels that infuse and ferment the wines, as well as the palates that touch the wine. Every commentary on the Song is different from the Song. If the grapes do not die, we cannot make good wine. The difference, however, should not rest in the dichotomy between subject and object, on the commentator's power over the text, or ultimately, in the violence of indifference. If the commentator should ask "Am I its keeper?" then chances are that the indifferently produced comments would not make good wine.

The difference rests on the non-indifference of the lyrical and ethical encounter. The Song retains its flavors through reader's unreflected impressions, which assume the proximity of alterity. An ethical encounter with the Song is a happening where humanness is aroused; and the goodness of its commentary is in the non-indifference that ferments grapes into wine, in the singularity of the subject's responding to poetry's touch. It is manifested in the commentator's unrelenting attention, which one gives without holding back oneself as the medium of poetry. In their differences, Levinas's writings, the Song, and my prosaic response "meet up" in a poetic space that is also an ethical proximity.[84] In substitution, the poems are resurrected; in resurrection, my ethical self is summoned, as Levinas quotes Paul Celan, saying:

Ich bin du, wenn ich ich bin.[85]

---

84. In a similar vein, Jabès writes of Paul Celan: "I love the man who was my friend. And, in their differences, our books meet up" ("The Memory of Words," 217).

85. Paul Celan, "Lob der Ferne" ("Praise of Distance"), in *Gesammelte Werke*, ed. B. Allemann and S. Reichert (Frankfurt/Main: Suhrkamp, 1983), 1.33; quoted in Levinas, *Otherwise than Being*, 100.

Chapter 2

Oneself as Awakened Sensibility (Song 4:1–7)

> The origin of eros has been traced to delight in the beauty of others. This luring of the self-absorbed ego out of itself makes knowledge of others possible.[1]

Nothing more readily expresses one's acute sense of self than a poem that proffers one's impression of the other's beauty, such as Song 4:1–7. Unlike definition, which suppresses acquired personal feelings in order to achieve objectivity, poetry remains open to the original touch with which the other had awakened oneself in the aroused sensibility. With the particular substance of each word played as sound, shape, color, or taste, Song 4:1–7 esthetically regenerates the arousing moment between the subject's seeing and saying beauty.[2] From sensibility that sustains the contraction of the lover's provoked feelings, the poem springs forth as his provoked response to her beauty.[3] It reverberates in the vulnerable exuberance of her beauty, with which she has greeted him.[4] Between seeing and saying, the lover is drawn by the beloved's beauty to continuously fine-tune his approaching steps, until the exuberance of her beauty is tenderly infused in him and expressed in his approaching. As he approaches her through the poem, he is awakened as a human self—

> Small is the theme of the following Chant, yet the greatest namely, One's–Self—that wondrous thing a simple, separate person.[5]

---

1. Wendy Farley, *Eros for the Other: Retaining Truth in a Pluralistic World* (University Park: Pennsylvania State University Press, 1996), 85.
2. The inherent deferring reference of words enhances the richness of the short lyric as the words invite more words through family resemblance into the reading experience, evoking words and what they as symbols would evoke.
3. "I cannot see any basic difference," Paul Celan remarks, "between a handshake and a poem" (*Collected Prose*, ed. Rosemarie Waldrop (Manchester: Carcanet, 1986], 26). Or in a Bedouin woman's words, "[t]hose who sing feel something strongly in their hearts ['*agl*]" (Lila Abu-Lughod, *Veiled Sentiments: Honor and Poetry in a Bedouin Society* [Berkeley: University of California Press, 1986], 182).
4. "Not Homer alone but also Plato, Aquinas, Plotinus, Pseudo-Dionysius, Dante, and many others repeatedly describe beauty as a 'greeting'" (Elaine Scarry, *On Beauty and Being Just* [Princeton: Princeton University Press, 1999], 25–26).
5. Walt Whitman, "Inscription" (1867), in *Leaves of Grass: A Textual Variorum of the Printed Poems*, 3 vols., ed. Sculley Bradley et al. (New York: New York University Press,

28   Chapter 2

A Snapshot of Song 4:1–7

In the way that I present this poem in physical shape—lines and stanzas—I have already begun to reveal my impression of the poem. Though lineation appeals to visual reception, it primarily concerns the sonic aspect of a poem. Rorbet Pinsky points out that "the poem is something that one hears aloud, and the poem in print is a notation designed to make what one hears as clearly apprehensible as possible."[6] As line ending plays along with or against other lyrical dimensions such as syntax and content, their confluence or tension provides tangible suggestions for the audience's emotional participation.[7]

It is likely that the poet had a preferred lineation for Song 4:1–7, especially when it was performed orally. However, the authorial lineation does not survive in the manuscripts.[8] In the history of reception, the lineation of the Song of Songs varies in different textual traditions. The Qumran fragments (4QCant[a] and 4QCant[b]) are written in running texts (as also in the Peshiṭta); the Old Greek (OG) text usually lineates according to the lines of the couplets or triplets; in the *Biblia Hebraica Stuttgartensia* (BHS, also the new *Biblia Hebraica Quinta* [BHQ]) edition of the Masoretic Text (MT),[9] the editors lineate by couplets. Take, for example, their witnesses to Song 4:3:

4QCant[b] III 2 ii 4–5

šklm mtʾmwt w[šklh ʾyn]bhm ³kḥwṭ
hšny śptwtyk wmdbrk nʾwh kplḥ hrmwn[10]

1980), 557. In this poem, which was the inscription to the fourth edition of *Leaves of Grass*, Whitman positioned himself as "waiting his readers with open arms" (Ezra Greenspan, *Walt Whitman and the American Reader* [Cambridge: Cambridge University Press, 1990], 222). He reworked this poem in 1871 and entitled it "One's-Self I Sing," and in 1888 as "Small the Theme of My Chant." The current critical collection chooses the 1888 version in the main text and notes the 1867 version in footnotes.

6. Robert Pinsky, *The Sounds of Poetry* (New York: Farrar, Straus & Giroux, 1998), 43.

7. James Longenbach, *The Art of the Poetic Lines* (St. Paul, MN: Graywolf, 2008), 14, 43.

8. Early manuscripts, such as the Masoretic and the Qumran texts, do not demonstrate lineation (James L. Kugel, *The Idea of Biblical Poetry: Parallelism and Its History* [New Haven, CT: Yale University Press, 1981], 121; Emmanuel Tov, "Special Layout of Poetical Units in the Texts from the Judean Desert," in *Give Ear to My Words: Psalms and Other Poetry in and around the Hebrew Bible—Essays in Honour of Professor N. A. van Uchelen*, ed. J. Dyk et al. (Amsterdam: Societas Hebraica Amstelodamensis, 1996], 115–28). The Old Greek version is the first to show consistent lineation; for the OG text with textual notes, see Jay Treat, *Lost Keys: Text and Interpretation in Old Greek Song of Songs and Its Earliest Manuscript Witnesses* (Ph.D. diss., University of Pennsylvania, 1996).

9. It should be noted that BHS and BHQ are not to be confused as a textual tradition in the same league with the OG and Qumran texts. I enlist them here more for the purpose of questioning the contemporary readers' assumption of its lineation. In other words, the ground of comparison among these three versions of lineation is the sphere of readerly reception instead of textual criticism. The base text behind BHS and BHQ, Codex Leningrad, does not lineate the Song.

10. Emmanuel Tov, "Introduction to 4QCant[a–c]," in *Les 'Petites Grottes' de Qumran (Plates), Discoveries in the Judaean Desert* 16 [Oxford: Clarendon, 2000], 213. 4QCant[a] has

All of them bear twins, and none is bereft. Like a scarlet
thread, your lips, and your mouth, lovely. Like a slit pomegranate . . .

OG

ὡς σπαρτίον τὸ κόκκινον χείλη σου,
καὶ ἡ λαλιά σου ὡραία.[11]
Like a scarlet thread, your lips,
and your mouth, lovely.

BHS/BHQ

kĕḥûṭ haššānî siptōtayik ûmidbārêk nāʾweh
Like a scarlet thread, your lips; and your mouth, lovely.

Without lineation, 4QCant[b] reflects the greatest gap between the oral performance and the written reference. However, its lack of inscriptional evidence for lineation does not mean that the poem is not perceived in terms of the aural experience that line endings suggest. More likely, to reconstitute the aural experience fully, readers of running text are required to know the text by heart, to allow the words to waft and morph in the mind's eye, to touch each other and gradually reach a configuration that is also congenial to the reader's sensibility. This process is comparable to that of oral poetry in that lineation is "a matter of degree and of judgment" in how to reproduce the poem.[12] In other words, lineation for poems that are not inscribed in lines (such as biblical Hebrew poetry) is more a matter of the performer's phonetic, syntactic, and thematic configuration of the poem. Of course, this judgment is not absolutely free of textual constraints, so relative boundaries can be drawn for the lineation of biblical Hebrew poetry based on stylistic, syntactic, and scribal indicators.

The OG and BHS/BHQ texts reflect just these sorts of attempts—to inscribe the hints of a meaningful configuration of the poem that the translators and editors hear. The lineation in OG gives more time and space to each line, so that the "scarlet thread" (4:3) colors and saturates the audience's senses with greater intensity, especially when the line briskly ends at "your lips." Prodded by this pausing, would not the audience desire more to come? This teased thirst, after being fermented in the silence (or the empty space) marked by the line ending is soothed with what resembles a velvety wine: "your mouth, um, lovely." The lingering thirst is temporarily quenched as the words glide down and reinforced as the second line ends. More attention to each line also allows the audience to savor the images more. But above all, the two syntactically complete lines find themselves

---

the first two words of this verse (except the *h*) in col. II frg. 5, line 10. The rest is reconstructed in line 11 (p. 202).

11. The text also shows one empty line above, indicating a stanza break (Treat, "Lost Keys," 60).

12. Ruth H. Finnegan, *Oral Poetry: Its Nature, Significance, and Social Context* (Cambridge: Cambridge University Press, 1977), 106.

thematically and stylistically dependent on each other by way of chiasmus. The formal straightforwardness that derives from the confluence between the line and syntax is ruffled by the tension between the line ending and the content. Evoked simultaneously in the reading, these effects subtly enhance the tease of the images.

In contrast, the lines structured in BHS/BHQ accentuate the thematic unity that usually requires a larger poetic unit (couplet or sometimes triplet). For example, in Song 4:3 a chiasmus unifies the two lines. Through "your lips" "and your mouth," the initial sensation of "a scarlet thread" is absorbed and then generalized as "lovely" at the end of the line. The dramatic line ending between the two lines in OG is reduced to a two-letter empty space, which, in its brief respite, enhances the chiasmus.

Furthermore, vertically, throughout the poem the lineation of BHS/BHQ helps to elucidate how the poem is structured along the beloved's seven bodily features.[13] The lyric body is formally marked by the sound play of the consonant *kap*. Marking both the pronominal suffix "your/you" (*-k*) and the preposition "like" (*k-*), this consonant adjoins the subjects and the metaphors in the first half of the couplets that describe the features. What are left out of these seven features (4:1a and 7) constitute an inclusio (4:1a and 7) that frames a bust portrait of the beloved.

In a closer reading based on this lineation, one also finds that the first two features encapsulate one couplet each, while the third ("your teeth") generates two couplets; the fourth and fifth features again involve one couplet each, while the sixth ("your neck") has two couplets. This micro tripartite structure, emphasizing the third as the last and the different, cultivates in the audience an expectation for the third stanza, the climax of the macro tripartite structure.[14] In the last stanza, one finds that, first, the word order in 4:5a–b reverts to the word order of the first stanza (bodily features metaphors). Hence, it creates a subtle sense of closure around the registry of her bodily members. Second, the couplets, decorous in form and syntax, give way to the only triplet of this poem. This formal shift emulates his peaking passion at visually caressing the seventh feature—her breasts: his control over rhythm is loosened as, it seems, his breath becomes irregular. Third, when the couplets resume in 4:6—functioning like the added couplet for the third and the sixth features (plus one more to extend the climax)—it seems that the lover has regained his control and stability after the short swirl. However, here the two couplets form an enjambed sentence. The overstretched syntax, in the same certainty that lines of couplets

---

13. The seven invocations of her bodily features appear in vv. 1b, 1c, 2a, 3a, 3b, 4a, 4b, and 5a. This counts "your lips" and "your mouth" in 4:3 as one, which is in part motivated by the need to use 14 times the pronominal suffix "you/your" that runs through the poem (except for v. 6).

14. The tripartite structure utilizes the common folk rhythm: "one, two, and the third, the different!" In the Song, the third *lô* ("not" letting him go) in 3:1–5 reverses the previous two ("not" finding him). One finds a similar rhythm in children's stories such as the "Three Little Pigs" and "Goldilocks and the Three Bears."

Oneself as Awakened Sensibility (Song 4: 31

have accumulated, resembles a wish cast in one long breath that only a desire of higher intensity can sustain. Finally, the generic constraint of *waṣf* —describing and praising the object—is exploded at the thematic front as the lover sets himself *in* the lyric picture, poised to "go to" that which he has so amorously praised (4:6).

Considering these inscriptional choices and their effects, I will present Song 4:1-7 in an eclectic manner, which is also familiar to the readers of English translations (e.g., the NRSV). I lineate by the lines to indicate the basic level of the poetic unit; and by indenting the second line of the couplet (and the third line, if it is a triplet), the thematic emphasis on the first line would still be marked. I also insert empty lines between the body of the poem and the *inclusio*, as well as between the stanzas. Such textual spatiality manifests in inscription, through the analogy of white space and silence, the aural experience that I recommend.

1a*hinnāk yāpâ rāyātî*	1aAh, you are fair, my dear,
b*hinnāk yāpâ*	bah, you are fair!
1c*'ênayik yônîm*	1cYour eyes, oh, doves,
d*mibba'ad lĕṣammātēk*[a]	dfrom behind your veil.
1e*śa'rēk kĕ'ēder hā'izzîm*	1eYour hair—like a flock of goats,
f*šeggālšû*[b] *mēhar gil'ād*	fthat cascade down from Mt. Gilead.
2a*šinnayik kĕ'ēder haqqĕṣûbôt*	2aYour teeth—like a flock of shorn ones,
b*šĕ'ālû min-hārahṣâ*	bthat come up from the washing;

---

a. We are uncertain what the veil looks like. Ancient translations vary in their understanding: "that which lies hid within" (Vulg.: *eo quod intrinsecus latet*), "your silence" (Syr.: *štqby*), "your laying" (Syh.: dsm' dylby; α': θεματός σου). The exact noun is used in the Song and Isa 47:2. Her dark face seems to imply that she does not veil (Dianne Bergant, *The Song of Songs*, Berit Olam [Collegeville, MN: Liturgical Press, 2001], 44). Or as M. Goulder suggests, she wears a transparent veil that covers the entire face, a "diaphanous muslin gauze" (*The Song of Fourteen Songs*, JSOTSup 36 [Sheffield: JSOT Press, 1986], 33). However, relying on poetic description for a representation of a real person is methodologically problematic. For instance, the lover also states that her neck is ivory colored (7:4). From a sociohistorical perspective, it was not common for women to wear veils in ancient Israel (Jill M. Munro, *Spikenard and Saffron: The Imagery of the Song of Songs*, JSOTSup 203 [Sheffield: Sheffield Academic Press, 1995], 53–54). In Assyria, wives and daughters of free men veiled themselves when going outdoors, while female prostitutes and slaves were unveiled (Othmar Keel, *The Song of Songs: A Continental Commentary* [Minneapolis: Fortress, 1994], 141). Israelite women had their heads, shoulders, and sometimes faces draped with a veil (*ṣā'îp*) on special occasions (Gen 24:65; 38:14, 19). A Lachish relief from Nineveh shows the women of a Lachish family wearing a long shawl framing the face on both sides and draping to the hem of their cloaks (Philip J. King and Lawrence E. Stager, *Life in Biblical Israel*, Library of Ancient Israel [Louisville: Westminster John Knox, 2001], illustrations 138, 267, 272). In short, the girl's shawl was probably left draping next to her face most of the time, when she went out and labored in the vineyards (Song 1:6). When she meets her lover, however, she might lift up her shawl to cover her face, as Rebekah veiled herself immediately before meeting Isaac (Gen 24:65). The way Bedouin women use their veils also confirms this practice (Abu-Lughod, *Veiled Sentiments*, 137, 161).

b. The reconstructed text of 4QCant[a] shows that the verb is a *qal* active participle ([*šglš*] *wt*). The OG and Vulg. manifest different Hebrew verbs: *šeggālû* (OG: ἀπεκαλύφθησαν) and *šĕ'ālû* (Vulg.: *ascenderunt*). Based on an Ugaritic cognate, S. S. Tuell proposes translating the

²ᶜ šekkullām matʾîmôt	²ᶜAll of them bear twins,
ᵈwešakkūlâ ʾên bāhem	ᵈand bereavement is not in them.
³ᵃ kěḥût haššānî siptōtayik	³ᵃLike a scarlet thread, your lips,
ᵇûmidbārēk nāʾweh	ᵇand your mouth, so lovely.
³ᶜ kěpelaḥ hārimmôn raqqātēk ᶜ	³ᶜLike a slit pomegranate, your palate,
ᵈmibbaʿad lěṣammātēk	ᵈfrom behind your veil.
⁴ᵃ kěmigdal dāwîd ṣawwāʾrēk	⁴ᵃLike the Tower of David, your neck,
ᵇbānûy lětalpiyyôt ᵈ	ᵇbuilt in courses;
⁴ᶜʾelep hammāgēn tālûy ʿālāyw	⁴ᶜa thousand of shields hang on it,
ᵈkōl šiltê haggibôrîm	ᵈall bucklers of warriors.
⁵ᵃ šěnê šādayik kišnê ʿŏpārîm	⁵ᵃYour two breasts—like two fawns,
ᵇ těʾômê ṣěbiyyâ	ᵇtwins of a gazelle,
ᶜhārôʿîm baššôšannîm	ᶜgrazing among the lilies.
⁶ᵃ ʿad šeyyāpûaḥ hayyôm	⁶ᵃTill the day breathes,
ᵇ wěnāsû hassělālîm	ᵇand the shadows flee,
⁶ᶜ ʾelek lîʾ el-har hammôr	⁶ᶜlet me go to the mountain of myrrh,
ᵈ wě ʾel-gibʿat hallěbônâ	ᵈand to the hill of frankincense.
⁷ᵃ kullāk yāpâ raʿyātî	⁷ᵃAll of you is beautiful, my dear,
ᵇ ûmûm ʾên bāk	ᵇand no flaw is in you!

verb as "to flow in waves" ("A Riddle Resolved by an Enigma: Hebrew *glš* and Ugaritic *glṯ*," *JBL* 112 [1993]: 99–104). Tremper Longman III adjusts Tuell's translation to "to stream down," since the subject is a flock of goats, not hair (*The Song of Songs*, NICOT [Grand Rapids, MI: Eerdmans, 2001], 142).

c. There are several opinions regarding how to translate *raqqâ*, which appears twice in the Song (4:3 and 6:7) and three times in Judges (4:21–22, 5:26). First, it is traditionally rendered "temples" (KJV). M. Rozelaar challenges this view by pointing out the number disagreement between the Hebrew singular and the English plural as well as the implied awkward position given the narrative situation in Judges. He suggests that the narrative situation in Judges makes the opened mouth a more felicitous choice, which also fits the downward movement in the poems of the Song of Songs ("An Unrecognized Part of the Human Anatomy," *Judaism* 37 [1988]: 97–101). Second, and similar to the first option, the OG and Vulg. translate the noun "cheeks." The Hebrew word "cheeks" is used in Song 1:10 (*lěḥāyayik*) and 5:13 (*lěḥāyāw*). Again, these usages of *lěḥî* are properly dual, in contrast to the singular state of *raqqātēk*. Third, 4QCantᵃ witnesses *mzqntk*, which is probably connected to *zākān*, "chin" (Tov, "Introduction to 4QCantᵃ⁻ᶜ," 200). However, 4QCantᵇ maintains *rqtk* (ibid., 214). Fourth, Keel points out that a slit (not slices) in the pomegranate is always present in Egyptian paintings. He proposes translating *raqqâ* as "palate" (*Song of Songs*, 138, 143–46). The girl's invitation for the boy to drink of *mēʿăsîs rimmōnî* ("the juice of my pomegranate"; Song 8:2b)—that is, to kiss her deeply—further supports this translation. Briefly, a slit pomegranate may visually resemble the girl's slightly open mouth, and its delicious taste that of her sweet palate. Last, the choice of this word may have been prompted by the strain of the vowel pattern *a-ā-ē* in conjunction with the rhyming *-ēk* in 4:3a–b.

d. Though the general sense of a tiered structure is agreed upon by all, its specific meaning is much debated (A. M. Honeyman, "Two Contributions to Canaanite Toponymy," *JTS* 50 [1949]: 50–52). For a historical sketch, see Marvin H. Pope, *The Song of Songs: A New Translation with Introduction and Commentary*, AB 7C (Garden City, NY: Doubleday, 1977), 170–73.

Though it would be a close analogy, a bust portrait could not fully capture the lyrical movement, as one follows the lover's visual tracing of his beloved's upper body and is led to an exit out of this tracing, to a leaping out of words preserved in words. Visual representation alone remains preliminary, for it stops the reader from being fully immersed in the poetic words, in its texture, affect, and significance. These aspects are important in the reader's reception of the poem, because they not only testify to the awakening of the lover's self at the sight of his beloved's beautiful body but also provoke the awakening of the reader's self, which comes in contact with another beautiful body—that is, the poem. There is no alternative other than diving into the poem to relive its originary moment.

In the following pages, therefore, I will spend more time on this poem than on subsequent poems in later chapters, in order to alert readers to the details of this groundbreaking moment. I will comb through the poem with four intertwined topics. Each reading will layer over and interact with the others to gesture toward the infinite richness of lyrical experience. In the first section, "Delight," I will deepen the reading of the poem by fleshing out the outline. In this process, the underlying pulsation of the lover's feeling that inspires and permeates the poem will be revived. The following section traces the caress, the "Touch" that arouses the lover before his saying (and the readers before listening to) the poem. The third section, "Approach," will then establish sensibility as the ethical ground where the other appears to the self, and the self approaches the other. Finally, by elaborating on the lover's wish to go to his beloved in Song 4:6, I will draw out an ethical approach to a beautiful other when one is aroused by the erotic "Desire." In contrast to other instances in Scripture (such as David and Bathsheba), where a man obscures a woman's and his own humanness by approaching her in an ultramaterial way, this poem embodies an ethical approach that summons oneself in response to the other's calling. So here we go.

Delight

If, as William Blake claims, "Exuberance is Beauty,"[15] Song 4:1–7 is a beauty praising beauty. Exuberance is felt immediately in the opening phrase: *hinnāk yāpâ rāyātî* ("Ah, you are fair, my dear"). The presentative particle *hinnê* opens the poetic space in vivid immediacy, in "the here-and-now-ness of the situation."[16] With such a full-blown exclamation, it also

---

15. William Blake, "The Marriage of Heaven and Hell," *Blake's Poetry and Designs*, ed. Mary Lynn Johnson and John E. Grant, 2nd ed. (New York: Norton, 2008), 73.

16. T. O. Lambdin, *Introduction to Biblical Hebrew* (New York: Scribner, 1971), 168; see also *IBHS*, 675. F. I. Andersen proposes categorizing the particle as a "perspectival presentative predicator": it signals a switch of perspective to the viewpoint of a character, presents a new element in a discourse in a quasi-verbal predicating function ("Lo and Behold! Taxonomy and Translation of Biblical Hebrew *hnh*," in *Hamlet on a Hill: Semitic and Greek Studies Presented to Professor T. Muraoka on the Occasion of His 65th Birthday*, ed. M. F. J.

emulates the dilation of the lover's pupils upon seeing his beloved. Were not a theatrical enthusiasm necessary to set the tone for this poem, the lover might say, without *hinnê*, as in Song 6:4: *yāpâ 'att rāyātî* ("fair are you, my dear").[17]

This initial sensation, which is short and repeated in a chiastic structure centering on *rāyātî*, reaches to an even higher level of affirmation in 4:7. There the closure is sealed in hyperbole[18] through the antithetical parallel of "all" (*kōl*) and "none" (*'ên*) that hinges on *rāyātî*. Visually and thematically, the two micro chiastic rings form a macro ring, an inclusio around the poem. The center of the two mini rings, the direct address *rāyātî*, simultaneously invokes "you" and specifies one of "your" identities that matters to "me." With the vocative being set like a diamond on a ring, this poem already reveals its underlying saying as a charged response to her beauty rather than a dispassionate observation.[19] Like the boy's arms embracing the girl (see 2:6, 8:3), the inclusio circles the body of the poem, situating every word in "my" infatuation for "you."[20]

In the main body of the poem, the upswing of exuberance is intriguingly mapped through the lover's downward gaze, which traces seven of the beloved's bodily features in three phases (4:1c–2d; 3a–4d; 5a–6c). Her bodily features juxtaposed to their respective metaphors consist of two vertical threads that are crossed horizontally by the seven threads of his extolment. The lover's ardent longing to adhere to her body and his outpouring of delight spilling into metaphors, therefore, constitute the warp and weft that interweaves this poem.

To begin with, the first stanza (4:1c–2d) invokes and praises three features: *'ênayik* ("your eyes," 4:1c), *śa'rēk* ("your hair," 4:1e) and *šinnayik*

Baasten, and W. T. van Peursen [Leuven: Peeters, 2003], 52–56). Moreover, as Robert S. Kawashima points out, *hinnê* adds an expressive force to the succeeding clause in biblical narratives (*Biblical Narrative and the Death of the Rhapsode* [Bloomington: Indiana University Press, 2005], 84–85).

17. Similarly, the presentations of Sarai's beauty happen both with *hinnê* in Abram's emotion-laden exclamation to her (Gen 12:11) and without *hinnê*, in the Egyptians' observation (Gen 12:14). Psalm 133 offers yet another example of the way that initial *hinnê* sets an exuberant tone for the whole poem; see F. W. Dobbs-Allsopp, "Psalm 133: A (Close) Reading," *JHebS* 8/20 (*Journal of Hebrew Scriptures* [2008]: 4–5, www.jhsonline.org/Articles/article_97.pdf [accessed on April 22, 2015]).

18. Compare the hyperbolic praise of Absalom's beauty in 2 Sam 14:25. At the beginning of Khalil Gibran's poem "A Lover's Call XXVII" (*The Khalil Gibran Megapack 43 Classic Works* [Rockville, MD: Wildside, 2013], 450–51), one also reads how, out of love's affection, the young lover praises the beloved as an ethereal perfection.

19. Emmanuel Levinas has contrasted personal speech with a vocative to impersonal discourse out of "a Universal Reason" (*Proper Names* [Stanford, CA: Stanford University Press, 1996], 130–31).

20. Taking the inclusio as a frame, the poem physically evokes the scene in 2:9, where the young man peeks at his beloved through the window (F. W. Dobbs-Allsopp, "The Delight of Beauty and Song of Songs 4:1–7," *Int* [2005]: 270).

("your teeth," 4:2a). The repeated second-person pronouns hark back to the introductory *hinnāk*, while the three individual features give flesh to the abstract "you." Standing at the beginning of the lines, these three words form key knots along the vertical thread, as well as torn openings to horizontal excursions. Fittingly, the excursions travel to the center from three spatial peripheries, which are marked by the preposition *min* ("from")."*From behind* your veils," your gaze comes to the front; "*from* Mt. Gilead," the goats cascade down; "*from* the washing," the shorn ewes come up. On the semantic level, these centripetal movements mime how at first, the eyes, wherever they have been, become attracted to the beloved, who will remain at the center of the beholder's vision. Furthermore, after the exuberant introduction, the first stanza easies the audience's way into the poem, selecting features that are black or white, which befit the images of gentle animals like rock doves, goats, and ewes. The audience soothingly strolls through balanced poetic lines[21] without feeling pressured to stir up sensations before the poem is ready.

When the poem unrolls the second stanza (4:3a–4d), however, the black and white painting is instantly plunged into a sensual splash of colors. Metaphors lead the similes that praise the second set of three features: *siptōtayik/midbārêk* ("lips" and "mouth," 4:3a), *raqqātēk* ("palate," 4:3c), *ṣammātēk* ("neck," 4:4a). The very first phrase, "like a scarlet thread" (*kĕḥûṭ haššānî*), drops and smears on the black and white background a provocative red that is limited by its thinness.[22] It provokes an enticing elusiveness that grows dizzyingly stronger by morphing into an abstract adjective: *nāʾweh* ("lovely"). Between waves of vivid images, this abstraction creates a pause, a deliberate ambiguity, alluding to a savoring beyond words (cf. Song 1:2, 4:6). While the double reference to lips and mouth shows the lover-admirer's emphatic attention to these features, it is of teasingly light strokes and is transitional in function: the dual noun *siptōtayik* assumes

---

21. The couplets about the eye (4:1b) have two words per line, with a syllable count of 5/7. The longer words in the second line smooth the transition from the short opening line to the longer lines in the main body. Also, each of the couplets in 4:1c and 2a has three words and similar syllable counts (15 and 17). However, 4:2a has more syllables in its first line: 3 + 3 + 4 // 3 + 1 + 3. This imbalance, in a way, prepares for the elaboration in 4:2b. Though in 4:2b the first line has three words and the second two, their syllable counts are very close: 3 + 3 // 4 + 1 + 2. All this being said, one needs to keep in mind that word and syllable counts are a means to reach a relative sense of the musicality of the poem, because Hebrew poetry does not conform to strict and/or sustained meter. For instance, a syllable can be ultra long (*-bôt*) or very short (*kĕ-*). The different values of these syllables are marginalized in this analysis.

22. Based on its physical image of thinness, "thread" derives the figurative meanings of "the least" (Gen 14:23) and "easily broken" (Judg 16:12, Qoh 4:12). The ultimate elusiveness of the mouth/lips is seen in its absence in 6:5b–7, which repeats 4:1c–3a nearly verbatim.

the duality of the teeth (4:2); in its polyvalence ("mouth" or "speech"),[23] *midbārêk* reintroduces her mouth as a delicious opening (4:3b). Then a slit pomegranate materializes the latter vision. The slit opening sucks the audience's attention into the delicious inside of the pomegranate and, in the same breath, the beloved's mouth, in terms of its deeper red color and its succulent taste that is like "spiced wine" (Song 8:2). In this line, the lover lingers on and intensifies his longing for her lips and mouth.[24] The repeated second line, *mibbaʿad lĕṣammātēk* ("from behind your veil"), furthermore, frames the face of his beloved,[25] as it stages the movements of drawing out her eyes (4:1b) and sinking into her mouth (4:3b).

After such sweet little talk, "the Tower of David" (*migdal dāwîd*) raises visual heights that solicit psychological respect. The sublimity shown in the posture of her neck restrains his erotic urgency from slipping into egoistic dominance over the other.[26] It is further reinforced through the military imageries depicting her necklace (*ʾelep hammāgēn* and *šiltê haggibôrîm*). The leaves of the necklace also serve as a metallic base to her face.[27] And what a glowing face it must be that needs a foil such as the glamor of thousands of shining pieces! In this stanza, a long-short rhythm also regulates the two lines of the couplets, swinging the audience's breath between the heightened image and its tender detailing.[28]

---

23. Though the former is in the foreground, the latter remains evocative and insinuates the opening of her mouth as she speaks. This contrasts the singular form of *ḥût* in 4:3a, which implies her closed lips.

24. Note the girl's wish to kiss the boy in two stages (8:1-2): *ʾeššāqĕkā* ("I would kiss you") and then *ʾašqĕkā . . . mēʿăsîs rimmōnî* ("I would let you drink . . . the juice of my pomegranate").

25. Bergant, *Song of Songs*, 45.

26. "Hebrew associates the neck with an attitude, not with a particular form"—for instance, "pride" (Ps 75:5-6), "proudly" (Job 15:26), and "inviolable" (Ps 48:12-13; Keel, *Song of Songs*, 147). "Tower of David" corroborates this cultural sentiment with its connotations of a proud dynasty and David as a great warrior. Because no literary or archaeological evidence of this tower has been found, this phrase may very likely be a lyrical creation that underscores the grandeur of the image (Robert W. Jenson, *Song of Songs* [Interpretation (Louisville: John Knox, 2005], 44). This is in contrast to the superficial arousal that Plato detests: one who looks upon beauty "with no reverence" is superficially aroused and thus goes about, after "the fashion of a four-footed beast" (Plato, *Plato's Phaedrus*, trans. R. Hackforth [New York: Liberal Arts, 1952], 250E, 96).

27. After praising her neck, the lover wishes to make beads for his beloved (1:10-11). The covert metaphor of shields, following the overt metaphor of the Tower of David, refers to the necklace worn over her neck (Keel, *Song of Songs*, 147; figs. 14-16, 44). The shields may refer to the gold leaves on the necklace, like those found on the "wreath of lapis lazuli and carnelian with gold poplar leaves from the 'Great Death Pit' (PG 1237)," which were worn by female attendants in the Ur III royal tombs (Lee Horne, "Ur and Its Treasures: The Royal Tombs," *Expedition* 40/2 [1998]: 4-11, fig. 6).

28. The word counts of the couplets are 3-2 in 4:3a-4a and 4-3 in 4:4b. Robert Gordis notes also that the 3-2 *kinah* rhythm predominates in the second *waṣf* (*The Song of Songs; A Study, Modern Translation, and Commentary* [New York: Jewish Theological Seminary of America, 1954], 87).

After repeating these two formally mirrored units (or stanzas), the climax is easily discerned, when the seventh feature appears in 4:5. Indeed climax comes as difference. The lover is able to mention the beloved's breasts. Then the inherent tension in the poem—intense seeing arouses a desire to touch but prevents its realization (because of the required visual distance)—explodes after the perfect cycle of seven. The erotic energy, which has been worked up to the rim as the lover's gaze moves down, bursts open the generic constraint of invoking and praising her bodily features and flows toward a poetically performed rendezvous in 4:6.

Though the invocation ceases at 4:5, the sense of wholeness is symbolized in the sevenfold invocation of her bodily features and the fourteen appearances of the second-person pronoun.[29] Also the wholeness of her body, which has been compromised in the metonymic unfolding of individual bodily members, is reunited in the concluding phrase "all of you" (*kullāk*; 4:7a). With these literary devices, the lover is able to invest the quality of perfect beauty in his beloved, without poring over a slavishly realistic portrait.

This investiture of perfection signifies, however, something other than that the beloved is perfectly beautiful. In fact, after introducing the young man as desirable and popular (1:1–4), the girl herself immediately juxtaposes her (culturally) undesirable complexion to his popularity: "I am dark and/but lovely" (*šĕḥôrâ ʾănî wĕnāwâ*; 1:5).[30] In spite of her confident tone, the fact that she defends herself at the very beginning of her self introduction betrays a sense of insecurity: "Am I good enough for him?" This twofold self-portrait becomes the initial page to the lover's following portraitures of her, which, by focusing on her loveliness, erases her insecurity buried under "I am dark." The significance of the hyperbolic assertions that permeate his praises, therefore, lies not in its possibility but its impossibility, for however much the real is short of the perfect, the lover's exuberant

---

29. The springboard of conventional symbolism assists the leap from the concrete parts to the conceptual whole, because the number 7 has the symbolic value of perfection. Just to name a few: the 7 days of the creation cycle (Gen 1:1–2:4); Jacob bowed to Esau 7 times when they met (Gen 33:3); the cultic calendar, such as the Sabbath day, the Passover offering, the festival of unleavened bread (Lev 23:3–8), is punctuated by the cycle of 7; the Israelites were confronted with 7 nations greater than them (Deut 7:1); all the men of war encompassed the city of Jericho 7 times in one day (Josh 6:4). What the 7 bodily features and the 14 pronominal suffixes meaning "you/your" symbolize, therefore, is that "your body is perfect; and as for you, you are doubly perfect!"

30. The conjunction *waw* effects a poetic ambiguity. It can be contrastive: I am dark, *but* I am lovely. This reading invests more self-defense into her self-introduction. Or it can be assertive: I am dark and lovely. This interpretation takes a cue from her celebrated independence that defies social norm (cf. F. W. Dobbs-Allsopp, "I Am Black *and* Beautiful": The Song, Cixous, and Écriture Féminine," in *Engaging the Bible in a Gendered World: An Introduction to Feminist Biblical Interpretation in Honor of Katharine Doob Sakenfeld*, ed. Linda Day and Carolyn Pressler [Louisville: Westminster John Knox, 2006], 129–30).

admiration compensates. His literally untrue statement[31] expresses most authentically the excess of sensation over sense. With hyperbole, he speaks more in significance and less in description. Saying "*all* of you is beautiful" (4:7) is already a confession and witness of love: "I truly love you, truly I do."[32]

As a matter of fact, one cannot, in expectation of a realistic representation, accuse the lover of being color-blind. What he sings to her is not an amatory memo or a pornographic slide show. A man in love describes his beloved so extravagantly, David Hume says, that you really can discern nothing of the real girl from his description:

> . . . so complete a shape; such well-proportioned features; so engaging an air; such sweetness of disposition; such gaiety of humour. You can infer nothing, however, from all this discourse, but that the poor man is in love; and that the general appetite between the sexes, which nature has infused into all animals, is in him determined to a particular object by some qualities which give him pleasure. The same divine creature, not only to a different animal, but also to a different man, appears a mere mortal being, and is beheld with utmost indifference.[33]

From the perfect state or qualities ascribed to his beloved, a sympathetic audience catches, above all, the intensity of the lover's feeling, which is consequential to having his living "appetite" pleased. When the aroused erotic energy implodes at the sight of the beloved, the lover's vision is blinded by excessive illumination from within.[34] It mingles and magnifies her radiance, hallowing her like a goddess who "looks forth like the dawn" (Song 6:10). Or "like a sun, which it was somehow possible to stare at and which was coming nearer and nearer, letting itself be seen at close quarters, dazzling you with its blaze of red and gold,"[35] says Proust of the face of a girl selling milk at the train station. Proust is dazzled, not because he does

---

31. Similar poetic manipulation of opinions instead of truths is found in regard to the volume of the girl's breasts. Her brothers think she has no breasts (8:8), while she contends that her breasts are voluptuous like towers (8:10).

32. There is circularity in the lover's perception of the beloved's beauty. Beauty invites love; love inflames beauty. Even if the beloved is not the most beautiful girl to other beholders, she can radiate beauty and exuberance when she sees her lover. The enflaming, transfiguring force of love qualifies the assertion that the idealness of the beloved in the lover's eyes is purely invested.

33. David Hume, "Of the Delicacy of Taste and Passion," *Selected Essays*, ed. Stephen Copley and Andrew Edgar (New York: Oxford University Press, 1993), 97–98. Stendhal (M. H. Beyle) calls this phenomenon "crystallization": the lover studs real perception with "a galaxy of scintillating diamonds," in the same way that the small twig is deposited with salt crystals in the mines of Salzburg (*Maxims of Love*, trans. Suzanne and Gilbert Sale [London: Merlin, 1959], 45).

34. Martha Craven Nussbaum, "'Faint with Secret Knowledge': Love and Vision in Murdoch's 'The Black Prince,'" *Poetics Today* 25 (2004): 691.

35. Marcel Proust, *Remembrance of Things Past*, trans. C. K. Scott Moncrieff and Terence Kilmartin (New York: Vintage-Random House, 1982), 1.706–7.

not see clearly enough, but precisely because he "devours every detail of the real presence." This is what happened to Bradley Pearson in Iris Murdoch's book *The Black Prince*. Pearson recalled years later in the following words the moment when he sat with Julian Baffin (who was then an ordinary teenage girl) in the restaurant on the top of London's Post Office Tower:

> Consciousness half swoons with its sense of humble delighted privilege while keen sight, in between the explosions of the stars, devours every detail of the real presence. I am here now, you are here now, we are here now. To see her among others, straying like a divine form among mortals, is to become faint with secret knowledge.[36]

Pearson's intense seeing unleashes a blinding joy, for as Martha Nussbaum says, "[I]rrigating oneself with the water of the loved one's beauty brings the summit of pleasure."[37] After each deep sip of her beauty, he is transported away, in the explosive force of eros, from the thought of perceiving her body. He cannot remain fully conscious in the presence of his beloved; but he always pedals back. The sensual upheaval streaming in through the eye temporarily satiates and simultaneously creates longing for more, since happiness demands its persistence.[38] The weakening of one explosion enables and prompts him to come back to take another sip, and another, and another. Thus the lover's vision is interrupted and brought together by erotic delight that pulsates between extreme receptivity and exuberant outburst. It is feeling at its fullest volume.

The rhythm of erotic vision, its keen sight between blinding explosions, is inscribed in Song 4:1–7 as the invocation of a series of bodily features and a de-centering elaboration on each feature. Juxtaposed with each bodily feature is a metaphor. Metaphor, in its etymological sense, means "to transport" (*meta-pherin*), that is, it "carries the thought beyond the theme thought."[39] Syntactically in our present poem, the metaphorical train to the beyond typically whistles away at the signal of the comparative preposition *kĕ-*, which is attached to the metaphors (4:1e, 2a, 3a, 3c, 4a, and 5a).[40] This preposition bridges a bodily feature to its metaphorical image while maintaining their difference.[41] Its simultaneous fissuring and annexing effect is further facilitated by the lack of copula between the bodily

---

36. Iris Murdoch, *The Black Prince* (London: Penguin, 1975), 239.
37. Nussbaum, "Faint with Secret Knowledge," 693.
38. Scarry, *On Beauty and Being Just*, 22–23, 29–30.
39. Emmanuel Levinas, "Exercise on 'The Madness of the Day,'" in idem, *Proper Names*, trans. Michael B. Smith (London: Athlone, 1996), 156. See also Julia Kristeva, "Le Cantique des cantiques," in *La Bible et l'autre: Les dialogues bibliques du Collège des Études Juives de l'Alliance Israélite Universelle tenus de 1998 à 2002 en collaboration avec l'Université de Paris IV–Sorbonne*, ed. Shmuel Trigano (Paris: Édition In Press, 2002), 71.
40. The lack of this preposition in 4:1c reflects a reaching back to 1:15 with intentional difference. I will discuss this feature in the third section of this chapter, "Approach."
41. Cf. Anne Carson, *Eros the Bittersweet* (Normal, IL: Dalkey Archive, 1998), 73.

member and its metaphor.⁴² Their juxtaposition enhances the eroticizing vacillation presented by metaphor before becoming a predication and being compressed into a single *gestalt*. The verbless syntax, the preposition *kĕ-* and the metaphor together inscribe a dynamic mental expansiveness beneath the grammatically configured predication, so much so that "the text is no longer to be considered in it[s] linearity, but in its spatiality, its volume."⁴³

Through this mental act of transportation, the lover of our poem drifts away from the real details of his beloved's body, as Pearson does, but, instead of encountering the explosion of stars, his vision is blinded by vivid images. The richly elaborated images overlay and obscure an actual perception of her bodily features.⁴⁴ The lover pours so much energy into detailing the image instead of the beloved, both because he can only see her between flashes of evoked images and because he is able to describe freely only what he has already acquired. The latter conforms to a cognitive function of metaphor: to bring close the distant, one associates it with personally experienced objects.⁴⁵ In conjunction with this rule, the objective visual details, such as the blackness of her hair, serve as the point of contact in the metaphorical flight.

---

42. Though the Hebrew verbless clause is grammatically equivalent to an English clause with a copula, the added copula in English does fill up the space between the two nouns (cf. Keel, *Song of Songs*, 139).

43. Marc-Alain Ouaknin, *The Burnt Book: Reading the Talmud*, trans. Llewellyn Brown (Princeton, NJ: Princeton University Press, 1995), 61. Being, in the semantic form of "to be," is presupposed in Hebrew logical sentences. Nothing logical can be said unless the subject *is* . . . or *does* . . . (verbs that assume the state of being). One observes the similar but more intentional omission of the copula in Levinas's works. He radically suppresses the verb "to be," especially in his later writings, though French literature is already more forgiving of the absence of copula. Phrases juxtaposed, piled, or standing alone form a rugged sense unit—or betray the lack of it. Though it is difficult for rational reading (grasping), this writing style reflects a natural ambiguity morphing around, eroding, and embracing the concepts and relations commonsensically taken as neat entities corresponding to the world. This physical, inscriptional awkwardness in Levinas's works places a cautionary curb on the reading process when one attempts to choose and assimilate the non-self elements into one's egocentric configuration based on the assumption that the parallel between word and world is objective and devoid of personal texture.

44. Passion has already prevented the man from directly comprehending his beloved's beauty. J. Cheryl Exum observes this effect and explains the breakdown of bodily descriptions with it, but she does not apply it to the metaphorical elaborations in each line (*Song of Songs: A Commentary*, OTL [Louisville: Westminster John Knox, 2005], 160). See also Francis Landy, *Paradoxes of Paradise: Identity and Difference in the Song of Songs* (Sheffield: Almond, 1983), 176. However, this blinding is physically modified if the words are inscribed in a single line, which allows the eyes to move back and forth. In the act of reading, the characteristic of the imagery flows back to the bodily feature through the undercurrent of understanding, which, in an effort to complete the sense unit, reverses the flow of the words. Therefore, a series of mini-loops are formed in this process of comparing, focusing, and understanding, traversing the downward visual movement laterally.

45. "Metaphor," in *Princeton Encyclopedia of Poetry and Poetics*, ed. Alex Preminger, Frank J. Warnke, and O. B. Hardison (Princeton: Princeton University Press, 1974), 490.

So the necessary aspects of a metaphor seem to be all present: the subject matter, the familiar object, and the point of contact. But it remains to be answered, what prompts and sustains the mental act of linking, of reaching beyond? In his study on "the feeling brain," Antonio R. Damasio provides the key to how images, instances, and situations are connected—emotion.[46] Experiences with similar emotional responses are grouped together in the brain and will be summoned when a new and similar feeling appears. In this poem, the generating force behind the metaphorical connection is found in "an inward pulsing of delight,"[47] a similarity more genuine than reality.[48] Through the emotional key of delight, the lover unlocks his memory of beauty, resounding with what will rise to the highest level of exuberance and also befit the chosen aspects of his beloved's features. In other words, the points of contact in these similes are twofold: the correspondences between the bodily features and the metaphors, and more essentially, their similar impressions upon the lover.[49] The beloved's features and their respective metaphors are united in the lover's delightful savoring: "Your eyes, *ah*, doves."

Juxtaposed in delight are not only the bodily features and their metaphors but also the asyndetic lines devoted to each feature. Absent of any connectives, they assemble a bust portrait of the beloved with open space between the bodily members. I venture to propose that, analogous to Salvador Dalí's *Madonna of Port Lligat* (1949),[50] the open space merges the bodily members together without erasing the discontinuity created by competing emphases on each feature's beauty. The physical separateness, moreover, allows the filling of the lover's spirit, which silently exudes adoring delight. For in Dalí's painting, it is not just any scenery, or for that matter, any female model. The female figure is Gala, his mistress; and the scene, the familiar and beloved view of Port Lligat that Dalí saw daily. It is as though a

---

46. Damasio, *Looking for Spinoza*, 71, 100, 200, and 204. Of course, the lover can access these romantic images as conventional symbols of stereotyped sentiments. But it remains true that they are based on concrete experiences with which the lover is familiar: "Emotionally competent objects can be actual or recalled from memory" (p. 57).

47. Bernard of Clairvaux, *On the Song of Songs*, trans. Kilian Walsh, 4 vols. (Kalamazoo, MI: Cistercian, 1971), 1.7. See also Damasio, *Looking for Spinoza*, 43–46.

48. Picasso wrote: "I keep doing my best not to lose sight of nature. I want to aim at similarity, a profound similarity which is more real than reality, thus becoming surrealist" ("Pablo Picasso," http://www.abcgallery.com/P/picasso/picassobio.html#Cubism [accessed October 22, 2007]).

49. Therefore, the male lover finds "riches, power, and strength" in the beauty of his beloved (Richard S. Hess, *Song of Songs* [Grand Rapids, MI: Baker, 2005], 124–25).

50. In 1950, Dalí created another painting of the same title and theme with different details. At this time, Dalí sought to synthesize Christian iconography with images of material disintegration inspired by nuclear physics. His fascination with discontinuous matter prompted him to create gaps even in physical phenomena (contra the gap between the phenomena and the thing-in-itself [*das Ding an sich*]). Even the transcendent status of Mary and Jesus is suggested through the rectangular holes in their torsos.

Fig. 1. Salvador Dalí, *The Madonna of Port Lligat*, 1949, oil on canvas, 19¼ in × 14¾ in, Marquette University, Milwaukee, Wisconsin. © Salvador Dalí, Fundació Gala. Reproduced with permission, Artists Rights Society (ARS), New York, 2016.

piece of Dalí himself is invested in the painting in the form of the spirited space that disconnects and connects the visible elements differently.

Like the scenery that at times fills the gap between Mary's bodily members, the metaphorical images in Song 4:1–7 refer to each other across the lines and constitute background scenery, the wonderful and powerful landscape of love. Their haze and traces ripple between the lines and infuse their tactile beauty into the beloved's body. The rock dove flutters its wings; the black goats streaming down the mountain; the white ewes coming up from the water; the scarlet thread and the juicy pomegranate pour on the canvas a shocking lusciousness and desirability; the shields reflect golden rays on the Tower of David; two fawns bounce amidst lilies in the loving gaze of their mother. In the waves of poetic lines, with glowing familiarity and affection, the land shows its chosen facets according to the lover's embodied memory. Its vast expanse and endless variations aptly express the lover's voluptuous and ever-fresh delight in the beloved's body.[51] Though the explosions of joy finish their visible courses at the end of each couplet, the lover's joyful exuberance is amassed and distilled between couplets until it is compressed into a fiercely unstable force. In short, the beloved's

---

51. The abundance of the lover's joy evokes the abundance of the metaphorical world (F. Gerald Downing, "Aesthetic Behavior in the Jewish Scriptures," *JSOT* 28.2 (2003): 143).

body is painted with the textures of the lover's particular memory of beauty and enshrined in his erotic delight, which, in place of a realistic painting of her dark skin, connects the textures.

As an oil painting brushed onto the canvas, as waves carrying sparkling sea creatures sustained by the ocean, the words of this poem are assembled against the white space. It is not an objective glossy surface of one's rational light that seeks to examine the meaning of his affection,[52] for, when one is immersed in the joy of seeing one's beautiful beloved, in the sweet taste of life that satisfies one's living appetite, one has no hollowness within to constitute the cold reflection. The constituting site of the poem instead recedes, through the pulsation of feeling, to one's receptivity. The thin red thread, the succulent pomegranate, the awe-struck tower. In their disarming greetings, these beautiful things have stroked one's exposed sensibility and spurred one to the focal point of feeling, the flame of being. "It is as though beautiful things have been placed here and there throughout the world to serve as small wake-up calls to perception, spurring lapsed alertness back to its most acute level."[53]

Before surfacing as a conscious result of pleasure and cognition, the esthetic moment first disentangles one from "the exteriorities" in which one seeks the basis of being.[54] Instead of securing one's being in his or her work, product, or heritage—in esthetic experiences one essentially and fullbodily *is*. The sheer intensity, not its warm and sweet taste, of the feeling aroused by beauty enables one to feel feeling. It is needless to say how the beautiful other, the beauty of all beauties, can awaken oneself in a blinding contact that overflows representation.

Feeling, once it has refused to embark on the ventures of the Idea—war and ownership, money and politics (the foundations of our being in Being, but also its alienation)—will, through its dialectic of the "fragmentary," "singular pulsations," obey a "logic of pure quality that would not enrich our view of the world," and lead us toward a "bare, blind contact with the Other."[55]

The poem's "fragmentary" and "singular" pulsations could not be assimilated into the cold reflection of reason. Through the expansion of feeling, which is resilient enough to sustain the tension of reaching back to

---

52. "The obsessive return to the same strategy shows us the lover again and again seeking to catch the meaning of his love by this exhaustive summary of the physical and sensuous items that make up the beauty of the loved one" (Harold Fisch, "Song of Solomon: The Allegorical Imperative," *Poetry with a Purpose: Biblical Poetics and Interpretation* [Bloomington: Indiana University Press, 1988], 82).
53. Scarry, *On Beauty and Being Just*, 81.
54. "Existing through civilization, the *I* becomes a concept" (Emmanuel Levinas, "Jean Wahl and Feeling," *Proper Names*, trans. Michael B. Smith [London: Athlone, 1996]), 112, 116).
55. Ibid., 116. The quotations within Levinas's writings are from Jean Wahl, *Traité de métaphysique* (Paris: Payot, 1953; Plon, 1955), 702.

sensibility in spite of the bend of time and reason to move forward into conscious grasp, the reader is awakened to his or her "inner substance."[56] At its descending into one's interiority, feeling inflames all the faculties that it passes. In Plato's words, when at the sight of eros the dried and sealed openings to the outside (senses) are revived and allow streams of beauty to pass down to "the parched roots of the soul's wings, . . . the soul recovers breath."[57] To see at this moment is not to grasp the other's beauty but to allow one's self to be caressed and aroused to the full volume of feeling alive.

As for this poem, it testifies and performs this delightful awakening for its reader, who is not to be left untouched. Such affective aspect, however, is underappreciated when Song 4:1–7 is regarded as an amatory description that represents the beloved. As an alternative, I will seek to restore the affect of lyrical touch in the following section.

Touch

As a poem that sequentially describes the beloved's features, Song 4:1–7 is often referred to as a *waṣf*.[58] This Arabic lyric genre characterizes the individual features of things, animals, and people for evaluation.[59] In the past, scholarly attention has often been given to the characterization of individual features in a *waṣf*; and so the saliency of *waṣf* has been defined narrowly as "description."[60] To make sense of Song 4:1–7, therefore, is often

---

56. Levinas, "Jean Wahl and Feeling," 114.

57. Plato, *Phaedrus* 251D–E; quoted from Nussbaum (in her translation), "Faint with Secret Knowledge," 693.

58. There are four of these poems in the Song: 4:1–7, 5:9–16, 6:4–10, 7:2–6. Based on J. G. Wetzstein's report that in Syrian weddings the groom sang songs that described the body of the bride ("Die Syrische Dreschtafel," *Zeitschrift für Ethnologie* 5 [1873]: 270–302), Franz Delitzsch first associated this genre with the Song of Songs (*Commentary on the Old Testament in Ten Volumes*, vol. 6: *Proverbs, Ecclesiastes, Song of Solomon*, trans. M. G. Easton [Grand Rapids, MI: Eerdmans, 1975], 162–75). Ancient parallels to this lyric genre can be found in the Sumerian letter "The Message of Lugindira to His Mother (Jerrold S. Cooper, "New Cuneiform Parallels to the Song of Songs," *JBL* 90 [1971]: 160), the Neo-Assyrian and Late Babylonian god-description texts (Alasdair Livingstone, *Mystical and Mythological Explanatory Works of Assyrian and Babylonian Scholars* [Oxford: Clarendon, 1986], 92–112), Egyptian deceased-king description hymns (Keel, *The Song of Songs*, 22–24; Alfred Hermann, "Beiträge zur Erklärung der ägyptischen Liebesdichtung," in *Ägyptologische Studien*, ed. O. Firchow [Berlin: Academie-Verlag, 1955], 124–33), Egyptian love song nos. 31 and 54 (Michael V. Fox, *The Song of Songs and the Ancient Egyptian Love Songs* [Madison: University of Wisconsin Press, 1985], 269–71), and the depiction of Sarah in the Genesis Apocryphon from Qumran (1QapGen XX 1–8; Joseph A. Fitzmyer and Daniel J. Harrington, *A Manual of Palestinian Aramaic Texts* [Rome: Pontifical Biblical Institute, 1978], 112–13). David Bernat also argues for the use of this genre in other biblical texts, such as Job 40–41 and Prov 31:10–31 ("Biblical *waṣf* Beyond Song of Songs," *JSOT* 28.3 (2004): 327–349).

59. Akiko Motoyoshi Sumi, *Description in Classical Arabic Poetry Waṣf, Ekphrasis, and Interarts Theory* (Leiden: Brill, 2004), 6. My exposition below is largely informed by Sumi's study of this poetic genre.

60. For instance, Gustav von Grunebaum contends that, if "the perfection of form and language" is set aside, the beauty of the lover's presentation "derives entirely from

equated with taming the fancy poetic language into rational predications that uncover the kernel of truth—that is, the beloved's image. With irony, Tremper Longman illustrates how this thematic preoccupation works through a paraphrase of v. 2: "To be banal about it, the verse basically has the man saying to the woman, 'Your teeth are white, and you even have all of them!'"[61]

Such thematic paraphrases pay no attention to the media that realize the contact between poetry and reader. Rather, it operates according to a hermeneutic of mimetic *verisimilitude*, which is to say that representation transcends "the differences between media" in the cognitive process.[62] Precisely due to the marginalization of media—both human sensibility and lyric language—interpreters are puzzled by the "bizarre, if not grotesque" images of the female lover so extracted.[63] It is like someone who believes that all mirrors should give faithful reflections and then is appalled at the grotesque images in a distorting mirror. The cause of "grotesqueness" lies neither in the authorial intention (as a parody) nor in radically different esthetic tastes.[64] Rather, it can be located in the interpretive lenses that transcribe the extravagance of the lover's impression as the ridiculousness of the beloved's qualities.

---

the fidelity of his observation, not from his reaction to the impressions that actually inspired his song" ("The Response to Nature in Arabic Poetry," *JNES* 4 [1945]: 139–40). See also Marcia Falk, "The *waṣf*," *Love Lyrics from the Hebrew Bible: A Translation and Literary Study of the Song of Songs*, Bible and Literature Series 4 (Sheffield: Sheffield Academic Press, 1982), 80; Longman, *Song of Songs*, 140. However, As Athalya Brenner points out, "[N]o 'description' is actually obtained" at the end of the poem ("'Come Back, Come Back, the Shulammite' [Song of Songs 7.1–10]: A Parody of the *waṣf* Genre," in *A Feminist Companion to the Song of Songs* [Sheffield: Sheffield Academic Press, 1993], 235, 239 n. 3); see also Fox, *Song of Songs*, 271 n. 5; Exum, *Song of Songs*, 159. In other words, instead of being a "pictorial description" of the beloved, the metaphors in the *waṣf* draw readers' attention to the "resemblance" between the lover's impressions of the beloved and the natural scenes (cf. Sumi, *Description in Classical Arabic Poetry*, 14–15).

61. Longman, *Song of Songs*, 144. However, even stripped of lyrical excess, the evaluative intent is inherent in careful descriptions. The dialogue between Zorba and Nousa is a good example: "She looks over me carefully. . . . 'You've got all your teeth, a big mustache, broad shoulders, massive arms. I like you" (Nikos Kazantzakis, *Zorba the Greek* [New York: Simon & Schuster, 1953], 101).

62. Charles Sanders Peirce, "On Representation," *Writings of Charles S. Peirce: A Chronological Edition*, 8 vols. (Bloomington: Indiana University Press, 2000; orig. 1886–90), 6.1; Sumi, *Description in Classical Arabic Poetry*, 10. Cf. Robert Eaglestone, "One and the Same? Ethics, Aesthetics, and Truth," *Poetics Today* 25 (2004): 606.

63. Leroy Waterman, *The Song of Songs: Translated and Interpreted as a Dramatic Poem* (Ann Arbor: University of Michigan Press, 1948), 63; M. H. Segal, "The Song of Songs," *VT* 12 (1962): 480; B. S. J. Isserlin, "Song of Songs IV: 4: An Archaeological Note," *PEQ* 90 (1958): 59–60. More recently, Fiona C. Black deliberately explores such a grotesque image ("Beauty or the Beast? The Grotesque Body in the Song of Songs," *BibInt* 8 [2000]: 311).

64. Contra Richard N. Soulen, "The *waṣfs* of the Song of Songs and Hermeneutic," in *A Feminist Companion to the Song of Songs*, ed. Athalya Brenner and Carole R. Fontaine (Sheffield: Sheffield Academic Press, 1993), 185.

As a plain grammatical analysis of a poem cannot give us more than the grammar of the poem,[65] rational distillation cannot meet poetry where it happens. Vain and frustrating, it is like polishing the ground, before we walk, into such a glossy state that we could no longer walk. We want to walk, so we need the rough ground.[66]

Poetry, more than any other discourse, embodies the materiality of language.[67] Materiality here does not refer to "the matter opposed to thought and mind, which fed classical materialism" but to the unreflected somatic impression that resists assimilation into rational reflection.[68] Like a rose that clings through its thorns to its recipient's sensitivity, poetry clings through lyrical forms to its audience's bodily senses and emotions; thus it prevents a smooth conversion into the universal critical language. Pinsky points out that "[t]he medium of poetry is a human body," and this body is not an expert's but "the audience's body."[69] The contact between poetry and its audience happens on the latter's embodied sensibility. Instead of thematizations about what the poem means, poetic meaning lies in the audience's altered sensibility through its contact with the poem.

Not only is it imprudent to regard the *waṣf* as objective representation, it is also unethical. Such a rational and reductive approach endorses the first injustice we do to an other, that is, describing the other by generalizing definition. We tend to tame others through generalizing definitions;[70] otherwise, "their sharp particularity would be too threatening, would give us too much pain."[71] In Martha Nussbaum's words, such descriptive definition is a "crude vision of people and things"[72]—crude in the word's basic mean-

---

65. Michael Riffaterre, "Describing Poetic Structures: Two Approaches to Baudelaire's *Les Chats*," *Yale French Studies* 36/37 (1966): 213.
66. Ludwig Wittgenstein, *Philosophical Investigations*, ed. G. E. M. Anscombe and R. Rhees, trans. G. E. M. Anscombe (Oxford: Blackwell, 1953), S.107, 3.
67. Mutlu Konuk Blasing goes so far as to claim that rational discourses are in fact based on these material media, which poetry embraces (*Lyric Poetry: The Pain and the Pleasure of Words* [Princeton, NJ: Princeton University Press, 2007], 2).
68. Emmanuel Levinas, *Existence and Existents*, trans. Alphonso Lingis (Boston: Kluwer, 1988), 57.
69. Pinsky further explains that "the column of air inside the chest [is] shaped into signifying sounds in the larynx and the mouth. In this sense, poetry is just as physical or bodily an art as dancing" (*The Sounds of Poetry*, 8).
70. Murdoch, *Sacred and Profane Love Machine*, 82.
71. Nussbaum, "'Faint with Secret Knowledge,'" 702. When Nazi soldiers categorized real people as "Jews," they were shielded from feeling the pain of the latter's plight and the horror of their death that they executed. Moreover, one's sensibility is often selectively open or closed to external stimuli and thus becomes compartmentalized. For instance, as portrayed in the movie *Shindler's List* (dir. Steven Spielberg, produced Branko Lustig et al., Universal Studios, 1993), the Nazi soldiers maintained their sensibility in response to Wagner's music, accompanied by which they insouciantly cleaned the ghetto of "the Jews'" remains.
72. Nussbaum, "Faint with Secret Knowledge," 702.

ing: it anesthetizes senses, first of oneself, then toward the other.[73] Hence, "[b]efore research begins, the method converts all *Other* into *Same*."[74] The conversion of *waṣf* into description is the conversion of the material body of a poem into universal critical discourse. This conversion uncannily betrays "a critic's willful impoverishment ensuring his or her immunity to the effect of literature."[75]

Contrary to beauty and poetry, which spurs the recipient's relaxed sensibility to an acute state, a rationalistic reading of Song 4:1–7 seeks to cross out any trace of the other's appearance on one's sensibility, as well as the act of its crossing-out, so that a correspondence between the object's qualities and the subject's representation may be construed. It bends readers' reception toward a caricature of the beloved as it compresses into the one-dimensional image of the beloved not only the lover's exuberant feelings but also the otherness of the beloved. This is not to say that rational analysis gets poetry all wrong, for what is at stake here cannot be explained with the terminology of true or false. Poetry enables one to speak of the other with the authentic breath that embodies one's somatic impressions of the other in poetic language. Hence, it maintains the fire of ethics as the signifying relation between one and the other before the fire turns into cold luminosity in rational reflection. Ethics matters in relation to the other before the question of truth arises, Levinas says:

> [E]thics does not replace truth with falsehood, but situates man's first breath not in the light of being but in the relation to a being, prior to the thematization of that being. Such a relation, in which the being [*étant*] does not become my object, is precisely justice.[76]

Guided by the ethical relation that precedes epistemology, now let me retrace my steps and approach this *waṣf* anew. Etymologically, though "description" is the core meaning of the nominal *waṣf*, the form 1 verb of *waṣf* (*waṣafa*) means both "to describe" and "to praise, laud, extol."[77] The distinctive verbal meanings suggest an intertwined texture: describe to extol, and extol by describing. The goal to extol adds an emotional timbre that description alone would have missed. This is particularly pronounced in

---

73. "When we do ill we anaesthetize our imagination. Doubtless this is, for most people, a prerequisite for doing ill, and indeed a part of it" (Isis Murdoch, *The Sacred and Profane Love Machine* [New York: Penguin, 1984], 170; Nussbaum, "'Faint with Secret Knowledge,'" 702). Linda M. Alcoff also writes that "the ethical seeing . . . is attentive to nonoppositional and fluid differences rather than repeating ready-made categories" ("Habits of Hostility: On Seeing Race" *Philosophy Today* 44/4 [2000]: 57).

74. Emmanuel Levinas, "Signification and Sense," *Humanism of the Other*, trans. Nidra Poller (Urbana: University of Illinois Press, 2003), 35.

75. William Waters, *Poetry's Touch: On Lyric Address* (Ithaca, NY: Cornell University Press, 2003), 145.

76. Levinas, "The Poet's Vision," 137.

77. Sumi, *Description in Classical Arabic Poetry*, 6.

the case of love poetry. The inflowing sensation provoked by the beautiful beloved, after vivifying the lover, reverts to an outpouring of exuberant praises. Thus, after a glance at the lovely lady has revived his "withered heart," Charles Baudelaire addresses himself "to singing her praises" by addressing her individual features in hyperbolic terms:

> What will you say this evening, poor solitary soul, what will you say, my long-ago withered heart, to the most-beautiful, the most-good, the most-cherished, from whose divine glance you have suddenly flowered again?
> —We'll set our pride to singing her praises: nothing excels the mildness of her authority; her spiritual flesh has the perfume of Angels and her eye clothes us anew in a garment of light. [78]

Impression, too full, turns into expression. The ground of metaphorical comparisons in his poem and in the present *waṣf* is not the neutrality of reason but the "flowered" sensibility of the lover. From this perspective, the exuberance that permeates the *waṣf* testifies to the unreflected impact of the beloved on the lover.

Moreover, according to Akiko Sumi's study on the Arabic *waṣf*, the most important aspect of this genre is to transport the audience into a state of *ṭarab*—that is, a "strong emotion of joy or grief."[79] The passion-infused descriptions do not cease at the point of expression but seek to provoke exuberance in their audience. A *waṣf*, in other words, emulates not only the qualities of the object but also their affectivity. In this sense, a *waṣf* resembles rhetoric in its "art of seduction,"[80] with the difference being that it stirs the audience not into accepting an idea or action but into a mode of emotion. Hence, Richard N. Soulen rightly calls for a hermeneutic that is attentive to the affective intent of this lyric genre: "A *waṣf* is a celebration of the joys of life and love and at the same time an invitation to share that joy."[81]

Human emotions are embodied responses, whether they are expressed in the creases around one's eyes or in the exact shape of a poem. The latter explains why Yeats exhausts himself in seeking the "appropriate body" that fully conveyed the emotional aura in his mind.

> It was not writing down the *content* of a germinating poem that troubled him; his prose sketches are sometimes eerily close in content to the fin-

---

78. Charles Baudelaire, "Altogether," *The Flowers of Evil*, trans. Keith Waldrop (Middletown, CT: Wesleyan University Press, 2006), 57.
79. Sumi, *Description in Classical Arabic Poetry*, 124; George D. Sawa, *Music Performance Practice in the Early ʿAbbāsid Era 132–320 AH/750–932 AD* (Ottawa: Institute of Mediaeval Music, 1989), 195.
80. Blasing, *Lyric Poetry*, 34.
81. Soulen, "The *waṣfs*," 224. Gillis Gerleman also notices that the imageries are designed to stir joyous emotion (*Ruth: Das Hohelied* [Neukirchen-Vluyn: Neukirchener Verlag, 1965], 64).

ished poem. But in the prose, spirit has not yet found its appropriate body. The stanza form remains to be chosen; the rhythms must be established; the rhymes await discovery; throughout, the envisaged 'emotional unity' demands the addition of this, the excision of that. It was the second phase of composition—in which an already-imaged theme found its poetics—that so exhausted Yeats. [Emphasis original][82]

As a good poet would do, the voice of the lover generates another beautiful body—Song 4:1–7—to express and invite participation in his joy at seeing his beautiful beloved.[83] In line with how the body of the beloved has provoked the lover's joy, the physical body of the poem provokes the audience's joy. The sensations that the audience gains by tracing the exquisite compositional structure, combing through the subtle sound plays, and holding its breath in the lucid images are not exactly like touching the beloved's skin or being caught in her tresses or succumbing to her glance. But facing this lyrical beauty is one of the closest means that the audience has of catching the fire of the beloved's beauty in her lover's eyes.

At a level that is often ignored, lyric poetry invites its audience "to take pleasure in the sound of words without necessarily worrying about their sense."[84] Such is the carefree function of the vowel pattern *a-ā-ē* in Song 4:3–4: *raq-qā-tēk*, *lĕšam-mā-tēk*, and *ṣaw-wāʾ-rēk*. In conjunction with the rhyming *-ēk*, they end three consecutive lines that do not form any thematic unity but do manifest a pleasant vocal string. In this unreflected sonic experience, the delight of the ear resuscitates the delight of the eye. These "pointless" plays should not be taken lightly, for sound and feeling have a profound somatic association that has been traced to the infantile stage of acquiring language. Toddlers express their feelings and intentions through sounds that are not yet language. These sounds, mostly preserved in the mother tongue, function as the unconscious foundation to linguistic emotion.[85]

---

82. Helen Vendler, *Our Secret Discipline: Yeats and Lyric Form* (Cambridge: Belknap, 2007), 3. The two versions of George Oppen's "Debt" offer yet another example. The content of these two poems is the same: the experience of manufacturing. The first, called "The Manufactured Part" tilts toward the end of narrative coherence. In the second version (published in *The Materials*), the poem's "calibrated turns of its lineation" prompt the readers to hear—not just comprehend, in reading and re-making the poem—the experience of manufacturing. That is, the (re-)making of the poem emulates the rhythm of the manufacturing (James Longenbach, *The Resistance to Poetry* [Chicago: University of Chicago Press, 2004], 40–42).

83. Scarry, *On Beauty and Being Just*, 5. Of course, the first-person voice in Song 4:1–7 does not mean that the lover is necessarily the poet. By naming only the lover, I focus on the performative force of the first-person voice in the poem.

84. Longenbach, *Resistance to Poetry*, 39.

85. Blasing, *Lyric Poetry*, 15–16. In the case of the audile aspect of the Song, a cautionary note is in place. The present study is based mainly on the vocalization of the Hebrew text in the MT tradition. It should be acknowledged that, compounded with the fact that Hebrew is not my mother tongue, the sonority of the Song could not be completely

Moreover, sound plays frequently direct attention to more than the sound itself. Take the couplet in 4:2c, d, for example. The first word of the first line, *šekkullām* ("all of them"), unravels into two strands in the second half, *šakkūlâ* ("blemish") and *bāhem* ("in them"). The latter two bracket the central *ʾên* ("none"), which negates on the semantic level the negative sense of the bracketing words. In 4:6c, the repeated sonic elements *e* and *l* in *ʾelek lî el* carve the texture of the subject as a "going toward" the other, while marking on the sonic level the two ends of the journey—"you" (-*k*) and "I" (-*î*). Following this rich intricacy, *har* is enhanced in the following *hammôr*; the rolling sounds sweetly manifest the semantic sense of this construct chain, "the mountain of myrrh." When their semantic and sonic qualities are summoned at different turns, poetic words become erotically full-bodied and slippery. Their significance can no longer be exhausted by their lexical meanings.

The repetition of sonic units also generates a bittersweet suspense between sense and sensation on a larger scale. The consonant *k* signifies both the pronominal suffix "you" (-*k*) and the preposition "like" (*k*-). As it weaves through the main body of the poem, the sound *k* adjoins the "you" that owns the bodily features and the metaphors that are led by "like." Thus, the sameness of this consonant marks this poem's thematic thread as a series of similes: "your x is like y." Along this stable main thread, the poem generates energy from the variety of metaphorical colors and textures, the different content playing off the permeating beat of *k*. Moreover, as a characteristic feature of the Song, repetition always arrives with a delicious difference. Appearing in two alternating patterns, this salient sonic feature refreshes the structured similes. With *k* being repeated back-to-back and separating the bodily features from the metaphors in the first and the third stanzas,[86] the beloved's body fades into the appearing scenery.[87] When the repeated consonants embrace the subject and the metaphor in the second stanza, the body and the image are on the verge of fusing together.

Aside from notifying the similes, the consonant *k* also begins another word, *kōl* ("all"). This word appears in the last couplets of the first two

---

reconstructed, because neither the Song's accompanying musical score nor the historical pronunciation of the words has been preserved.

86. Structurally, the "breast-fawn" simile compensates the omission of the *kĕ-* ("like") in 4:1c in hindsight. This reaching back beyond the immediate past is also enhanced by the choices of image. The image of the fawn reverts to animal imagery as in the first stanza, instead of the insensate objects in the second stanza. I suggest that, in both form and metaphor, the description of the breasts emulates the first stanza. For a different stylistic preference, or due to the fluidity of memorization, 4QCant[a] converts the word order in 4:1c–2a to that of 4:3, forming alliteration in these lines with the preposition *kĕ-* (Tov, "Introduction to 4QCant[a-c]," 200).

87. There are three lines that do not elaborate on the metaphor: the double reference to the lips and mouth in 4:3ab facilitates the audience's longing to capture it; the image of veil in both 4:1d and 3d frames her face.

stanzas (4:2c, 4d). Its semantic sense helps to wrap up the individual stanzas, while its sonic repetition reinforces the correspondence between them. Through the phonetic link of *k*, "all" further joins in the wordplay of "you" and "like" to frame the conclusion in 4:7:

kullāk yāpâ raʿyātî
ûmûm ʾên bāk
All of you is beautiful, my dear,
and no flaw is in *you*!

This sonic inclusio embodies the completeness of the beautiful body of the beloved (and by extension, that of the poem), which coheres with the semantic sense of *kōl*.

The pleasant fusion of structure, sense, and sound is further exhibited in the regulated pattern of the consonants that begins the couplets (and the triplet) of the three stanzas. In the first stanza, the rough guttural *ʿayin* is followed by three *šîn/śîn*s; in the second stanza, the consonant *kap* plays the leading role three times, while the last couplet is led by the smooth guttural *ʾālep*; the third stanza then opens by returning to *šîn* and wraps up the three stanzas by picking up both *ʿayin* and *ʾālep* in the following two couplets.

Repeated words also teasingly draw attention to their different surroundings. *Kĕʿēder* ("like a flock of"), for instance, weds two couplets (4:1c–2b) that contrast in all other aspects: the downward and upward verbal movements (*gālšû* and *ʿālû*); the explicit masculine-plural noun "the goats" (*hāʿizzîm*) and the implicit feminine-plural noun "the shorn ones" (*haqqĕṣûbôt*); the explicit mountain Gilead (*har gilʿād*) and the implied water in "the washing" (*hārahṣâ*). Tied around the sameness of *kĕʿēder*, the two images unify in a picture of contrast and harmony: a flock of black goats cascades down Mt. Gilead, forming a free, bouncy movement along the slope; a flock of white ewes, of "one size" and in two rows, neatly marches "with one step"[88] from the water, shining with sparkling water drops under the morning sun. As *kĕʿēder* sustains and accentuates the contrasts of color, movement, texture, and grammatical elements between the lines of the balanced antithetical parallel, its semantic meaning is textured differently by its surrounding words.

I hope by now it is clear that the significance of reading this *waṣf* lies not so much in what concept or structure the readers can extract as in how their senses are vivified by coming into contact with the poem. This is to say that one ought not allow the moments to pass so quickly when words signify otherwise than the message, for in a slippery simultaneity, a poem interweaves words through their different aspects. Reading a poem

---

88. Levi ben Gershom, *Commentary on Song of Songs*, trans. Menachem Marc Kellner (New Haven, CT: Yale University Press, 1998), 55.

is therefore not translating, footnoting, or summarizing its content. Before understanding and comprehension, it is resurrection;[89] it is giving one's living breath to sound another voice.

As the poem's words touch those of its audience in the resurrection of sense and signification, they are attracted to and rub against each other through verbal similarities, as "flock" welcomes and yet differs from "flock." In so doing, poetic words also discreetly alter, enrich, and ramify the pre-existing texture of the audience's words. In the audience's reception, layers and facets of meaning converge, morph, and waft, exquisitely and firmly tied together by the thread of the physical shapes and sounds of the words.

Never does the meaning of these symbols fully dismiss the materiality of the symbols that suggest it. They always preserve some unexpected capacity for renewing this meaning. Never does the spirit dismiss the letter that revealed it. Quite the contrary, the spirit awakens new possibilities of suggestion in the letter.[90]

The contact between a reader's individualized language and the poem reveals the erotic undertone of all poetic readings. As words resurrect in the audience's sensibility the sounds, colors, and tastes of what the lover has experienced, they synaesthetically[91] caress the audience. In this linguistic contact, the audience's receptivity is evoked beyond thematic reception. In *A Lover's Discourse*, Roland Barthes describes two kinds of erotic linguistic contact. First, the singular emotion of "I desire you" is resuscitated individually in each reader and yet tinted by that which permeates the poem.

> Language is a skin: I rub my language against the other. It is as if I had words instead of fingers, or fingers at the tip of my words. My language trembles with desire. The emotion derives from a double contact: on the one hand, a whole activity of discourse discreetly, indirectly focuses upon a single signified, which is "I desire you," and releases, nourishes, ramifies it to the point of explosion (language experiences orgasm upon touching itself); on the other hand, I enwrap the other in my words, I caress, brush against, talk up this contact, I extend myself to make the commentary to which I submit the relation endure.[92]

The second kind of the linguistic contact, enwrapping the other in one's words, fittingly summarizes another somatic aspect of the present *wasf*. In-

---

89. Emmanuel Levinas, "Poetry and Resurrection: Notes on Agnon," *Proper Names*, 10.

90. Idem, *Nine Talmudic Readings*, trans. with an introduction by Annette Aronowicz (Bloomington: Indiana University Press, 1990), 8.

91. Verbalization stimulates other sensory effects and fuses them into a "multi-sensory force" (Sumi, *Description in Classical Arabic Poetry*, 140). Synaesthesia transfers or equates different sensations to generate a fluid and abundant perception, such as "love is sweet like honey." It "enables the lover to combine the power of several sense-impressions into one collective impression" (Erika von Erhardt-Siebold, "Harmony of the Senses in English, German, and French Romanticism," *PMLA* 47 [1932]: 584).

92. Roland Barthes, *A Lover's Discourse* (New York: Hill & Wang, 1978), 73.

stead of mimetic representation, what connects the words to the beloved's features is the lover's savoring embrace. The lover wraps his beloved in his words, just as the inclusio (4:1 and 7) enwraps the body of the poem, just as his right and left hands embrace her (2:6, 8:3). First he enwraps, and then he caresses her body one feature at a time with words that are "fingers." When the climactic seventh feature is touched, his words even become lips. "Your breasts are two fawns, twins of a gazelle, grazing among lilies" (4:5). Since lilies are also his lips (5:13),[93] the image becomes slippery with regard to whether the fawns graze among lilies, or lilies kiss the fawns. Retrospectively, would not the consonants š/š that lead the lines in 4:1c–2d also evoke a lingering taste on the lips of the much-desired kisses, which begin the first and last chapters of the Song (1:2, 8:1)? Invoking and tracing her symmetric beauty, the lover verbally caresses and kisses that which so attracts him. "When nothing comes between the lover and the beloved," remarks Ann Townsend, the erotic is "in their kisses."[94]

The embracing arms hold the individual characterizations, not only within the lover's hyperbolic evaluations (4:1, 7), but also within the relation that fuses "I" and "you" in rā'yātî. In this repeated central phrase, "I" am identified as "your" keeper, while "you," as "my dear," provide the noun to which to attach "myself" (-î).[95] "You" and "I" thus become irreplaceably significant to one another. In Richard A. Cohen' words, "the-other-put-into-the-same, converts firstness—the for-oneself . . . into an actual *relationship*."[96] "I" am not speaking from an indifferent neutral ground but out of the love relationship with "you," whom "my" song aims to delight, even as "your" beauty has delighted "me."

Out of (and feeding back to) this relationship, the lover sings the *waṣf* to his beloved. On this lyric occasion, the beloved is the audience, the addressee, and the object of praise all at once. Across the separation between "you" and "I," the effect of the lover's verbal caress is realized in the beloved's reception as the primary *audience*. Moreover, in the manner that a yogi's voice guides the students in waking attention to their body, the beloved, as *the addressee*, is awakened to her bodily beauty that is *the object of*

---

93. The young man's lips are praised as lilies in 5:13; cf. 1:1. Falk suggests that, "because the garden and its flowers are associated with female sexuality, pasturing is usually symbolic of male sexual activity" (*Love Lyrics from the Bible*, 104). Tom Gledhill also notes that grazing has erotic overtones (*The Message of the Song of Songs: The Lyrics of Love* [Leicester: Inter-Varsity, 1994], 108).

94. Ann Townsend, "Meretricious Kisses," in *Radiant Lyre: Essays on Lyric Poetry*, ed. David Baker and Ann Townsend (Saint Paul, MN: Graywolf, 2007), 57.

95. "The identity of the subject comes from the impossibility of escaping responsibility, from the taking charge of the other" (Emmanuel Levinas, *Otherwise than Being: Or, Beyond Essence*, trans. Alphonso Lingis [Pittsburgh: Duquesne University Press, 1998], 13).

96. Richard A. Cohen, "Introduction," in Emmanuel Levinas, *New Talmudic Readings*, trans. Richard A. Cohen (Pittsburgh: Duquesne University Press, 1999), 9.

praise; only now, her awakening is sweetened by his touching, of his fingers and lips in her imagination, and of his voice in her ear.

In a touch that arouses, the *waṣf* offers its affective invitation. As the beloved accepts this invitation and participates in her lover's lyrical emotion, she is persuaded into a state of delight that resurrects his delight at seeing her beauty. Beyond this immediate circle, the rest of the audience, including you and me, come in contact with the poem through our bodily experiences, which the poetic words evoke. In this linguistic contact, we are touched and provoked to respond. Will we respond in accord with our aroused emotion, our awakened sensibility? The answer to this question determines how we approach the poem.

Approach

At this juncture, the poem may be revisited as a provoked initiative, in the sense that it provokes its audience with the sensation that has provoked the lover to sing praises.[97] It derives energy not only from the materiality of the words and the lines but also an assumed caress that precedes the poem. For, before becoming the thematic thread, the lover's visual tracing reveals a prior touch—that is, her body caresses his eye. The resultant passion of this visual caress explains the lover's unmediated exuberance in 4:1 and the delight that sustains the poem. Considering its generative significance, an excursion on the prior caress is appropriate, for it raises awareness of the relationship that begets the poem.

Common sense has it that vision is an active grasp of the given objects and that it leads to understanding and knowledge, as expressed in the metaphor "I see."[98] But before and besides projecting into cognition, seeing is being caressed: the visible given objects caress the eye.

> Sight is, to be sure, an openness and a consciousness, and all sensibility, opening as consciousness, is called vision; but even in its subordination to cognition sight maintains contact and proximity. The visible caress the eye. One sees and hears like one touches.[99]

To maintain, here, means to sustain without being able to assimilate or erase.[100] "It is a matter of a lingering attentiveness rather than a thematiz-

---

97. Levinas, *Otherwise than Being*, 10.
98. George Lakoff and Mark Johnson, *Philosophy in the Flesh: The Embodied Mind and Its Challenge to Western Thought* (New York: Basic Books, 1999), 53.
99. Emmanuel Levinas, "Language and Proximity," *Collected Philosophical Papers*, trans. Alphonso Lingis [Dordrecht: Nijhoff, 1987]), 118. Also, in Classical Latin literature, "The eye is primarily a passive, receptive organ" (Suzannah Biernoff, *Sight and Embodiment in the Middle Ages* [New York: Palgrave Macmillan, 2002], 49).
100. Alphonso Lingis, "Introduction to *Otherwise than Being*," in *Otherwise than Being*, xxiii.

ing, all-encompassing gaze."[101] Ethics as a way of seeing is embodied in the passivity of seeing as being caressed, regardless of the forms of the visible givens. One's tuning in to the other is a prior "gesture of recognition of the other," important because of this attention.[102] It cannot be shown in a representative description of the other, for it happens after a sensibility that "does not turn into perception."[103] Attention is the saying that subtends the said: the handshake, before denoting agreement, is already peace; "the caress, awakening in the touch, is already affection."[104] The subject becomes attached—by way of the friction upon sensual contact (even one that is subtle and distant like vision)—to the other through the subject's provoked attention.

Attention is most readily shown in erotic vision. The lover's attention is sustained, as the radiant beauty of his beloved saturates his sensibility to its full capacity and overflows, while the accompanying streaming delight prevents him from turning his eyes away. So overwhelmingly is he drawn to her beauty that he can only pretend to comprehend, while in reality he short-circuits this task and eagerly scurries back to the eyes, feasting on the sheer sensation. The unutterable tenderness from the eye to the heart delightfully confounds the thinking mind and this sweet confounding reveals a glimpse even into the infinite!

I cannot but be wounded: such is the nature of the wounding gaze often seen in love literature. The overwhelming sensation at the sight of a beautiful boy produces extraordinary physical pain in Plato's *Phaedrus*.[105] In the twelfth-century French romance *Eneas*, the heroine Lavine is wounded by gazing at the handsome Eneas.[106] What she sees is not assimilated as her object of esthetic judgment; rather, it retains its sensual impact that caresses her beyond what she can bear. Rumi also testifies: "It was just a glance, but it became a fountain that drowned my heart."[107] Or as Petrarch confesses: "I did not defend myself against it, for your beautiful eyes, Lady, bound me."[108]

---

101. Paul Davies, "The Face and the Caress: Levinas's Ethical Alterations of Sensibility," in *Modernity and the Hegemony of Vision*, ed. David Michael Levin (Berkeley: University of California Press, 1993), 25.

102. Emmanuel Levinas, "Paul Celan," *Proper Names*, 43.

103. Philippe Crignon, "Figuration: Emmanuel Levinas and the Image," in *Encounters with Levinas*, ed. Thomas Trezise, trans. Nicole Simek and Zahi Zalloua, Yale French Studies 104 (New Haven, CT: Yale University Press), 121.

104. Emmanuel Levinas, "Sensibility," in *Ontology and Alterity in Merleau-Ponty*, trans. Michael B. Smith, ed. Galen A. Johnson and Michael B. Smith (Evanston, IL: Northwestern University Press, 1990), 64.

105. Plato, *Phaedrus*, 251.

106. Biernoff, *Sight and Embodiment*, 49.

107. Rumi, "The Face of That Beauty," in *Love's Ripening: Rumi on the Heart's Journey*, trans. Kavir Helminski and Ahmad Rezwani (Boston: Shambhala, 2010), 103.

108. Judy Sproxton, *The Idiom of Love: Love Poetry from the Early Sonnets to the Seventeenth Century* (London: Duckworth, 2000), 41.

The salient mark of the wounding gaze is not a passive acceptance of abuse but a sincere exposure of one's vulnerable self to the other, whose beauty has provoked one's unremitting attention. It traumatizes, as lightening tears open oneself from without and spreads the shock down to the soul's root. In this vehement sensation, the beholder is stripped "beyond nudity, beyond forms,"[109] until an anterior susceptibility to the lover's touch is exposed. What matters most here is the emotional susceptibility, without which love, poem, music, and morality just do not *mean* anything.[110] This irresistibly imposed danger of the "loss of self" generates an emotional tension between the lover's unprotected vulnerability and the beloved's armed loftiness, aptly conveyed through the military metaphors (e.g., 4:5).[111] These military images are cohesive to the lover's emotional texture, though they would pose a vexing problem for readers who seek to reconstruct the sociopolitical background.[112]

Without attaching one's attention to the other's beauty, one would not realize, through the sustained seeing-as-caress, how the other has always already wounded oneself. Awakened to this exposure that does not hold back or close up, one is brought back to sincerity, a nudity "exposed to the point of outpouring, effusion and prayer."[113] "Thus there is both relation and rupture, and thus awakening: awakening of the Self by the Other. . . . An awakening signifying a responsibility for the other."[114]

The responsibility for the other has always been incumbent upon the self, but until I am awakened, I have eyes but do not see.[115] The ethical turn is realized at an esthetic moment—esthetic in its etymological sense of "sensitive" (αἰσθητικός). Allowing oneself to be brought up short by the other's appearance and passively to sustain the impact, one is opened to the other at the level of sensibility, which provides ground for ethical relation.

What then is sensibility? In Andrew Gibson's concise portrait of this "richly suggestive term," he finds three elements: "a disposition to refined

---

109. Levinas, *Otherwise than Being*, 15. De-nuding is thus a pre-original experience that transcends contexts.

110. Appreciation of music, for example, requires both perceptual abilities and emotional susceptibility. After physical trauma has disabled a person's emotional responses to outside stimuli, the music that he or she had enjoyed previously becomes utterly meaningless, even though he or she is perfectly capable of hearing it (Oliver W. Sacks, *Musicophilia: Tales of Music and the Brain* [New York: Knopf, 2007], 287).

111. Carson, *Eros the Bittersweet*, 39.

112. Cf. Carol Meyers, "Gender Imagery in the Song of Songs," HAR 10 (1986): 215. On the conventional contrast between the lover's defenseless attachment and the beloved's armed loftiness, see also Judy Sproxton, *The Idiom of Love*, 41.

113. Levinas, *Otherwise than Being*, 72.

114. Idem, "Foreword," *Proper Names*, 6.

115. Riera observes that Levinas regards ethics as "an abyssal and infinite anteriority" and retracts it "from the space of theoretical thinking and from fundamental ontology into that of sensibility" (Gabriel Riera, *Intrigues: From Being to the Other* [New York: Fordham University Press, 2006], 90).

or delicate emotion," "an education in or formation of feeling," and "a mode of openness and attentiveness."[116] Even though all of these are relevant in reading the *waṣf*, the most essential one is the third: sensibility as one's exposedness to the other's touch. In the following pages, I will continue to focus on the aspect of attentiveness, in light of Levinas's writings on sensibility, which often appears in conjunction with an erotic relationship.

Levinas's conception of an erotic relationship in fact goes through a paradigmatic shift from *Totality and Infinity* to *Otherwise than Being*.[117] In the former, an erotic relationship with a heterosexual other (in his case, the feminine) is construed as a carnal sphere beside the ethical realm. In the latter, not only is this contrastive construction abandoned, but also the erotic sphere is converted into a fundamental stratum to describe the ethical relationship:

> The highly original concepts that were elaborated to formulate the erotic relationship—. . . the concept of contact by sensuousness contrasted with the signifying aim, even the theme of skin caressed contrasted with face addressed—are now the basic concepts with which the ethical relationship of responsibility with the other is formulated.[118]

The key factor behind this shift is a redefinition of sensibility. In *Totality and Infinity*, Levinas ascribes sensibility to the sphere of enjoyment, in which "the ego pursues its own closure and contentment."[119] In *Otherwise than Being*, sensibility is deepened and takes root in vulnerability, susceptibility, and exposedness to alterity. It is deeper than a physical impression, along with its pleasure or pain, which is below the radar of cognition. It is a passivity lurking "hidden in the depths of all activity," even consciousness and language,[120] for perception and emotion are impossible without a prior

---

116. [F]rom the early eighteenth century onwards, it meant quickness or acuteness in emotional apprehension, a particularly keen susceptibility to emotional influence, indicating a specific kind or quality of emotional capacity, 'the soft sense of the mind' that Mackenzie regarded as feminine or feminizing. This is sensibility as a disposition to refined or delicate emotion, including compassion. In fact, the more significant conception or sensibility implies *Bildung* (in a very particular sense), an education in or formation of feeling. At its most sophisticated, the concept of sensibility invokes a subtilization or complexification of feeling, a mode of feeling in the midst of feelings. But, at the same time, the term properly designates an ethical faculty. Sensibility is to be understood as distinct from cognition in that it does not direct itself at an object with the intention of mastering it, but is rather characterised by a mode of openness and attentiveness. (Andrew Gibson, *Postmodernity, Ethics, and the Novel* [London: Routledge, 1999], 162)

117. John E. Drabinski offers a book-length analysis of how Levinas's idea of sensibility evolves from the incipient works to the more mature ones, especially from the perspective of phenomenology (*Sensibility and Singularity: The Problem of Phenomenology in Levinas* [Albany: State University of New York Press, 2001]).

118. Lingis, "Introduction," xxi.

119. Ibid., xxii.

120. Levinas, "The Servant and Her Master," *Proper Names*, 140. See also Drabinski, *Sensibility and Singularity*, 184.

susceptibility to being affected. Cognitive, esthetic, and ethical experiences originate in sensibility as responses to intrigue, as the impression upon sensibility provokes answerability. It boils down to an anterior exposedness, "by which the subject opens itself to objects and to things."[121] The essential characteristic of being alive is that I am responsive to those that are not "I." The true antithesis of life is not death but anesthesia, of which death is but one manifestation. Sensibility thus grounds the self, which is already for-the-other and "otherwise than an ego."[122]

Meanwhile, sensibility is not to be understood as merely spontaneous and pre-reflective kinesthesia, waiting to be selectively processed by consciousness. In his later essay "In Memoriam Alphonse de Waelhens," Levinas ponders the ambiguity of the mind as being conditioned by the body. To reflect the continuity, he substitutes the traditional dichotomy of the mind and the body with "the mental and the extended." The mental is epitomized in the constituting initiative of the consciousness, the "I think," while the extended refers to the constituted thought fleshed by the body. The mental capacity is operated by the body and responds to the body's sensual responses to external stimuli. Neither mind nor body is the absolute origin in this living experience. Rather, there is already a synthesis between the constituting and the constituted before the genesis of constitution, when the *I* of "I think" produces intention that shapes the given: "[T]he texture of the *constituting* is stitched together with *threads* that also come from the realm of the *constituted*, without that origin having to correspond to any 'intentional aim'" [emphasis original].[123] This synthesis is realized upon sensibility, which, not metaphorically, is "the very flesh of the mind": "Sensibility . . . might it not be . . . an original transcendental synthesis accomplished by the *I think* . . . of this *I think* itself and of extension via this already construed *I think*?" [emphasis original].[124] In less complicated language and without grounding in the synthesis of sensibility, William James observes, at the behavioral psychological level, the same intriguing knot that the constituted is also the constituting. Using the pair of action and feeling, he says: "Action seems to follow feeling, but really action and feeling go together; and by regulating the action, which is under the more direct control of the will, we can indirectly regulate the feeling, which is not."[125] Sensibility reveals that the mental initiative of the

---

121. Lingis, "Introduction," xxiv.
122. Riera, *Intrigues*, 91.
123. Levinas, "Sensibility," 61.
124. Ibid., 61–62; idem, "Signification and Sense," 16.
125. William James, "The Gospel of Relaxation," in *Talks to Teachers on Psychology, and to Students on Some of Life's Ideals* (Cambridge: Harvard University Press, 1983), 118. Or according to Damasio, individual feelings are found to build up the collective emotional system, which becomes key to grouping and interpreting future feelings that accompany new situations (Damasio, *Looking for Spinoza*, 145–47).

subject is already conditioned or embodied through the subject's bodily receptions.

To illustrate the intrigue better, Levinas applies the language of time and trace. The contact with the other that had stroked the chord of sensibility, that gives rise to perception and knowledge, was always already a past and "never stabilized in any present, never available to my thinking." Thus it remains an irretrievable intrigue unable to be re-presented.[126] The ego, coinciding with the intentionality of consciousness, cannot reach back to that contact, which resists the assimilation of the consciousness. It is like an itch in my body that I cannot reach, a wound that I cannot heal. In fact, the "nontransparency of one's presence to self" and "the nonrepresentable" other[127] are found in the same untraceable trace: "I sense myself in sensibility but it is also by way of sensibility that the other comes to me."[128]

"Between seeing and saying,"[129] one is caught in a synthesis that precedes the conscious "I think."[130] Here lies the subjectivity of the subject in diachronic perspective: the appearance of the other has already provoked me with affection before I perceive the image. Susceptibility to the other, which upon the self's realization is already too late to cease, forces the self to acknowledge not only its vulnerability to the other, but also the burden to catch up with this provocation so as to restore wholeness.[131] In the case of this *waṣf*, the response to the provoked affection is expressed in the writing of a poem that arises from and appeals to susceptible sensibility. Such is an ethical writing that responds to the other "without assimilating

---

126. "Such pastness is not merely a lingering of the previous notes in the final chord, not a retained phase, but a lapse, a past of this present. . . . the past has escaped my memory already, and so was never stabilized in any present, never available to my thinking" (Robert Gibbs, *Why Ethics? Signs of Responsibilities* [Princeton, NJ: Princeton University Press, 2000], 347).

127. Levinas, "Sensibility," 66.

128. Leora Batnitzkey, "Encountering the Modern Subject in Levinas," in *Encounters with Levinas*, ed. Thomas Trezise, trans. Nicole Simek and Zahi Zalloua, Yale French Studies 104 (New Haven, CT: Yale University Press), 20.

129. Emmanuel Levinas, "The Servant and Her Master," 148.

130. Jean Jacques Rousseau vividly describes a moment of gapping the burdened past and the active response: "A sentiment takes possession of my soul with the rapidity of lightning, but instead of illuminating, it dazzles and confounds me; I feel all, but see nothing; I am excited, yet stupid; to think, I must be cool . . . and when I read that anecdote of a Duke of Savory, who turned himself round, while on the road, to cry out, 'À votre gorge, marchand de Paris!' (Charles-Emmanuel I.) I said, 'Here am I'" (*The Confessions of Jean Jacques Rousseau* [London: Gibbings & company, 1901], 166).

131. Elisabeth Weber summarizes that "it was a wound that brought the subject to expose his thoughts. . . . As writing and testifying ego is, however, already 'late' to that which affects, which touches it. The ego's speech preserves at most the trace of being affected, and the trace of being possessed" ("The Notion of Persecution in Levinas's *Otherwise than Being, or Beyond Essence*," in *Ethics as First Philosophy: The Significance of Emmanuel Levinas for Philosophy, Literature, and Religion*, ed. Adriaan Theodoor Peperzak [New York: Routledge, 1995], 74).

or reducing it to the same." It does not prevail over knowledge and vision but approaches in dedication.[132]

> If vision and knowledge consist in *being able* over their objects, in dominating them from a distance, the exceptional reversal brought about by writing comes down to being touched by what one sees—to being touched from a distance. The gaze is seized by the work [*l'œuvre*], the words look at the writer.[133]

To catch up with the untouchable touch, in other words, is to revisit the original site where the other has impressed one as beautiful, with the lingering feeling as the key to resuscitate, differently, the full volume of the other's beauty. Willingly emulating the anterior visual action in the verbal caress, the lover's original feeling is resurrected and exposed to the beloved (the addressee), sustained by an attentiveness that can be given again and again, even though the original moment provoked by her beauty is but a trace. Sensibility in this poetic endeavor is evoked in terms of sensual experiences and their associated feelings in embodied memories, which function as the friction to attach one's language to another's. It is also shown in the baring of one's interiority in its prayerful attention toward the other.

The beloved, "who is unique to the affection and who, by virtue of that uniqueness, is no longer a simple individual among individuals . . . cannot be represented and given to knowledge," save that she is "approachable" in his dedicated saying.[134] The dedication itself is the fountain of a love poem, even though what is said may be nothingness.[135] With it the original touch is reenacted, as the lover restages himself in "the quasi-narrative dimension of" approaching the beloved again, desiring to touch her through words in which she vividly appears.[136]

Writing to the beloved is, therefore, to approach her. This constant approaching is best illustrated by and also illustrates the characteristic repetitions in the Song. More precisely, it is not repetition that renews: the original bliss is renewed in every new wave of sensual experience. Take the initial exclamation in Song 1:15 and 4:1, for example. *Hinnāk*: "here-and-now, you!" João Salgado comments that the subject "I" is manifested in the

---

132. Cf. Riera, *Intrigues*, 1, 85.
133. Levinas, "The Poet's Vision," 132.
134. Idem, "Sensibility," 66.
135. Barthes, *A Lover's Discourse*, 77, 157.
136. Riera points out that "the other is an event that exceeds the grasp of consciousness and of its present-oriented temporality, thus overflowing the frames of narration" (*Intrigues*, 85, 88). Approaching the other is the "original experience" that Levinas notes in Blanchot's writing. "Literature, in Blanchot's view, is foreign to the World and the worlds-behind-the-world; it presupposes the poet's vision, which is an original experience in both senses of the adjective: a fundamental experience, and an experience of the origin. All artistic 'disinterestedness' toward things has already been that experience" (Levinas, "The Poet's Vision," 130–31).

constituting power of the here-and-now, which is the site of the world according to the subject.[137] By giving you the here-and-now, I empty myself as the site for your appearance, "like a spider dissolving in the constructive secretions of its web."[138] I give you my fully illuminated consciousness, not in order to see your qualities but to prohibit the evasion of my attention.[139]

Hinnāk yāpâ: the *a* vowels, as in a delightful exclamation "ah," rise up from the trace of *hinnāk* and crescendo into a plateau of *raʿyātî*. Then gently it thins into an *i* vowel that evokes again the trace of *hinnāk* differently. Hence a vocalic unity is formed at the line ending of Song 1:15a: *hinnāk yāpâ rāʿyātî*. It is soon torn open, however, as another *hinnāk yāpâ* appears and insists on paralleling its double: *hinnāk yāpâ, raʿyātî, hinnāk yāpâ*! Now what has been thinned into a closure is attenuated and again reopened to a resounding "ah!" Centered in the couplet is "my dear," who inspires the subject to praise, and praise again.

The next line, *ʿênayik yônîm*, signals a new direction in augmenting the same. It first recalls the lover's initial exclamation (1:15):

hinnāk yāpâ rāyātî	Oh you are beautiful, my dear
hinnāk yāpâ ʿênayik yônîm	Oh you are beautiful, your eyes doves

Up to *ʿênayik*, there seems to be a perfect formal parallel: a rhythmic pattern across the line break (syllable counts 2–2–3 // 2–2–3), the chiming *a* vowels and *i* vowels, and a focusing from the general ("you") to the specific ("your eyes"). But the last word, *yônîm*, interrupts this closed parallelism. In completing what *ʿênayik* expects, it transports *ʿênayik*, through the remembrance of the lover (and the addressee), toward a concrete evocation of another beautiful image, which remains in the making since the readers bring into the weaving their own visions of the doves fluttering their wings. *Yônîm*, an outsider and a lead word, imparts mobility in rhythm, vision, and signification to the otherwise overly sweet and stable formal parallel.

When the reader reads up to *ʿênayik yônîm* in 4:1, the memory of 1:15 conditions the present expectation and tempts the reader to make a line break here.[140] But the lover again reinvents the trace of *hinnāk yāpâ* by

---

137. The subject "I" is "defined as the center of the here-and-now experience" (João Salgado, "The Feeling of a Dialogical Self," in *Otherness in Question: Labyrinths of the Self*, ed. Lívia Mathias Simão and Jaan Valsiner [Charlotte, NC: Information Age, 2007], 59).

138. Roland Barthes, *The Pleasure of the Text*, trans. Richard Miller (New York: Hill & Wang, 1975), 64.

139. Levinas, "Paul Celan," 43.

140. So does BHS/BHQ. It should be noted that small divergences exist in the making of the rabbinic tradition. For instance, in the Mishnah (m. ʿAbodah Zarah 2:8), Joshua and Ishmael debate whether *myyn* in Song 1:2 should be read with the following verse (Ludwig Blau, "Masoretic Studies, III: The Division into Verses," *JQR* 9 [1896]: 140–41). Robert Alter also agrees with this lineation (*The Art of Biblical Poetry* [New York: Basic Books, 1985], 199). His poetic analysis, however, focuses on the second part of ch. 4.

adding new and decisive words—*mibba'ad lĕṣammātēk*. The weight of this aditional detail pulls the simile down from the framed exclamation (4:1ab) to form a new lyrical structure (simile and its elaboration) between these two lines (4:1cd). The latter then inaugurates the sevenfold simile-elaboration formation in the main body of the poem.[141] As this new lineation overlays one's memory of 1:15, one is caught in an aporia, unable to reduce the words to one single configuration.

The tension between repetition and renewal desires and yet decidedly precludes a conclusive comprehension. Through re-writing, writing over the previous, the lyrics embody an erotic longing that inspires, but will not be contained in, the words. Solicited by the alteration of the other and/or oneself, and embodying the unfaltering proximity between one and the other, repetition-with-renewal is meaningful beyond being a poetic technique, for it testifies to one's "restaging" to the trace of the other.[142]

The same saying that inspires the lover's variations on *hinnāk yāpâ* is resuscitated in his verbal approaches to the beloved. To say it is "Darling, how I adore you" is still a reduction and betrayal. Not to be confused with the tautology of reason that drives at the closure of being, poetic repetition with renewal does not lead to an ever more precise description. Rather, in the altering expressions of the same caress, it emulates how one's sensibility is being constantly vivified by the other's beauty, now as it has been at first. It is the remembrance of the initial perfect bliss in newly found joys.

In short, the meaning of the poem is intricately tied to the moment of its birth. The other's beauty caresses and wounds the subject's sensibility through one's unguarded eyes. Between seeing and saying arises one's provoked initiative, which embodies one's responsibility to the other. This haunting responsibility would not subside until its inspired response measures up to the texture and depth of one's aroused sensibility, that is, the trace of the other upon one's sensibility, which is ever altering. There is no solitary peace for oneself, from which one can establish one's sovereignty and objectify the other. Rather, the initiative in one's approaching the other is always already a response to the intrigue of alterity that needs to be updated. The next question is in whether such approach is responsible to the ethical imperative of the other, especially in the heat of one's erotic desire.

---

141. A fine difference, worthy of attention, is that the elaboration on the veil in 4:1c and 4:3c refer back to the bodily feature, but in the following lines of descriptions the elaboration refers to the metaphor.

142. As true as it is in creative writing, this constant alteration is also seen in the reader's approaches to the text from Levinas's rereadings, or "long frequenting," of Husserlian works (Drabinski, *Sensibility and Singularity*, 10) to the proliferating commentaries on the Song.

Desire

Not only does the lover approach the beloved through renewed verbal repetitions in Song 4:1–7, his approaching is staged at the climax of this poem. His seeing will no longer return to her body, but *he* will go toward her (Song 4:6). The subject that has been describing the object lets go of its lofty position and enters his own words. This gesture enacts the highest praise, like the hand that paints dropping the paintbrush and reaching across the visual distance to touch the painted.

At the apex of the poem, the fluid visual trace of her features and metaphors is replaced by a plateau of parallelism: the day breathes and the shadows flee; he will go to the mountain of myrrh and the hill of frankincense. The verbs transform time as meaningful events: the day will overtake the night of the longed-for rendezvous at the threshold of dawn.[143] The anxiety of ending, however, is preemptively suspended by the leading compound adverbs *ʿad še-* ("until") and serves but to generate an erotic intensity for the following main clause. Bracketed by *ʿad še-*, the antithetical parallel of time seals a perpetual presence for the desired encounter, which responds with a synonymous parallel of space that localizes a sweet spot worthy of this eternity. Situated at the center of time and space is the lover's self adjuration: "Let myself go!" (*ʾelek lî*). In contrast to the nominal clauses in 4:1–5 and 7, this is the only verb in the main clauses of this poem.[144] The

---

143. From a grammatical perspective, *ʿad še-* can be either "until" or "while" (*DCH*, 6.266). The former signifies that the action in the subordinate clause precedes that of the main clause (e.g., Song 2:7; 3:4, 5; 8:4; Judg 5:7; Ps 123:2), while, less frequently, the latter indicates simultaneity (Song 1:12). Since all commentators agree that the rendezvous in the main clause should happen at night, the time referred to in the temporal clause may evoke either end of the rendezvous. Consequently, this verse may be paraphrased as either "until daybreak, I will keep going" or "when it is twilight, I will go." As daybreak, it refers to the time when the day regains life force, and the sun drives out the shadows (J. P. Fokkelman, *Reading Biblical Poetry: An Introductory Guide* [Louisville: Westminster John Knox, 2001], 194; Duane A. Garrett, *Song of Songs*, WBC 23B [Nashville: Thomas Nelson, 2004], 162). As twilight, it describes the time when the day blows cool winds and the shadows grow longer (Leonard S. Kravitz and Kerry M. Olitzky, *Shir Hashirim: A Modern Commentary on the Song of Songs* [New York: URJ, 2004], 49; Exum, *Song of Songs*, 156; Falk, *Love Lyrics from the Bible*, 121). Though the day's breathing can easily refer to both settings, the fleeing shadows fit less congruently with twilight. Fox argues that the shadows "do not 'flee' as the sun sets, but stretch out, *niṭṭim* (Jer 6:4; Ps 102:12), and linger until they cover the earth" (Fox, *Song of Songs*, 115; see also Gordis, *The Song of Songs*, 82–83; Hess, *Song of Songs*, 99). Moreover, in other biblical texts, shadows are used as a synonym for nighttime (Isa 16:3, Jer 6:4), and the fleeing of the shadows means that they are no more (Job 14:2; Yair Zakovitch, *Das Hohelied*, HThKAT [Freiburg im Breisgau: Herder, 2004], 162 n. 121). In consideration of these textual references, I propose that the temporal clause refers to the end of the rendezvous—that is, daybreak.

144. Four other finite verbs are used in this poem, but they appear in subordinate clauses in 4:1c (*šeggālšû*), 2a (*šeʿālû*), 6a (*šeyyāpûaḥ*, *wĕnāsû*). One exception is that 4QCantª has a partially reconstructed participle ([*šglš*]*wt*) in 4:1c (Tov, "Introduction to 4QCantª⁻ᶜ," 200).

yqtl aspect accentuates desire instead of its consumption: perpetually riding this verb, the lover approaches but never arrives at the fragrant hills. This pose constitutes "one of the hallmarks of the erotic":[145] "together, but not yet."[146]

The implied image of night not only corroborates the conveyed erotic desire but also solicits the ethical significance of "let myself go." In the night, nothing is awaited; it is "tranquility in waiting.[147] From this nocturnal element emerges a forgetting of oneself, without pretension or retention, renouncing oneself without losing identity, a relaxed self beyond being's drama of being tensed in itself. Awakened by your beauty, I estrange myself in this erotically ambiguous moment: the "I," that abiding biological impetus, pursues happiness, is submerged and saturated by the sweet happiness that swells to the brim of my receptivity, and in the overflowing I feel exposed in an acute sense of being brought up short, not by happiness's insatiability that insists on another satisfaction, but by the touch of an other that is always already a trace. Eros, the choice wine, intoxicates and sobers up, in that the intoxication of the "I" of *I think* sobers up subjectivity qua sensibility.

Indeed, people have a prior singular desire for happiness, like an organism's simple desire to be alive and thriving.[148] In Biblical Hebrew, *nepeš*, which often denotes the life force that makes an individual person, is found to have the meaning of "a living appetite." It is an infant-like appetite for sweetness, a fundamental desire for the body and soul to taste sweet,[149] as in "desire is a reaching out [*orexis*] for the sweet."[150] That sweet taste makes life desirable, the lack of it makes Melinda say, "I want that I want to live."[151] Conversely, if one did not have such a predetermination for pleasure, there would be no suffering.[152]

To many, the living appetite for sweetness comes closest to its fulfillment in the burning sensation of mutual erotic love. "Remembering her brings my love to life again,"[153] Baudelaire writes. You, whom my desire loves (*šeʾăhăbā napšî*; Song 1:7; 3:1, 2, 3, 4), make possible the plateau of being alive: "I am here now, you are here now, we are here now."[154] The

---

145. Anne Carson, *Eros the Bittersweet* (Normal, IL: Dalkey Archive, 1998), 26, 63; Jackson, "Eros and the Erotics of Writing," 72.
146. Blanchot, *L'attente L'oubli*, 76; quoted from Levinas, "The Servant and Her Master," 146.
147. Ibid., 145.
148. Cf. Damasio, *Looking for Spinoza*, 40–42.
149. Job's outcry, in this perspective, is that of an infant betrayed by its mother with a bitter taste instead of sweet milk (J. Gerald Janzen, "Lust for Life and the Bitterness of Job," *Theology Today* 55 [1998]: 154).
150. Aristotle, *Rhetoric* 1.1370a5 (quoted from Carson, *Eros the Bittersweet*, 63).
151. *Melinda and Melinda*, dir. Woody Allen, Fox Searchlight Pictures, 2005, DVD.
152. Levinas, *Otherwise than Being*, 73.
153. Baudelaire, *Flowers of Evil*, 46.
154. Murduch, *The Black Prince*, 239.

bodies caress and the souls embrace, in a movement like fine oil poured out, choice wine gliding down the palate, the spring garden wafting its scent in the wind, myrrh and honey dripping, doves chirping and fawns leaping. . . . At its height, the cathartic wash of erotic energy, like death, exposes the insubstantiality of World, History and Identity, which are the armors and manifestations of one's pursuit of happiness.[155] In his letter to his wife, Gisèle, Celan expresses his coming toward her as "leaving behind" the world, as authenticity beyond "false clarities," as significance that gives meaning to time:

> You see, in coming toward you I feel I'm leaving a world behind, hearing doors bang shut behind me, door after door, for they're so many, the doors in this world made of misunderstandings, false clarities, scoffings. . . .
>
> I'll be there next to you in an instant, in a second that inaugurates time.[156]

In this sweet plateau of erotic encounter, one cannot coil back on oneself after enjoying the other's beauty, for one is no longer able "to be complacent" *in* oneself.[157] "The 'I' separate from itself," discovering "a place in which the person, in grasping himself as a stranger to himself, emerges."[158] One is detached from oneself and drawn toward where the other is. Or in Carson's words, "The self forms at the edge of desire."[159] Precisely in tasting sweet eros, one frees oneself out of the customary shell of self-protection and genuinely tastes the significance of human life, which overflows the sweetness of the egoistic happiness.[160] The self has been awakened and reckoned its unicity: ". . . there is no one else to replace myself, for you. . . ." At the very root of the self, after blowing out the fog of egoism, there already is a voice calling, "let myself go to you."

This separation of self is inscribed in the form of *lî* in Song 4:6b. Here "myself" is a reflexive, as *se* in French, "as-for-oneself" (*quant-à-soi*). It physically differentiates the "I" who is absorbed in the action (*'elek*) and the self for whom this action becomes meaningful. I am outside of and thus able to summon myself, in reference to, as a consequence of my response to the other. This occasions the birth of the human self, an awakening by an other. Fittingly, such reflexive use of "for myself" is referred to as the "ethical dative" grammatically.[161]

---

155. Levinas notes that, indeed, "this World produced by work and history" must come, but its "ultimate meaning" must be decided ("The Poet's Vision," 135).

156. Paul Celan, "Letter to Gisèle Celan—Lestrange"; quoted from John Felstiner, "The One and Only Circle: Paul Celan's letter to Gisèle," *Fiction* (New York: Department of English, City College of New York, 2008), 39.

157. Levinas, *Otherwise than Being*, 72.

158. Idem, "Paul Celan," 43; cf. Celan, *Collected Prose*, 46.

159. Carson, *Eros the Bittersweet*, 39.

160. Nussbaum, "Faint with Secret Knowledge," 702.

161. *GBH* §133d; *GKC* §119S. See also Exum, *Song of Songs*, 154.

I would like to add quickly that this ethical significance does not mean that the self's initial desire for sweetness is wrong. The meaning of being human is often shown in overriding my natural desire for the sake of caring for another's desire. It is precisely through the energy of deliberately substituting my self-concern with the care for you, in giving what I myself cherish, that human freedom shines forth. I tear the bread that I am hungry for to give to you, bear the murder charge and am sentenced in place of your mother,[162] jump in front of an oncoming train to cover your unconscious body between the rails[163] so you will live and thrive. That is freedom from the inertia of being.

Furthermore, new facets of the climactic approach emerge when it is read in relation to surrounding texts. Together, they embody the way that ethical awareness is brought to the language of desire. First, the seemingly imposing and aggressive proclamation of approach is tenderized when compared to the girl's previous invitation.

2:17 ʿad šeyyāpûăḥ hayyôm	Till the day breathes,
wĕnāsû haṣṣĕlālîm	and the shadows flee,
sōb dĕmēh-lĕkā dôdî liṣĕbî	turn, make *yourself* like, my love,
ʾōr lĕʿōfer hāʾayyālîm	a gazelle or a fawn of a deer,
ʿal hārê bāter	upon the *mountain* of halves.[164]
4:6 ʿad šeyyāpûaḥ hayyôm	Till the day breathes,
wĕnāsû haṣṣĕlālîm	and the shadows flee,
ʾelek lî ʾel-har hammôr	let *me* go to the *mountain* of myrrh,
wĕʾel-gibʿat hallĕbônâ	and to the hill of frankincense.

Attracted by verbal similarities, his words merge with hers as he answers her invitation; and thus the thematic content—their desired union—is manifest on the verbal level. The lover borrows words from his beloved's invitation, offering his lips as the site of her words to express a shared desire. Substituting "you" (*lĕkā*) for "me" (*lî*), his proclamation in 4:7 becomes a reply. And his bold tone is but a passion matching his beloved's. Moreover, through the same image of the fawn (2:17; 4:5), their erotic longing to be

---

162. Commenting on *The Black Prince*, Nussbaum writes that it is for Julian's sake, Pearson "conceals the true facts concerning her mother's murder of her father and takes the conviction and sentence with staggering courage" ("'Faint with Secret Knowledge,'" 703).

163. When Wesley Autrey, a construction worker and a Navy veteran, saw a stranger, Cameron Hollopeter, who had suffered a seizure and had fallen onto the tracks, he jumped in front of a Manhattan subway train to cover him with his own body. For the full report, see Cara Buckley, "Man Is Rescued by Stranger on Subway Tracks" (web pages: *New York Times*, http://www.nytimes.com/2007/01/03/nyregion/03life.html [accessed March 20, 2008]).

164. The root *btr* means "to cut in pieces" (*BDB*, 126). It is used to refer to two halves of cut animals (Gen 15:10) and two halves of the cut calf (Jer 34:18–19). In this context, it is a euphrasy for the girl's breasts (Longman, *Song of Song*, 147).

one flesh is poetically achieved. In the way the gazelle bounces on the hills, may he be on her breasts (her vision in 2:17, 1:13); as the fawns are caressed between lilies, so may her breasts be between his lips (his vision in 4:5, 7:9). The fusion on verbal and imagery levels stays evocative of the sensual impression of delight when the audience comes into contact with the lyrics, but it remains as a "not yet" to the lovers' union. Thus it further inflames rather than consuming eros.

Second, the visual tracing assumed in the *waṣf*, which can potentially give rise to the illusion of dominance over the other, is also conditioned by the lines that follow this poem. Though I see your body (4:1–7), *you* are as far as Lebanon (4:8). Moreover, instead of the domesticated or gentle animals appear in the *waṣf*, the wild lions and leopards roam in your dwelling (4:8). The psychic distance, which I come to acknowledge at the height of my desire to go to you, reveals a radical separation between you and me. The only way to reach you, I realize, is to entreat you—"come with me from Lebanon!" (4:8)[165] In other words, the beloved's body so extolled in the *waṣf* cannot be reduced to an "It" as the object of reason or lust, for the "you" that transcends the sum of the bodily parts evokes transcendence:

> Even though 'you' are attached to the body, which the demonstrative 'that' can point toward, the part of 'you' that does not presuppose the 'that' reveals the trace of the 'you' par excellence—God. This is the part of 'you' that resists the reduction of I-Thou into I-It. This is the meaning of 'you;' 'you' do not rest on the neutrality of 'there is.' To mean does not refer to being.[166]

Were the body exposed without "you," it would bear the cruelty of "ultramateriality," of a person reduced to a body: "what *therefore* remains hidden even when uncovered."[167] Beauty invites partaking. At the moment of beholding a beautiful person, many stories lie latent. Though itself a basic biological need like eating and drinking, provoked sexual initiative can result in dark and tragic consequences if the person is seen as an ultramaterial object. "You shall not murder!" God's thunderous voice ripples in the background when David has Bathsheba brought to him, when Shechem seizes Dinah, when Amnon enters Tamar, when the Levite's concubine is consumed to death. For in God's image "you" are created.

The other "appears without appearing"[168] when the beholders "have eyes but do not see" (Jer 5:21) due to anesthesia. Nullifying one's sensibility

---

165. Cf. Alter, *The Art of Biblical Poetry*, 71. Like a garden enclosed, the *waṣf* prepares for the invitation, the approach, and the joyful banquet in the following poem (4:12–5:1).
166. Emmanuel Levinas, *Alterity and Transcendence*, trans. Michael B. Smith (New York: Columbia University Press, 1999), 91.
167. Crignon, "Figuration," 109 (emphasis original). Crignon traces how Levinas himself evolves and softens his stance on the non-phenomenality of the face. He also points out that Levinas's ostensible resistance to the image is rooted in his Jewish iconoclasm.
168. Emmanuel Levinas, *Totality and Infinity: An Essay on Exteriority*, trans. Alphonso Lingis (Pittsburgh: Duquesne University Press, 1969), 257.

of a provoked tenderness to care for the other's bodily frailty results in nullifying the other. Is it not a murder of the other *and* the self? "They have ... departed" (Jer 5:21): even though incense still burns and sacrifices are still brought into the House of God, *they* have departed. They as humans have departed, existing in profanation, a modality of being without signification. Is not the abandonment of sensitivity, "a semi-deliberate inattention,"[169] the root of all guilt?

Love poems such as this *waṣf* tame raw physical need with a humanist awareness of facing an other. The lover's erotic energy, pent up within the periphery of praising by characterization, reveals a voluntary submission of desire to the generic strain of the *waṣf*. The desire to seize the other for oneself is seized and transformed by the linguistic contact with the other. The lover's desire is sustained in the pose of ever coming to and never consuming the beloved, no matter how close physically she is to him. Resisting both Platonic and "phallic illusions of totality, finality or fullness," the verbal caress eternalizes "a hand that seeks without ever finding."[170] This poetically sustained desire becomes "a desire that desires beyond desire while remaining desire,"[171] a touch that feels touched without grasping. It therefore evokes in the audience the feeling of the way the other as a whole person impresses oneself. This is the precise difference between the saying of eros and sex.

> We talk more about the how-to of sex than any other generation, yet I fear we know less. We exaggerate the importance of technique over feelings and imagination. We refer to 'having sex' as though sex were a commodity, whereas the older expression, 'making love,' emphasizes the journey and the emotional closeness.[172]

From the initial outpouring of desire toward another, one can let oneself go in different directions. Song 4:1–7 illustrates an ethical way of approaching the other: "by treating the beloved, the other, as prior to and more important than I, the lover practices ethics and shows the fundamental spirit of ethics—love—without aiming."[173] This is a humanist approach that looks up to the other as a body with a face, a face with a body.

> [T]he one-for-the-other, exposure of self to another, immediacy in the caress and in the contact of saying—the immediacy of a skin and a face,

---

169. Murdoch, *Metaphysics as a Guide to Morals* (New York: Penguin, 1992), 189.
170. Crignon, "Figuration," 110.
171. Richard Kearney, *The God Who May Be: A Hermeneutics of Religion* (Bloomington: Indiana University Press, 2001), 59–60.
172. Naomi H. Rosenblatt, *After the Apple—Women in the Bible: Timeless Stories of Love, Lust, and Longing* (New York: Hyperion, 2005), 253.
173. Stella Sandford, "Levinas, Feminism and the Feminine," in *The Cambridge Companion to Levinas*, ed. Simon Critchley and Robert Bernasconi (Cambridge: Cambridge University Press, 2002), 144.

a skin that is always the modification of a face, of a face that is weighed down with a skin.[174]

In the skin of sensibility, the ethical face and the erotic body are connected; the other is neither pure idea nor merely flesh. In sensibility, as provoked initiatives that seek to resuscitate the originary intrigue of the beautiful beloved, the subject achieves a synthesis between the desire for the primordial sweetness of life and the responsibility demanded by the face of the other.

Ending Invitation

Poetry, like a beautiful other, is essentially erotic: it provokes a desire that precludes possession or consumption. It is the delicious, sweet, cold plum that one tastes without eating.[175] Though given to the beloved, for instance, this song is not hers to possess.[176] Like a wafting fragrant breeze that passes through her fingers, it touches her and is gone, leaving the trace of sensualized feeling in her embodied mind. Coming into the public domain of poetry, it looks over her shoulder to greet and arouse other audiences. Moreover, lyric materiality is not exterior to a feeling person. Words are before my eyes but beyond my grasp. I can touch the space where the physical shapes are, I can even tear the paper where they dwell; but I fall in a dizzy hunger in the pursuit of possession, because I cannot grasp the words in the full weight with which they take hold of me. I can only caressingly resurrect them with my breath and blood.

Experiencing Song 4:1–7 as a reader is to sensualize and not sexualize oneself. The droning of a sweet chant in silence escapes the mind's control and keeps evoking oneself. The reading, a caressing of the poem that is also caressed by it, tenderizes one from within through feelings, from which the poem floods over oneself. As the tide embraces the tide. Then mixes. Then passes by. The reader receives love, while the poem receives life. And the two are no longer the same.

The caress does not leave a perceptible mark on the skin but it alters, from the original root of sensibility, how the reader's self feels and responds. Like musical form, poetry's touch results in a new perceptive equilibrium, which, having reconfigured one's pain and pleasure, is posed to respond to future experiences. Samuel Barbar's *Adagio for Strings*, for instance, awakens in the audience one's own dull, massive, unnamed, and condensed emotion of sorrow. The audience is provoked to grasp this pain, in the ability to revive a trace of the past, to relive the feelings distilled and condensed in emotion. Yet the hand that grasps does not exclusively belong to the

---

174. Levinas, *Otherwise than Being*, 85.
175. "Beauty: a fruit which we look at without trying to seize it" (Simone Weil, *Gravity and Grace* [London: Routledge & Kegan Paul, 1952], 150).
176. Waters, *Poetry's Touch*, 23.

audience. It is readjusted, reconstituted by instilling and ingraining esthetic forms from *Adagio for Strings*, in the way they interrogate, caress, and give voice to Samuel Barbar's personally textured sorrow. With the newly gained formal traces, the audience rewrites its previous configuration of sorrow. The performative participation in art, in its grasping as releasing,[177] is to have one's sensibility opened to the trace of an other. Touched and "breath-turning," the estranged I is set free, and so is the other.[178]

Just like the lover's wounding gaze that locates its significance in the susceptibility of sensibility, the poem greets and wounds its recipient, who is an "open, inhabitable, an addressable . . . *you*,"[179] who can offer a site of here-and-now for the resurrection of the poem. It is an extended hand that greets and is waiting to be greeted.

If one sets aside the third-person critical stance, one can greet the poem personally and resuscitate the original contact between "you" and "I." Each reader approaches the poem with his or her unique blend of memory and experience. Each reading is a substitution: giving one's life force to resurrect significance from the poem. Like a handshake, you and I together weave the poem, where we touch, and are touched:

> I feel through every leaf the pressure of your hand, which I return.
> And thus upon our journey link'd together let us go.[180]

---

177. Peter Schmiedgen, "Art and Idolatry: Aesthetics and Alterity in Levinas," *Contretemps* 3 (July 2002): 152.

178. Paul Celan, "The Meridian," *Paul Celan: Selections*, ed. Pierre Joris, trans. Rosmarie Waldrop (Berkeley: University of California Press, 2005), 162.

179. Waters, *Poetry's Touch*, 159.

180. Whitman, "Inscription," 557.

Chapter 3

Restlessness and Responsibility for the Other

> My exposure to him, antecedent to his appearing, my delay behind him, my undergoing, undo the core of what is identity in me.[1]
> It [the psyche] is an undoing of the substantial nucleus of the ego that is formed in the same, a fission of the mysterious nucleus of inwardness of the subject by this assignation to respond, which does not leave any place of refuge, any chance to slip away, and is thus despite the ego, or, more exactly, despite me.[2]

Besides framing the poem, the first-person pronoun (*'ănî*) appears four times in Song 5:2–8[3] and counts for one-third of its total occurrences in the Song.[4] Meanwhile, this poem relates the subject's experience from her vantage point. It seems reasonable, therefore, to deduce that this is a poem about the "I."[5] Yet when probed, the "I" is not presented as an autonomous entity that can be exhausted in the process of interiorization. Rather, the "I" is fissured by a vigilance regarding the other in the beginning (5:2); her bosom and soul are subjected to the other's intrigue and withdrawal (*bĕdabbĕrô*); and at the end, the "I" speaks of herself as one who is faint with love (5:8). Additionally, the poem about the "I" moves along a fine

---

1. Emmanuel Levinas, *Otherwise than Being: Or, Beyond Essence*, trans. Alphonso Lingis (Pittsburgh: Duquesne University Press, 1998), 88–89.
2. Levinas, *Otherwise than Being*, 141.
3. Although Song 5:2–8 is the first unit of the larger poem that constitutes Song 5:2–6:3 and so its interpretation will not be complete without taking into consideration the following two units (5:9–16 and 6:1–3), there are sufficient textual indicators to justify its relative independence. Aside from the change of scenes in the beginning and the abjuration at the end, the inclusio of *'ănî* neatly envelops Song 5:2–8.
4. Richard S. Hess, *The Song of Songs* (Grand Rapids, MI: Baker, 2005), 166. The independent first-person pronoun used exclusively in the Song is *'ănî* (Song 1:5, 6; 2:1, 5, 16; 5:2, 5, 6, 8; 6:3; 7:11; 8:10). This linguistic feature highlights the subjective function of the speaker (Yair Zakovitch, *Das Hohelied*, HThKAT [Freiburg im Breisgau: Herder, 2004], 216).
5. For instance, Dianne Bergant summarizes that this poem shows that the female lover is "self-possessed, . . . neither afraid of nor ashamed of strong emotion or of its physical manifestation" (*The Song of Songs: The Love Poetry of Scripture*, Spiritual Commentaries [Hyde Park, NY: New City Press, 1998], 96).

line between "I" and "my lover" (*dôdî*), which the seven occurences of the conjunction *waw* epitomize visually and symbolically (5: 2, 4, 6 [3×], 5 [2×]). Is it too unthinkable to say that her lover, in his capricious otherness and through her unalienable obsession, is the soul of the poem about the "I?"

At times one must go through an extreme situation to see the truly important, more profound even than the essential. In this poem, an insomnia that destabilizes the subject's consciousness irreversibly fissures her interiority, which is the foundation of her self-sustaining entity. When the undoing of the ego morphs into an undergoing, the "despite me"—the subject in the accusative—reveals subjectivity as a vulnerability pre-originally exposed to the other. Instead of interiority and substance, the unicity of the "I" is revealed as its responsibility for the other, "because he's more myself than I am." [6] Or, "The poem that spoke of me speaks of '*that which concerns another; someone entirely other.*'"[7]

Listening beside the Said

Otherwise than being the said, the "I" of the poem signifies the drawing out of the subject as she speaks of her state. In the manner of a "divergence of the identical from itself," the "I" grasps herself through speaking of her state, which is "already separate from" yet "remaining whole with the 'I.'"[8] The spoken state—her sleep torn by wakefulness—manifests "an unextinguishable insomnia of consciousness,"[9] which mobilizes the "I" to speak. Through the fissure in the said that is marked by the first *waw*, insomnia emits the first light of the night, "the *original dissipation* of opaqueness."[10] A nocturnal vigilance destabilizes the consciousness of consciousness, because the latter cannot contain insomnia in its thinking, because insomnia, as self-destabilization, exposes the subject's original exposure to the other through her irrepressible internal fissure. "Insomnia in the bed of being, the impossibility of curling up and forgetting oneself."[11] Instead of beginning from consciousness and proceeding in a translucent reflection of her failed self-identification, her speaking dwells on the very restlessness that separates and connects the pre-original trace of the other and her consciousness of its unsettling burden, which interrogates the pre-verbal pulling force of the-other-in-herself in her verbal expression.

---

6. Emily Brontë, *Wuthering Heights* (New York: Arc Manor, 2007), 63.

7. Emmanuel Levinas, "*Paul Celan*," *Proper Names*, trans. Michael B. Smith [London: Athlone, 1996]), 42. The quotation within is from Paul Celan, "The Meridian," *Paul Celan: Selections*, ed. Pierre Joris, trans. Rosmarie Waldrop (Berkeley: University of California Press, 2005), 48.

8. Levinas, *Otherwise than Being*, 30; idem, "The Other in Proust," *Proper Names*, 101.

9. Idem, *Otherwise than Being*, 30.

10. Ibid.

11. Idem, "Paul Celan," 45.

Similar to the way that the constituted night (5:2) constitutes the poetic space of Song 5:2–8, insomnia ties the thematic knot of the poem that scatters the reader's thematization of the poem. The nocturnal dark light permeating the poem neither illuminates nor clarifies; instead, it embodies the subject's inability to synchronize the other in her words. Hence, in a vigilance that does not lead to or rest in coherence, the "I" speaks from a site other than her enclosed interiority in response to the other who had intrigued her and is withdrawn.

²ᵃ*ʾănî yĕšēnā wĕlibbî ʿēr*   I am asleep, but my heart is awake . . .

Now a preliminary question begs the reader's attention: from where does one begin? Or, on what ground does the reader constitute this poem? The beginning of the poem makes this inquiry particularly relevant. Renita J. Weems even claims that "[t]he entire meaning of the unit seems to hinge upon how one interprets the opening scene in 5:2–8."[12] Is it a dream, fantasy, or reality?

Commentators often begin by defining the female lover's initial state. "Was she asleep and awakened by the knock on the door, or was she sleeping lightly and dreaming the contents of the poem that follows?"[13] When difficulties of rationalizing the happenings as actual events mount up, especially given the unexpected beating in 5:7, efforts are made to rationalize the whole poem as dream or fantasy. Even scholars who first treat it as a poem are found recoiling back to rationalization in order to comprehend it, by reducing it to "lyrical formulations" of a theme.[14]

These approaches betray their constituting grounds as either narrative linearity, which is the dominant conceptual metaphor in everyday life, or

---

12. Renita J. Weems, "Song of Songs," in *The New Interpreter's Bible* (Nashville: Abingdon, 1997), 5.409.

13. Tremper Longman III, *The Song of Songs* (Grand Rapids, MI: Eerdmans, 2001), 165. For readings that consider the poem a dream, see Marcia Falk, *Love Lyric from the Hebrew Bible: A Translation and Literary Study of the Song of Songs*, Bible and Literature Series 4 (Sheffield: Sheffield Academic Press, 1982), 121; Roland E. Murphy, *The Song of Songs: A Commentary on the Book of Canticles or the Song of Songs* (Minneapolis: Fortress, 1990), 165; Hess, *The Song of Songs*, 167–78; Wilhelm Rudolph, *Das Hohe Lied*, KAT 17/2 (Gütersloh: Mohn, 1962), 155. In contrast, Michael V. Fox reads the poem as an actual event: "In 5:2–8 the Shulammite tells the girls of Jerusalem about a nighttime visit by her lover and the events that followed" (*The Song of Songs and the Ancient Egyptian Love Songs* [Madison: University of Wisconsin Press, 1985], 141); see also Othmar Keel, *The Song of Songs: A Continental Commentary* (Minneapolis: Fortress, 1994), 188; Duane A. Garrett, *Song of Songs*, WBC 23B (Nashville: Thomas Nelson, 2004), 409; Michael D. Goulder, *The Song of Songs*, JSOTSup 36 (Sheffield: JSOT Press, 1986), 40–43.

14. While Longman insists that "we understand the poem as a poem, not as a dream or an event," the difficulty in understanding the violence in 5:7 forces him to admit that "the movement of this part of the poem is better understood as a dream than as an actual event" (*Song of Songs*, 169). Instead of toiling along the lines of narrative as Longman, Keel summarizes this poem in abstract terms as "lyrical formulations of a typical relational fantasy describing the missing of the opportune moment" (Keel, *Song of Songs*, 186).

the singular perspicuity of reason, which is believed to be able to discern the core of the subject matter. Yet, even though infinite writings may be generated on these grounds, they remain within the light of consciousness, of *I think*. Even though the shades of each "I" that interprets differ, all derive from "the same morning light."[15] Readings built upon these grounds, though instructive with respect to knowledge, do not move beyond the first word of the poem ("I"). "Again, again walking and always in the same place—another country, other towns, the same country."[16] In the same way that the "I" seeks and finds not her lover, the interpretive words so derived "could no longer mean anything but that closure," the closure of *I think*.[17] It is as though one were seeking darkness by holding a lantern high, or seeking otherness by colonizing another country.

If the subject is posited as consciousness, whatever event occurs within it (whether consciousness is overwhelmed, jolted, or wounded) comes from this subject who becomes conscious, who thus exists on its own, and so is separate. Philosophy becomes, to use one of Husserl's terms, an egology.[18]

Alternately, in his essay "Lyrical Theology," Tod Linafelt discredits the preoccupation with narrative when approaching lyrical poetry. He proposes reading Song 5:2–8 as a "pseudonarrative," that is, "a plot without context and without consequences."[19] The characters and settings of this poem are stripped of any reference to concrete, sociocultural reality. In other words, though this poem uses narrative elements, the atmosphere, the "What?" and "Why?" of a story, is rarified.

"Tell us '*just* exactly' what happened," the reader anxiously asks; in response to this request, the poem refuses to tell the story (*l'histoire*).[20] Exactly what happens in Song 5:2–8 is beside the point. The story line is flirtatiously sketchy. The scarce presence of narrative elements in the poem does not weigh on the presence of a preparatory sketch that awaits the reader to complete a fictional universe, but on the scarcity that forces the reader's attention upon the making of language (*poesis*).[21] Poetry is not so transparent that it allows what it says to pass through the words them-

---

15. Maurice Blanchot, *Awaiting Oblivion*, trans. John Gregg (Lincoln: University of Nebraska Press, 1997), 26.

16. This is Levinas's rendition of Blanchot's text ("The Servant and Her Master" *Proper Names*, 144; Blanchot, *L'Attente l'oubli* [Paris: Gallimard, 1962], 14). Cf. Gregg's translation of this text: "Time and time again, walking and always marking time, another country, other cities, other roads, the same country" (Blanchot, *Awaiting Oblivion*, 5).

17. Quoted from Levinas, "The Servant and Her Master," 144; Blanchot, *Awaiting Oblivion*, 13.

18. Levinas, "Martin Buber and the Theory of Knowledge," *Proper Names*, 19.

19. Tod Linafelt, "Lyrical Theology: The Song of Songs and the Advantage of Poetry," in *Toward a Theology of Eros: Transfiguring Passion at the Limits of Discipline*, ed. Virginia Burrus and Catherine Keller (New York: Fordham University Press, 2006), 293, 299.

20. Maurice Blanchot, *The Madness of the Day* (Barrytown, NY: Station Hill, 1981), 18.

21. Regarding this line of thinking, J. Cheryl Exum discards the "discussion of the degree of reality and fantasy in these verses" in favor of "the double entendre" that allows

selves. If one were to read poetry with justice, one ought to begin with the decision of breaking from "the anecdotal or social curiosities" that seek poetic meaning in "the narrative or fictive element,"[22] and focus on the verbal body, the words that refuse to fade away in the morning light.

Of the Hebrew verbs related to sleep, *škb* and *yšn* are often paired in poetic texts to mark the two stages of sleep: "to lie down" and "to fall asleep" (Ps 3:6, 4:9; Job 3:13). In the Song, this pair also provides a subtle link between two nocturnal scenes (3:1, 5:2), wherein the paired verbal roots morph into a noun (*miškābî*) and an adjective (*yěšēnā*), respectively. Though these new forms have gained independent force in their present syntactic functions, their link via the etymological roots remains active. Moreover, the nominal and adjectival forms, in comparison with verbs, better resemble the two *states* of her sleep that consecutively set up the pair of poems. While the former poem begins as she is lying on her bed, in the latter, she is in a state of sleeping. What happens while she lies in bed in the previous poem—that is, her seeking of her lover (3:1)—hints at the unspoken cause of her restlessness in the latter poem: his physical absence. This reading is strengthened by the repetition of the keyword ʿwr ("to wake," 4:16, 5:2), which links her heart's wakefulness to the wakening of the north wind and suggests that the trace of her lover has already destabilized her heart. Pondering on such vigilance before consciousness, Levinas affirms that love antecedes *cogito* and ego.

> Love is not consciousness. It is because there is a vigilance before the awakening that the *cogito* is possible, so that ethics is before ontology. Behind the arrival of the human there is already the vigilance for the other.[23]

Behind, beneath, and before the arrival of her lover as well as her perception of his arrival, there already is her vigilance for him.

Speaking of her state of sleep torn by wakefulness, the subject reveals an internal fissure between the "I" of *cogito* and "my heart" (*libbî*), which is signified by the contrastive *waw*. Out of this fissure arises her voicing of her present poem, which demonstrates that at the very beginning the *I* is already obsessed with the other, afflicted by lack of a trace of the other, provoked to give "a voice that rises within before all verbal expression, in the mortality of the *I*, from the depths of my weakness."[24]

---

this poem to be read as it slips between literal and figurative levels (*Song of Songs: A Commentary*, OTL [Louisville: Westminster John Knox, 2005], 190–91).

22. Levinas, "Poetry and Resurrection," *Proper Names*, 10. I should also sound a note of caution that this criticism of a narrative presumption does not entail a divestiture of narrative elements in lyrical experience.

23. Emmanuel Levinas, "The Proximity of the Other," *Alterity and Transcendence*, trans. Michael B. Smith (New York: Columbia University Press, 1999), 98.

24. Levinas, "The Proximity of the Other," 103.

²ᵃ⁾ănî yĕšēnā wĕlibbî ʿēr   I am asleep, but my heart is awake . . .
    ᵇqôl dôdî dôpēq   The voice of my dear—he is pounding!

Amidst her heartbeats, which pound in restless desire, an ambiguous voice (*qôl*) appears—ambiguous, because it is not self-evident at first reading whether *qôl* is exclamative²⁵ or normative, whether it is in absolute or construct state,²⁶ whether it is the voice of her lover, who is pounding, or the sound of her lover's pounding,²⁷ and whether it is literally a startling sound or a metaphorical "knocking on the door of the heart."²⁸ All possibilities flash through this short line: the "I" does not speak clearly the content of the voice, but she speaks clearly of her excitement at hearing the voice. This ambiguous sound is immediately followed by *dôdî* ("my dear"), as in a case of extreme obsession in which one attaches every stimulus to what preoccupies one's heart, in a trance during which one cannot hear anything except through an ear for the beloved. This arrangement clarifies not so much what the voice really is but, rather, by what kind of excitement the voice topples the subject's divided self. That is to say, the voice of the other "interrupts the saying of the already said."²⁹

Such excitement can be heard in her voicing of the voice: *qôl dôdî dôpēq*. The tripling of the *o* sound in the three words not only mimics the pounding, but also enacts the opening of her mouth in excitement. When read together, the first two words (*qôl dôdî*) further revive the scene of his previous coming (2:8). There, the initial excitement is carried through a series of participles that convey the immediacy of her perception: *mĕdallēg, mĕqappēṣ, ʿômēd, maṣgîăḥ, mēšîš*. Similarly in 5:2, a participle follows *qôl*

---

25. The exclamative use of *qôl* (*GBH* §162e) is variously explained as a "virtual imperative" (Fox, *Song of Songs*, 112) or an "interjection" (Murphy, *Song of Songs*, 165) that requests quietness or attention (Zakovitch, *Hohelied*, 213). Following this interpretation, many scholars translate it as "Listen!" or "Hark!" (Exum, *Song of Songs*, 183, 121; Keel, *Song of Songs*, 185; Marvin H. Pope, *The Song of Songs: A New Translation with Introduction and Commentary* [Garden City, NY: Doubleday, 1977], 512; Robert Gordis, *The Song of Songs: A Study, Modern Translation, and Commentary* [New York: Jewish Theological Seminary, 1954], 62). Alternatively, this noun may be elliptical for "I hear the voice" (Fox, *Song of Songs*, 112; Zakovitch, *Hohelied*, 213).

26. Cf. Garrett, *Song of Songs*, 203. The potential syntactical confusion is shown by the need of a *paseq*, "a sign denoting a slight pause" (Emanuel Tov, *Textual Criticism of the Hebrew Bible*, 2nd rev. ed. [Minneapolis: Fortress; Assen: Royal van Gorcum, 2001], 68). Its placement after *qôl* indicates that the Masoretic editors do not read *qôl* and *dôdî* together as a construct chain. For the use of *paseq*, see also William Wickes, *A Treatise on the Accentuation of the Twenty-One So-Called Prose Books of the Old Testament* (Oxford: Clarendon, 1887), 116; Bleddyn Jones Roberts, *The Old Testament Text and Versions: The Hebrew Text in Transmission and the History of the Ancient Versions* (Cardiff: University of Wales Press, 1951), 33; L. Himelfarb, "The Exegetical Role of the Paseq," in *Biblical Studies and Teaching*, ed. M. Arend and S. Feuerstein (Ramat Gan: Bar-Ilan University Press, 1997), 117–29 [Heb.].

27. Longman, *Song of Songs*, 119, 162.

28. Hess, *Song of Songs*, 167.

29. Levinas, *Otherwise than Being*, 182.

dôdî and thus emulates her previous excitement on the syntactic level. The developing excitement is further heard in how *dôpēq* sonically builds upon *qôl dôdî* and anchors this line: besides the persisting *o*, the consonant *dālet* (tripled in the middle) chains the last two words through alliteration, while the consonant *qôp* enwraps the clause.

However, while the aural pleasure drums up, the semantic meaning of *dpq* ("to beat, drive, knock") drives the excitement to an overbearing level. In Gen 32:13, Jacob said that, if the children and flocks "are driven" (*děpāqûm*) too hard on one day, they will die. More ominously, the men of a town "were incessantly pounding" (*mitdappěqîm*) on the door out of which the Levite's concubine would be cast, raped, and reduced to a corpse (Judg 19:22). Against the backdrop of her internal fissure, the excitement both appeals to her heart and drives too hard the sleepy "I." Thus, the "I" who speaks intertwines her pain and pleasure at hearing her lover's pounding voice through her voicing of his voice, through the commingling of the reader's phonetic and semantic receptions.

Man and woman, in love and across a door, speaking without seeing the other and often at night: this is a "type-scene"[30] in ancient Near Eastern love lyrics: cast in his gendered role, a man arrives at a woman's doorstep and asks to enter.[31] He waits on the outside, uncertain of the coming of death—

> I passed her house befogged.
> I knocked. It was not opened
> to me. A wonderful night
> for our keeper of the door!
> Bolt, I'll open you!
> Door, you are my death,
> an evil spirit for me.[32]

Or heavenly joy—

> Dumuzi pushed open the door.
> Came forth into the house like the moonlight,

---

30. For the concept and examples of biblical "type-scenes," see Robert Alter, *The Art of Biblical Narrative* (New York: Basic Books, 1981), 47–62.

31. Roland Barthes, *A Lover's Discourse* (New York: Hill & Wang, 1977), 13–14. In conjunction with this stereotype, other traces of gendered sexual experiences are noticeable in this poem. Male sexual experience, in terms of "a phallic teleology with implications of conquest and undertones of potential violence," can be found in Song 5:4, 7. Female sexuality, in terms of a "more diffuse *jouissance*" is especially celebrated in Song 5:5: "Foreplay, afterplay, and all the possible measuring distinctions of stages, amounts of arousal, and degrees of intensity blur; one can no longer say that the sex takes place at a single moment or in a single event" (Linda Williams, *Hard Core: Power, Pleasure and the "Frenzy of the Visible"* [Berkeley: University of California Press, 1989], 261).

32. This is an excerpt from "the Nakhtsobek Songs" (Barbara Hughes Fowler, *Love Lyrics of Ancient Egypt* [Chapel Hill, NC: University of North Carolina Press, 1994], 74).

> He gazed at her, rejoiced in her,
> embraced her, *kissed* her.[33]

It should be noted that, in Song 5:2, the door is not named,[34] subtly suggesting that the opening (*ptḥ*) evokes more than the opening of the physical door. Its pregnant non-presence suppresses the "natural" imagination of the physical door and directs the reader's attention to the space that it symbolizes, that is, the separation and connection between one and the other. At stake here is not merely the opening of the door but the opening by/of the addressee. This is expressed in that, what follows the imperative is not the object of the action (cf. "the door" in Judg 19:22) but the speaker and the addressee.

²ᶜ*pitḥî-lî ʾăḥōtî raʿyātî*	"Open for me, my sister, my dear,
ᵈ*yônātî tammātî*	my dove, my perfect one!
ᵉ*šerrōʾšî nimlāʾ-ṭāl*	For my head is drenched with dew;
ᶠ*qĕwwuṣṣôtay rĕsîsê lāylâ*	my locks, the drops of the night!"

"Open for me, my sister!" What he asks does not stop "at the simple act that could have appeared to be adequate to the request," which, "once accomplished, would still remain to be accomplished."[35] For, more profound than the opening of the door or her body (Song 8:9), what "remains to be accomplished" in the request is *her* opening to *him*—her willingness, responsiveness, and responsibility for him.

Because only a voice can penetrate the interruption that the invisible door stands for, it takes central stage in 5:2–3. Its naming (*qôl dôdî*) is followed by its content (5:2c–f) and response (5:3d). This link between the leading lines (5:2ab) and their development (5:2c–3d) is further enriched through other connections. "My heart" (5:2a) is morphed (up and out) into "my head" and "my locks" in his speech (5:2e, f), which is squarely met with her concern over "my robe" and "my feet" (down and out; 5:a, c). Her reference to "my lover" explodes in his words into a torrent of epi-

---

33. "Dumuzi's Wedding," ii 19–22, quoted from Yitschhak Sefati, *Love Songs in Sumerian Literature: Critical Edition of the Dumuzi-Inanna Songs* (Ramat Gan: Bar-Ilan University Press, 1998), 288, 292; cf. Thorkild Jacobsen, *The Treasures of Darkness: A History of Mesopotamian Religion* (New Haven, CT: Yale University Press, 1976), 32–33. For more examples whereby the door-entering is a double entendre for sexual consummation, see Julia Assante, "Sex, Magic and the Liminal Body in the Erotic Art and Texts of the Old Babylonian Period," in *Sex and Gender in the Ancient Near East: Proceedings of the 47th Rencontre Assyriologique Internationale*, 2 vols., ed. Simo Parpola and Robert M. Whiting (Helsinki: Neo-Assyrian Text Corpus Project, 2002), 1.39 n. 55.

34. Against the witnesses of the MT, Vulg., and Syr. The OG and OL supply "the door" (τὴν θύραν; *fores*) as in Judg 19:22. This amplification is best taken as an editorial effort to clarify and limit the possible references of the pounding because the subject of the action can be the lover or his voice, and the object can be the door or her body.

35. Blanchot, *Awaiting Oblivion*, 40–41.

thets—*'ăḥōtî ra'yātî yônātî tammātî* ("my sister, my dear, my dove, my perfect one")—which evaporates completely in her calculated response.

His pounding voice is also conveyed through the sevenfold drumbeats of *-î* ("me/my").[36] To soften the intrusive request that opens his speech, he attaches to it the most intimate epithet ("my sister").[37] This initial invocation opens up a series of epithets that cascade down and fill the next line. The piling up of four invocations glorifies the intrusiveness of his petition as uncurbed passion. Nevertheless, through the repeated *-î*, the invocations are realigned to the antecedent purposive preposition "for me" (*-lî*) and suggestively bring the addressee to the realm of his possession ("my") through the following two nouns (*rō'šî, qĕwwuṣṣôtay*).

He calls her but speaks of himself. The emphasis on *-î* ("me/my") only thickens the separation between them, not only by disallowing his better self to pose, but also by provoking an echo from her. "Already he allows me an 'as for me.'"[38] His self-bound voice does not speak so that she can talk to him, so she talks like him.

³ᵃ*pāšaṭṭî 'et-kuttontî*	"I have taken off my robe,
ᵇ*'êkākâ 'elbāšennâ*	how could I put it on?
ᶜ*rāḥaṣtî 'et-raglay*	I have washed my feet,
ᵈ*'êkākâ 'ăṭannĕpēm*	how could I soil them?"

"Enveloped in herself," she turns "toward and away from him."[39] Her four-line speech balances and develops his four-line speech. While his words were cascading down passionately into a smooth river of self-reference, hers spin off the second part of his speech and maximize the tension between the paralleled riverbanks of sleep and restlessness, which have consumed her attention. Her lines alternate between two modes of speech (predication and question) which verbalize her initial fissure. Congruent with this formal difference is the thematic dichotomy. She endorses her actions that are fitting for sleep (undressing and washing feet) and questions those that disrupt it (dressing and soiling feet). The alternating lines are further shown in the rhyming *-tî* (5:3a, c) and the alliterating *'-* (5:3b, d). Directly or indirectly, the phonetic repetitions bind attention to herself. Moreover, the two halves of her speech (5:3a–b and c–d) match impeccably in structure. Both, for instance, are framed by two verbs.[40] This allows an interesting wordplay between the first and the last words of her speech: the first and last consonants of *pāšaṭṭî* (*p-š-ṭ*) reverse in *'ăṭannĕpēm* (*ṭ-n-p*).

---

36. Keel also notes that "[t]he push is expressed . . . even more in the torrent of addresses that follow" (*Song of Songs*, 188).
37. Compare with the girl's use of the intimate reference of "my brother" in 8:1.
38. Blanchot, *Awaiting Oblivion*, 25.
39. Levinas, *Otherwise than Being*, 89.
40. For a more complete comparison, see Hess, *Song of Songs*, 170.

Simultaneously, therefore, on the phonetic, semantic, stylistic, and inscriptional levels, she speaks in a closed circle. Her speech mirrors and supersedes his in terms of egocentric contraction, which takes the form of "the insatiable turning back to self."[41]

The immediate juxtaposition of his speech and her response, without a conjunction, allows a continuation of the first-person-singular pronoun in this vocal exchange: "I, me, and my." The same egoistic concern "for-myself" gives coherence to their words but prevents the opening that gives peace to them. Speaking of and for oneself, their languages are closed;[42] so does what he has asked to open.

Though their language has failed to penetrate the separation, their mutual attraction grows stronger as it is denied in a delicious way. Barthes says, "I can do everything with my language, *but not with my body*. What I hide by my language, my body utters."[43] In this dialogue, the bodies that hide in language reveal differently. His reasons for his request (led by the particle *še-*) are to present his body to her, for as her lover he knows that, just as her body "is the very place of this attraction" for him, his body "exerts over her through the return of attraction."[44] For instance, his hair-locks: the provocative sensuality of a man's hair-locks as an ancient literary trope cannot be underestimated. In the *Epic of Gilgamesh*, Gilgamesh's beauty is epitomized in his wet locks as he washes himself. Sighting this, Ishtar is so aroused that she proposes marriage to him.

> He washed his matted hair, he cleaned his equipment,
> he shook his locks down over his back,
> . . .
> The lady Ishtar looked covetously on the beauty of Gilgameš:
> "Come, Gilgameš, you be the bridegroom! . . ."[45]

In Song 5:2, the man's drenched head and locks not only evoke his current bearing, which appeals to her compassion, but also seduce her with the projected steaming rendezvous that would wet his hair differently.[46] In her counterreasoning, she masterfully mirrors the art of verbal seduction. Under her thematic refusal is the tantalizing act of undressing. Her body is metonymically and sensually revealed through her washed feet, which enhance the erotic nuance by enabling only a limited visual imagination of

---

41. Levinas, "The Servant and Her Master," 146.
42. Cf. ibid., 144.
43. Barthes, *A Lover's Discourse*, 44 (emphasis original).
44. Blanchot, *Awaiting Oblivion*, 30.
45. *Gilgamesh* VI 1–2, 6–7; quoted from A. R. George, *The Babylonian Gilgamesh Epic: Introduction, Critical Edition, and Cuneiform Texts*, 2 vols. (Oxford: Oxford University Press, 2003), 1.619.
46. Hess also notices that, at "a second level of meaning," the dampness of the male lover's head and locks provides "the greatest sexual interest" (*Song of Songs*, 171).

her nakedness.[47] The interrogative particle (*'êkākâ*)[48] declines with a hidden allure: her naked body lying in bed—is it not what he desires?[49] Not only is the said erotic but also the way it is said. Given the seductive offering of their bodies, all is not lost in their self-bound speeches. The bodily enticement flirtatiously caresses the thematic messages at their unfolding and sinks without being assimilated into the poetic space, which absorbs it and becomes erotic.

"Two utterances clinging tightly to each other, like two bodies but having indistinct boundaries."[50] His and her utterances, separated by the boundary of self-reference, attract each other across the indistinct boundary between the said and the saying. Speaking in rhetorical questions and indirect explanations, she does not refuse him; she refuses his self-bound language by mirroring it. But her refusal turns against itself. Provoked by her alluring refusal, his initial pounding is escalated into a transgression.

De-Coring: Between Intrigue and Interruption

After his words have reached her but failed to arouse her to open to him, the lover quickly implements his second action: he thrusts his hand through the keyhole of the Egyptian-styled lock.[51] Her description of his

---

47. The erotic timbre is further enhanced if one takes into consideration the euphemistic use of *regel* (Exod 4:25; 2 Sam 11:11; Ruth 3:4, 7) as well as the pairing of lexemes derived from *ṭnp* and those from *zn'* ("harlotry") in Syriac literature (F. W. Dobbs-Allsopp, "Late Linguistic Features in Song of Songs," in *Perspectives on the Song of Songs*, ed. Anselm C. Hagedorn [Berlin: de Gruyter, 2005], 56 n. 166).

48. Though used both in true questions and in exclamatory questions (*IBHS* §18.4.d), these questions are rhetorical in the only two biblical occurrences (Song 5:3 and Esth 8:6).

49. Thus she indirectly gestures to her lover that she is ready for him (Zakovitch, *Hohelied*, 215). In terms of erotic imagery, a naked woman lying in bed is a classic motif seen in Egyptian erotic paintings, as well as sculptures (frequently found in graves) that were endowed with magic power to enable love (Keel, *Song of Songs*, figs. 68–69, 123; 113–15, 186–87). A naked woman on a terra-cotta model bed is also a common find in Mesopotamian erotic art (Assante, "Sex, Magic and the Liminal Body," 40, fig. 8–9). This motif is also found in Canaan, noticeably in Deir el-Belah (Miriam Tadmor, "Female Cult Figurines in Late Canaan and Early Israel: Archaeological Evidence," in *Studies in the Period of David and Solomon and Other Essays* [Winona Lake, IN: Eisenbrauns, 1982], 149). A cautionary note is due because the plaque and footrest, which are believed to represent a bed in the Deir el-Belah plaques, may just be the background of the figurine (Othmar Keel and Christoph Uehlinger, *Gods, Goddesses, and Images of God in Ancient Israel*, trans. Thomas H. Trapp [Minneapolis: Fortress, 1998], 186).

50. Blanchot, *Awaiting Oblivion*, 18.

51. Hess, *Song of Songs*, 161 n. 1; Philip J. King, and Lawrence E. Stager, *Life in Biblical Israel* (Louisville: Westminster John Knox, 2001), 32–33; Keel, *Song of Songs*, 193, figs. 117–18. The preposition *min* is used as in Song 2:9, whereby the lover peers *through* the lattice. There are undeniable erotic overtones in this picture, of course, even if one is unaware of the well-known association between "hand" and penis in ancient Near Eastern literature (Garrett, *Song of Songs*, 209). This not-so-subtle erotic evocativeness explains and is further strengthened by the choice of a general term *ḥōr* without giving technical specifics ("hole"; cf. Ezek 8:7; 2 Kgs 12:10).

response is straightforward: subject, verb, object, and locative adverb. It runs its orderly course in one clause and one line. There is not much left to the words themselves—or to the voice that says them. Her voice is reduced from rhetorical sophistication (5:3) to undivided attention.

⁴ᵃ*dôdî šālaḥ yādô min-haḥōr*
My lover extends his hand from the hole

His hand in the hole, though transgressing the still-unmentioned door, stops at the edge of the separation, which is manifested through the convergence of the line break, syntax, and content of 5:4a–b. Like his words, his hand cannot overcome the radical separation between him and her. Even as the words reached her ears, even if his hand could physically force the door open, he would still fail to arouse her to open for him. One never reaches the other by the extension of egoistic interest, which only converts the other into a thing deprived of its otherness.

On her side of this lyrical gap (5:4b), the second *waw* of the poem introduces a new subject, "my vitals" (*ûmēʿay*).⁵² Together with the *waw*, the fronting of "my vitals" marks a disjunctive clause that enhances the separation between the other and the "I." From this line on, her focus shifts to her feelings, while leaving him on the outside. Meanwhile, the fronting of "my vitals" embodies the shock that denudes the subject to her innards, which most keenly responds to his hand's movement. "His-hand-through-the-hole" cannot reach her physically, but, mediated through her perception, it makes her churn inside. From her wakeful heart to her aroused vitals, she now grasps the source of her turmoil: "because of him" (ʿālāyw)!

Stylistically, the *waw* is the pivot of a chiastic structure that sustains his action and her reaction.

⁴ᵃ*dôdî* (A) *šālaḥ* (B) *yādô* (C) *min-haḥōr* (D)
ᵇ*ûmēʿay* (D′) *hāmû* (B′) *ʿālāyw* (A′)

My lover (A) extends (B) his hand (C) from the hole (D)
And my vitals (D′) are churning⁵³ (B′) 'cause of him (A′)

---

52. In general, *mēʿeh* means "(the) inside" (*DCH* 5.382). It can denote the external view of the belly (Song 5:14), the womb (Gen 25:23, Isa 49:1, Ps 71:6; pair with *beṭen*), the seat of emotions (Isa 16:11, where *mēʿay* is paired with the same verb *hāmah* and parallels *qirbî* ["my heart"]). In Song 5:4, the parallel with *ḥōr* suggests a euphemistic reference to "vagina" (*DCH*, vol. V, 382). Without giving up either the emotional or the physical aspects of the sensation implied in the present context, I propose translating it "my vitals," in light of a comparable expression in Egyptian love lyrics—the "love of you is mixed deep in my vitals" (John L. Foster, *Love Songs of the New Kingdom* [New York: Scribner, 1974], 67).

53. Etymologically, the root *hāmāh* "may go back to a bilateral onomatopoeic root *hm*, used to describe an unarticulated confusion of acoustical and optical effects" (*TDOT* 3.414). Used in reference to inward agitation, it depicts the state of internal tumult due to overwhelming stimuli (e.g., Jer 4:19; Isa 16:11; Ps 43:5). *Hāmāh* is used together with *mēʿeh* in three other texts (Isa 16:11; Jer 31:20; MS B [the Cairo Genizah of the Hebrew of Sirach 51]). For an analysis of the latter, see Pancratius Cornelis Beentjes, *The Book of Ben Sira in*

The euphemistic connotation of "the hand," the mirroring of "the hole" and "my vitals," and the contrast between the former's having "the hand" and the latter's having-not transcend the separation of the door as well as the line and syntactic break. Poetic language is not merely enclosed sentences; it generates signs that provoke beyond the syntactic and grammatical totality. Her lover's hand gives an intriguing sign, the realization of which is withheld. Aroused and unfulfilled "because of him," therefore, the subject rises to open to him.

Her rising features an ingressive use of *qwm*[54]—that is, the accent of her present action is not on the rising but on the beginning of her opening (*liptōăḥ*). The process of opening, in her vision, will have finished penultimately in 5:6a (*pātaḥtî*) before the climactic encounter. These two actions demarcate the passing of time required for her to open, which is emphatically marked by the second and third *ʾănî* of the poem.[55]

From her rising to her opening, she enjoys the time between the arousal and the consummate opening. The four lines in 5:5 are tightly knitted into a semantic and syntactic web that is richly fluid. Two *waw* conjunctions are employed here to build up her enjoying of the enjoyment. First, the *waw* in 5:5b leads a circumstantial clause,[56] whereby her arousal is externalized from her vitals to her hand. Through a second thought, which drifts along the echoing sounds between *ûmēʿay* and *wĕyāday*, the predicate of the latter, the dripping myrrh, is indirectly applied to the state of the former.[57] Her decision to open in 5:5a, therefore, is caused by and further generates her erotic delight. Furthermore, the noun "hand," which is left out of the chiasmus of 5:4a–b, reappears in 5:5b–c with a reinforcing double—"fingers" (*wĕʾeṣbĕʾōtay*). Along the lexical thread of "hand," her myrrh-dripping hand and fingers respond to his-hand-through-the-hole. Second, the *waw* in 5:5c not only reinforces the word pair "hand" and "fingers"[58] but also epexegetically marks the ellipsis of the main verb, *nāṭpû*.[59]

Hebrew: A Text Edition of All Extant Hebrew Manuscripts and a Synopsis of All Parallel Hebrew Ben Sira Texts, VTSup 68 (Leiden: Brill, 1997), 5 n. 12 and 93.

54. F. W. Dobbs-Allsopp, "Ingressive *qwm* in Biblical Hebrew," *ZA* 8 (1995): 43–44.

55. The independent pronoun *ʾănî* that is used in these two occasions accentuates the agency of the self, comparable to "a meditating philosopher's ego" in Qoh 1:16; 2:1, 11, etc. (*GBH* §146b). T. Muraoka proposes reading the two independent pronouns in Song 5:5–6 "as a means to give an expression to the agitated, excited self of the maiden" (*Emphatic Words and Structures in Biblical Hebrew* [Jerusalem: Magnes; Leiden: Brill, 1985], 49).

56. Cf. *GBH* §159d.

57. In Sumerian love lyrics, the state of female arousal is indicated by references to the vulva's "wetness" (Gwendolyn Leick, *Sex and Eroticism in Mesopotamian Literature* [London: Routledge, 2003], 93).

58. "Hand" and "fingers" form a standard pair in Ugaritic and Hebrew poetic texts; e.g., Isa 2:8, 17:8, 59:3; Ps 144:1; CTA 14 [*krt*]: 157–58; CTA 3 [*ʿnt*] II 32–35 (2×) (Yitshak Avishur, *Stylistic Studies of Word-Pairs in Biblical and Ancient Semitic Literatures*, AOAT 210 [Kevelaer: Butzon & Bercker; Neukirchen-Vluyn: Neukirchener Verlag, 1984], 365–66; Pope, *The Song of Songs*, 521). They form a general-to-specific relationship (Avishur, *Stylistic Studies of Word-Pairs*, 302).

59. *IBHS*, §39.2.4; David T. Tsumura, "Vertical Grammar: The Grammar of Parallelism in Biblical Hebrew," in *Hamlet on a Hill: Semitic and Greek Studies Presented to Professor*

| ᵇwĕyāday (A) nāṭpû (B)-môr (C) | while my hands (A) *drip* (B) myrrh (C) |
| ᶜwĕʾeṣbĕʾōtay (A') môr ʿōber (C') | —and my fingers (A'), flowing myrrh (C') |

Retrospectively, the pivotal word *nāṭpû* ("drip") playfully melts away her previous resistance of *ʾăṭannĕpēm* ("soil"), through reshuffling the three radicals of the root from *ṭ-n-p* to *n-ṭ-p*. In other words, the vocal change gives a clue about her changed mind-set:[60] the anxiety about soiling her feet, which had kept him outside, has been replaced by the dripping joy that attracts her hand to the handle.

From *môr* to *môr ʿōber*, the fragrant fluid is intensified sonically and semantically.[61] It even overflows the settled parallelism in 5:5b–c at the heart of her celebration. By the gravity of syntax and the semantic force of the participle *ʿōber*, the poetic line in 5:5c flows across the line break down to the next line, 5:5d.

⁵ᵃqamtî ʾănî liptōăḥ lĕdôdî	I rise to open for my lover,
ᵇwĕyāday nāṭpû-môr	while my hands drip myrrh,
ᶜwĕʾeṣbĕʾōtay môr ʿōber	and my fingers, flowing myrrh
ᵈʿal kappôt hammanʾûl	upon the handles of the bolt.

As the substance of the first two lines has melted and dripped, the lyrical flow finally rests on the object that can give rest to her desire, though provisionally. The locative phrase in 5:5d is framed by *ʾl* and its playfully stuffed double, *-ʾwl*, which together resonate with her arousal "because of him" (*ʿālāyw*). In conjunction, the sonic elements of *hammanʾûl* ("the bolt") evoke those of her arousal (*ûmēʿay hāmû ʿālāyw*). Therefore, the thread of the second thought discreetly links her wet hands to him. The flowing myrrh that falls on the handle of the bolt is also attracted by his sound, sensation, and thematic anticipation to flow "because of" and "upon" him (*ʿālāyw*). Unlike her mirroring of his words, which perpetuates their separation, her hand mirrors the movement of his hand and draws her toward him.

In contrast to the brisk description of his thrusting hand, the passing of time between her rising up and opening is ceremonially thickened because of the density of its significance. The second appearance of *ʾănî* in this poem, redundant after the inflected finite verb *qamtî*, emphasizes the beginning of the subject's new trajectory from the bed of insomnia toward where her lover appears. In fact, an undisturbed process in which she unites herself through the enjoying of enjoyment is necessary in her opening to him, not least because it suits female erotic experience. More

---

T. Muraoka on the Occasion of His Sixty-Fifth Birthday, ed. M. F. J. Baasten and W. T. van Peursen, OLA 11 (Leuven: Peeters, 2003), 488–89. The couplet in 5:4a–b has the same grammatical structure, which substitutes *waw* for the gapped word *yādô*.

60. Cf. Zakovitch, *Hohelied*, 216.

61. For another sound play on *môr*, see Song 1:17.

essentially, it is the condition for her opening to him. Levinas points out that "[e]njoyment in its ability to be complacent in itself, exempt from dialectical tensions, is the condition of the for-the-other involved in sensibility, and in its vulnerability as an exposure to the other."[62] Fenced within two appearances of the disjunctive *waw* in 5:2 and 6, highlighted by the circumstantial *waw* conjunctions in 5:5, the subject safely savors the details of her erotic delight. Her accumulated joy gradually overwrites the memory of her internal fissure. Thus, refreshed and in the wholeness of herself, she is ready to open for him. But is the initial fissure really made whole?

In the likeness of someone who is ready to enjoy the bread at her mouth, the third *'ănî* of the poem effectuates her opening in 5:6a. At this point, the most recent memory of the *waw* has been congenial to her joy. When another *waw* attached by *dôdî* appears to introduce the line after her opening, the subject (as well as the audience) expects another "and," only to find that this *waw* realizes itself as an adversative "but." It separates the *dôdî* to whom her joy flows, from the *dôdî* whose withdrawal removes that which can receive the flow. Together with the line break, the fifth *waw* accentuates the unbridgeable interruption between the other-in-oneself and the other who remains on the outside.

⁶ᵃ*pātaḥtî 'ănî lĕdôdî*	I open for my lover,
ᵇ*wĕdôdî ḥāmaq ʿābar*	but my lover has turned away and is gone.

The flowing (*ʿōber*) myrrh that has betokened her readiness for the encounter is devastated by *ʿābar* (5:6b). In 5:5c–d, the participial form of *ʿbr* conjoins the enjambed lines through the fluidity of its image and grammatical aspect. In retrospect, however, the *qtl* form of *ʿbr* reveals another side of this fluidity—uncertainty. Can the flowing fall through the vacant line break to rest not only on the bolt handle but also on *him*? The unsecured line break between "flowing" and "upon," which has been sustained by her intention, in fact relies more critically on his response. Her fragrant liquid drips toward him like Whitman's patient spider launching filament out of itself, like the soul flinging a gossamer thread in hopes of catching the other.[63] When his trace is found not to coincide with his appearance, her sweet and erotic "flowing" is "gone."

Her emotional rupture is also reflected in the sound and syntax of this line (5:6b). In contrast to the lucid and complete details of his second initiative (5:4a), *ḥāmaq* and *ʿābar* pound the single beat without conjunction. It is as though she cannot believe it when *ḥāmaq* registers in her mind, and so she semiconsciously adds *ʿābar* to verify this painful reality. Further

---

62. Levinas, *Otherwise than Being*, 74.
63. Walt Whitman, "A Noiseless Patient Spider," *Leaves of Grass*, ed. Harold W. Blodgett and Sculley Bradley, Comprehensive Reader's Edition (New York: New York University Press, 1965), 450.

enhancing her unsettling pain is the sound play embedded in *ḥāmaq*, which reverberates with her arousing (*hāmû*) and his pounding (*dôpēq*) until (and in spite of) the semantic sense of *ḥāmaq* renders both in vain: "he has turned away."[64]

Now looking back, while the second and fifth ocurrences of *waw* protect the time of her undisturbed enjoyment (5:4b, 6b), they also predicate the meaningfulness of her enjoyment on the precarious acts of his intrigue and withdrawal, of herself on the otherness of her lover. The central, sweet time of her enjoying the enjoyment is necessary for her to unify her fissured self as a responsible human being in order to catch up with his intrigue, for how can she respond to his request when tension is warring within her? Yet this lapsed time also constitutes the unclosable gap between his intrigue and her response in the present, in her consciousness. "I opened . . . he had disappeared."[65] This lyrically embodied belatedness, as Levinas observes, instantiates an ethical burden laid on the human subject, on everyone who pronounces the word "I": "My presence does not respond to the extreme urgency of the assignation. I am accused of having delayed."[66]

Her internal fissure, which their common self-interest has covered and her enjoyment has filled, finalizes itself as the separation between the self and the other, as the diachrony between the "I" who cannot but be late and the other whose intrigue is always a pluperfect event. The other cannot be brought into the self's present time, and so he is always withdrawn in her synchronic re-presentation.

> The one and the other separated by the interval of difference, or by the *meanwhile* which the non-indifference of responsibility does not nullify, are not bound to rejoin one another in the synchrony of a structure, or be compressed into a "state of soul."[67]

More important than the commonsensical spatial divide between one and the other, which in visual representation can be synchronized and assimilated into a greater structure, the diachronic difference separates one from the other by a temporal lapse that is beyond historical reconstruction, that extends outside the wall of being.

---

64. Though there are only a few occurrences of this verb in the Bible, one can make an educated guess at its semantic sense. The passive participle of *ḥmq* in Song 7:2 suggests the curvature of her thighs. It is conceivable that it is derived from a basic sense of turning. The reflexive form of this verb in Jer 31:22 uses the motion of turning in a metaphorical sense, "turn oneself, perverse." The latter usage finds an echo in the Arabic cognate of this verb, "to be stupid," which "might develop from an original sense of 'turn away (from good)'" (Pope, *Song of Songs*, 525). Furthermore, the asyndetic construction of *ḥmq* and *ʿbr* recalls that of *ḥlp* and *hlk* in Song 2:11, "the rain is done and gone." The latter enhances the factuality of winter's disappearance and accentuates the joyous tone. Hence, I translate *ḥmq* in this context as "to turn (away)."

65. This is Levinas's quotation of Song 5:6 (*Otherwise than Being*, 88).

66. Ibid., 88–89.

67. Ibid., 141.

The void that his withdrawal carves under her enjoyment is not that of annulment, for the enjoyment remains sweetly flowing within its fences. Rather, it de-cores her enjoying of her own appetite. The enjoyment, which could have taken his presence as a means to satisfy her aroused desire and so recoil back to self-complacency, reveals its core at the moment when the other is most desired but—gone.[68]

> Sensibility can be a vulnerability, an exposedness to the other or a saying only because it is an enjoyment. The passivity of wounds, the "hemorrhage" of the for-the-other, is the tearing away of the mouthful of bread from the mouth that tastes in full enjoyment.[69]

There is no place to rest her flowing outside her time and being. Because of this void, the lyrical gravity weighs down the subject with such force that her initial fissure is abruptly torn open, and from this opening pours her soul. Indeed, "without egoism, complacent in itself, suffering would not have any sense."[70] It is only after one knows of the sweet appetite of life that one is capable of suffering. The following assault of her body dramatizes this pain of having been de-cored of her enjoyment, of "an attack made immediately on the plenitude of the complacency in oneself."[71] What makes the attack possible, in other words, is not just the perpetrators' action but also her vulnerability that is exposed when, hopeful of tasting delight, she opens to the outside.

Exposedness beyond Wounding

The contour of her going out, despite vigorous attention to the details that are redundant from a narrative perspective, remains all-together undeterminable. These details—the leading image of her failing soul, the doubling of "and not," the tripling of the assaults, the framing "watchmen" around the assaults—inscribe on the reader not only the thoughts that are presented in the poem but also the dimension of second thoughts. The second thoughts, which are the source of illumination and coherence, are not secured within the luminosity of daytime and consciousness. They are neither "a subjective vision of reality" nor "any metaphysical basis that might be sensed behind the allegorical, symbolic, or enigmatic appearances."[72]

---

68. Ibid., 73.
69. Ibid., 74.
70. Ibid.
71. Ibid.
72. Idem, "The Other in Proust," 101. Without opening the floodgate of allegorical interpretations, I will quote Jenson's paraphrase of Song 5:2–8 to illustrate how the assumed key of theological framework unlocks the "sense" of this poem by first and foremost regarding it as a "story," readily comparable with Israel's history of salvation.

> As with 3:1–8, the story quickly makes sense when read theologically. Israel is asleep, and the Lord is absent. She is not entirely insensible, and awakens when the Lord summons her; this scene too cannot but recall 'Behold, I stand at the door and knock.' But she

Like the hand thrusting through the hole that does not reach but touches, they are incantatory. The dramatic moment in 5:6c–7 flirts with dream and fantasy while remaining a lyric of sincerity. In a "dream-guise,"[73] it becomes more concrete than reality, letting itself be obsessed by what is important. The separation between one and the other situates "the real in a relation with what for ever remains other—with the other as absence and mystery."[74] By subtracting the unimportant without abstracting, it resuscitates her feeling of exposed vulnerability to the other. The felt intensity of these lines springs from thematic and generic ambiguities that bathe poetic meaning in the nocturnal light. In fact, ambiguity already shrouds the leading line of this unit:

⁶ᶜ*napšî yāṣě'â bědabběrô*   My soul[75] goes out because of his departure.

Does her soul's going out signify the absence of her life force, the evaporation of her appetite that is comparable to death (Gen 35:18; Jer 15:9)? Or does it refer to her going out the door, which initiates the following search? In fact, does she or her soul go out? Or does she go out after her soul goes out? To address these ambiguities, we shall again return to the poetic words.

When her expected bliss evaporates in the emptiness that his withdrawal has created, her soul is poured out, *bědabběrô*. Semantically, *bědabběrô* can refer to either his words ("at his speaking") or his withdrawal ("at his

---

delays turning to the Lord until his knock turns to actual invasion: then she is wrenched within—the phrase in verse 4b appears to be a quotation from Jeremiah, where it evokes the *Lord's* anguish for Israel (Davis). But it is too late and he has departed, whereupon her lovesickness overwhelms her prudence. She encounters the prophets in their role as watchmen, who this time offer no comfort but only judgment. After the woman's confession that she is faint with love, the outcome of the story remains open. We again have before us a pattern of Israel's history as the prophets sometimes proclaimed it, different from the version evoked by the similar poem but equally authentic. (Robert W. Jenson, *Song of Songs*, IBC [Louisville: John Knox, 2005], 54; emphasis original).

In spite of its confessional value, the allegorical sense attached to the narrative sequence steers the reader away from the poem itself and from encountering the poetic significance.

73. Resembling a dream, a poem can reduce the narrative content and devote its energy to the details that carry poetic significance. Helen Vendler describes Yeats's poem "His Dream" as follows: "The ballad, in this dream-guise, becomes a Symbolist poem in which narrative content has been reduced to a minimum" (*Our Secret Discipline: Yeats and Lyric Form* [Cambridge: Belknap, 2007], 114).

74. Levinas, "The Other in Proust," 105.

75. It should be acknowledged that *nepeš* entails more than "soul" does in English. In the present context, *nepeš* shares with "soul" in directing attention to the interior of the subject, but it does not evoke the dichotomy between body and soul, as the latter would, given the deep impact of Greek philosophy on English literature. In fact, harboring what "desire" and "life force" stand for, *nepeš* is inextricably embodied in the carnal person. Moreover, with the pronominal suffix, *napšî* can function as a reflexive pronoun; e.g., Gen 12:13, 19:20, 27:4 (*DCH* 5.732; 19; Aaron D. Rubin, *Studies in Semitic Grammaticalization*, HSS 57 [Winona Lake, IN: Eisenbrauns, 2005], 19).

flight").⁷⁶ Although his words "open for me!" have been realized in 5:5–6, and while the sound of his words still rings in her mind when she opens, he is already gone. The two possible readings of *bĕdabbĕrô* express her irreconcilable feelings at the turn from expectation to disappointment. In her rising toward and being emptied of enjoyment, her sensibility, which sustains the movement, is exposed to intense feelings of nothing but her attachment to the other.

Intermingled in the going out, therefore, is her disappointment at the empty space where he had intrigued her (reading with the previous line), and her determination to follow his trace that is still incumbent upon her fully awakened sensibility (reading with the following line). Her soul that animates herself is drawn out, her life force is emptied, and the color of all that is in her world is drained. Yet her soul is not poured into nothingness; rather, it follows the immense pull of the soul of her soul and the core of her enjoyment—the other who had intrigued her and is withdrawn.

She would not feel the pain of revealing the core of her soul if she had lightly opened to him before she was ready. Her soul would not be exposed, if the opening only concerned the door and her body. The masculinist interpretation of her pain, such as "punished coyness,"⁷⁷ falls short of paying attention, not only to feminine sexual experience, but also to the opening of her soul. In love and poetry, a happiness that does not touch the soul is inferior to a suffering that does. Elinor Wylie spells out in the following poem the painful superiority of a soul ravished by the other's withdrawal.

---

76. The most common meaning of *dbr* is "to say." With a necessary revocalization, *bidbārô* instead of *bĕdabbĕrô*, some commentators translate this phrase as "when he speaks," "upon his speaking," or "for his word" (Gordis, *Song of Songs*, 63; Zakovitch, *Hohelied*, 217; Garrett, *Song of Songs*, 213; Longman, *Song of Songs*, 163; Kravitz and Olitzky, *Shir Hashirim*, 63). Exum further renders this interpretation as "because of him" (*Song of Songs*, 185; see also Falk, *Love Lyrics from the Bible*, 124). Garrett argues that this root does not have the meaning of "to turn away" in the Hebrew Scriptures, for in his judgment, the examples of *dbr* meaning "to turn away" in *HALOT* could be "either intelligible with the normal meaning of speak" (Ps 75:6) or based on "conjectural emendations"(Ps 56:6; Garrett, *Song of Songs*, 213; see also Longman, *Song of Songs*, 168). Indeed, some texts can be rendered with either translation (Ps 75:6, 78:19; Job 19:18). But in other cases (e.g., Gen 34:13; Jer 31:20), *dbr* in the *piel* meaning of "to turn back," which is related to the Akkadian D-stem *duppuru* ("to turn, to flee," *CAD* D 186–88), is a more favorable option (cf. *DCH* 2.396). The latter facilitates another common translation, "at his flight," "at his leaving" (Pope, *Song of Songs*, 526; Murphy, *Song of Songs*, 165; Hess, *Song of Songs*, 162; Keel, *Song of Songs*, 194). Theophile J. Meek suggests that this phrase can be translated with either meaning ("The Song of Songs: Introduction and Exegesis," in *IB* 5.128).

77. Rudolph, *Das Hohe Lied*, 154. In this regard, Andrew Marvell's poem "To His Coy Mistress" exemplifies men's propensity for immediate sexual gratification, which is disguised in the *carpe diem* argument (cf. Diane Ravitch and Michael Ravitch, *The English Reader: What Every Literate Person Needs to Know* [Oxford: Oxford University Press, 2006], 65–66).

A Lodging for the Night[78]

If I had lightly given at the first
The lightest favors that you first demanded;
Had I been prodigal and open-handed
Of this dead body in its dream immersed;
My flesh and not my spirit had been pierced;
Your appetite was casual and candid;
Thus, for an hour, had endured and ended

My love, in violation and reversed.
Alas, because I would not draw the bolt
And take you to my bed, you now assume
The likeness of an angel in revolt
Turned from a low inhospitable room
Until your fiery image has enchanted
And ravished the poor soul you never wanted.

Although the reason for the man's departure in Song 5:2–8 is not spelled out (which is different from Wylie's poem), the female lover's experience provides a felicitous comparison. If the woman had opened the door and given her body before she was ready, it would have been no more than a casual encounter that would have violated her love. But in his withdrawal, her love is inflamed in its integrity, though painfully so. He has left; yet inflamed by his absence, his trace becomes unbearably enchanting.

⁶ᶜ*napšî yāṣ'â bĕdabbĕrô*	My soul goes out because of his departure.
ᵈ*biqqaštîhû wĕlō' mĕṣā'tîhû*	I seek him but do not find him,
ᵉ*qĕrā'tîw wĕlō' 'ānānî*	I call him but he doesn't respond to me.

The going out—the "I" after "my soul"—marks the critical movement whereby the "I," wedged into her deepest being, goes out of herself.[79] Her first action follows the pull of her soul to go to him, whose presence would stop the hemorrhage of her soul. But the repeated adversative *waw* conjunctions together with the central negation block this possibility, try as she might.

Under this dominating shadow, fine differences emerge that reveal a lyrical progression in this couplet. Morphologically, *biqqaštîhû* and *mĕṣā'tîhû* in 5:6d may both be broken down into a combination of one verbal root (with its embedded vowel pattern) and two suffixes. When the reader's attention is also extended to the phonetic aspect via the passing of syllabic units, he or she hears in the first two syllables the verbal root, while the third and the fourth (-*tî*- and -*hû*) signify the subject "I" and the object

---

78. Elinor Wylie, "A Lodging for the Night," *Last Poems of Elinor Wylie*, ed. Jane D. Wise (New York: Knopf, 1943), 62.
79. Cf. Paul Celan, "Snowpart," *Paul Celan: Selections*, 131.

"him," respectively. Though cohering with her desire, the inscriptional proximity of "I" and "him" is nullified by *wĕlō'* ("but not"). Coming down to 5:6e, *qĕrā'tîw* similarly has four syllables: the first two denote the act and the last pair denotes the agents. The *-tî-* of the subject "I" persists, but the third-masculine-singular objective suffix *-hû* morphs into its alternative spelling, *-w* (cf. 3:2).[80] Given the semantic and syntactic similarity of this verb to its two predecessors, this alteration expresses not so much a grammatical necessity as the trace of "him" fading vocalically in her speaking, after her failed seeking in 5:6d.

That is to say, the sonant fading embodies the diminishing possibility of pronouncing him as the object of her action. This vocalic transition also prepares for the following subversion. The fourth and last verb, *'ānānî*, has only three syllables: two of the root and one of the objective suffix. The "I" that enables the previous actions reduces her self from the thrice-repeated subjective suffix *-tî-* to the objective suffix *-nî*. Meanwhile, her lover is no longer the object but is restored to the initiating "he." Consequently, the third-masculine-singular pronoun is no longer inscribed explicitly but is implied in the verbal pattern. From the doubled *-hû* to the weakened *-w*, to the evaporation of any inscriptional trace of "him," this lyrical progression verbally performs her reception of his absence. She seeks, but she does not find him; she calls, but *he* does not respond to *her*. The wakefulness at the beginning of the poem now realizes its full force "as awakeness to the precariousness of the other."[81] An awakeness to one's irreplaceable singularity summoned by the other's alterity, which the "I" cannot control but must bear.

The two rhythmic lines 5:6d–e do not proceed toward a solution of the problem; instead, by embodying the fierceness and futility of her search, they unravel her initiative. Denuded of the self-sustaining illusion in which the ego exercises its intelligence and power toward self-interest, the "I" (*-tî-*) reduces herself to the passive recipient "me" (*-nî*).

> Not includable in the present, refractory to the thematization and representation, the alterity of the neighbor calls for the irreplaceable singularity that lies in me, by accusing this ego, reducing it, in the accusative, to itself.[82]

---

80. The suffix *-w* mainly appears in postexilic literature. The poet of the Song might have had the choice of both forms. For additional discussion on the morphology of the third-masculine-singular suffix, see Carl Brockelmann, *Grundriss der Vergleichenden Grammatik der semitischen Sprachen* (Hildesheim: Olms, 1961), 311–12; W. Randall Garr, *Dialect Geography of Syria–Palestine, 1000–586 B.C.E.* (Philadelphia: University of Pennsylvania Press, 1985; repr. Winona Lake, IN: Eisenbrauns, 2004), 110–11.

81. Emmanuel Levinas, "Peace and Proximity," *Emmanuel Levinas: Basic Philosophical Writings*, ed. Ariaan T. Peperzak, Simon Critchley, and Robert Bernasconi (Bloomington: Indiana University Press, 1996), 167.

82. Idem, *Otherwise than Being*, 153.

With subjectivity qua passivity, she experiences her lover as too close and too far—touchable not through her grasp but through the hollow of her soul. Through her passivity more passive than his non-responsiveness, she clings to his trace instead of shedding intelligible light over his disappearance.[83]

The despair is affirmed semantically; yet a latent hope sparkles through a nearly verbatim reiteration of Song 3:1c in 5:6d, which also follows a reference to her soul. The happy ending of her previous seeking makes it possible to hope: if I recite, "I seek him but do not find him," would I not find him next, as it was before? However, the next line moves in a different direction according to the current state of her soul. The interruption of her flowing myrrh is interrupted by her soul that goes out, which, in spite of the active seeking and calling that her soul inspires, is interrupted by his silence. In this silence, she comes to the end of her active control, where the other's response is needed to make herself meaningful.

Silence, the "without-response" of the other, interrupts calling and response. In Derrida's *Adieu* to Levinas, he uses "interruption" to denote the separation between one and the other, which erupts in the form of "the silence or disappearance," as shown in phone conversations:

> I cannot speak of the interruption without recalling, like many among you no doubt, the anxiety of interruption that I could feel in Emmanuel Levinas when, on the telephone for example, he seemed at each moment to fear being cut off, to fear the silence or disappearance, the "without-response," of the other whom he tried to call out to and hold on to with an "allo, allo" between each sentence, and sometimes even in midsentence.[84]

Unanswered, the subject's calling opens up the interruption that marks the lateral extreme of being. Pouring out attention and receiving no response, calling and not being answered[85]—would not the silence signify what death does? Would not the significance of interruption weigh heavier across the proximity of one toward the other than one's being toward its extinguishment? "Don't leave me, don't; that would be worse than death."[86] One's suffering at the other's non-responsiveness reveals that subjectivity is first a vulnerability to the other. To be or not to be—that is the *essential* question, but not the most important one. The significance of subjectivity that overflows a being's self-preservation is revealed in the interruption between one and the other.

What becomes of the other who is silent? Jean-Dominique Bauby, then the editor-in-chief of the French *Elle* magazine, testified from the other side

---

83. Ibid., 63.
84. Jacques Derrida, *Adieu to Emmanuel Levinas* (Stanford, CA: Stanford University Press, 1999), 7.
85. See also Prov 1:28, 21:13; Isa 65:12; Jer 7:27.
86. Blanchot, *Awaiting Oblivion*, 49.

of this silence. After a massive stroke at the peak of his life, he suffered the "locked-in" syndrome, during which he was "locked" inside his body and could communicate only by blinking one eyelid. When his friends called on the phone, and while his body, mind, and soul were there, he could not be certain whether he was there as a responsible "you."

> Sweet Florence refuses to speak to me unless I first breathe noisily into the receiver that Sandrine holds glued to my ear. "Are you there, Jean-Do?" she asks anxiously over the air.
> And I have to admit that at times I do not know anymore.[87]

Without response, the "you" falls short of humanness, and so does the "I." Interrupted communication is not only a failure of the message; more importantly, it is a failure of living out the ethical unicity of "I" and "you." As the subject, doesn't one come to the lateral end of being (contra the linear termination in death) to realize that, without the other's response, the filament of one's soul will not find a resting place?

The female lover's wound, lacerated by her lover's non-responsiveness, remains raw because her giving without holding back keeps the wound open and because of the extreme consciousness that her feeling of pain evokes and suffocates. The latter grows into an "obsession, suffocation, oppression, being crushed against a wall."[88] Her soul goes out, for it is bound to him (Song 3:1) before being tied to her body.[89] It seeks to recover the soul of her soul that had destabilized her in her sleeping, that had had the core removed when he withdrew. He attracts her movement toward the wall of her being, which stops and therefore intensifies the attraction. Crushed between attraction and interruption, she finds no way out. Not even death: "the hole of nothingness—previously the only way out—is blocked by being tied [*noué*] in a knot [*nœud*] without dénouement, losing the meaning that tragedy still conferred upon it."[90] The absolving of her life force does not absolve her desire for him; his leaving is worse than her death.

In the dark shadow of the central phrase *wĕlō'* lurks another semantic thread of *'nh*, "to persecute" (*piel*), which does not participate in the present semantic formation. His non-responsiveness inflicts her soul, which animates her actions. Since she cannot hold back what she has given, she cannot help but be persecuted by the "without-response" of the other. "It is being torn up from oneself, being less than nothing, a rejection into the negative, behind nothingness."[91] With poetic license, she undergoes a null-site beneath the depths of her interiority, exposing a passivity anterior to her active going out.[92]

---

87. Jean-Dominique Bauby, *The Diving Bell and the Butterfly*, trans. Jeremy Leggatt (New York: Vintage, 1998), 41–42.
   88. Levinas, "Exercises on 'The Madness of the Day,'" in idem, *Proper Names*, 162.
   89. Idem, *Otherwise than Being*, 76.
   90. Idem, "Exercises on 'The Madness of the Day,'" 162.
   91. Idem, *Otherwise than Being*, 75.
   92. Ibid.

Following the line of passivity, her seeking goes down into an extreme situation, where she cannot find but is found, wounded and exposed. How could such an "amorous catastrophe" relate to an indignant physical assault, apart from the apparent absurdity of the narrative's perspective? Through the optic of an "extreme situation," which psychologist Bruno Bettelheim has introduced, Barthes has helpfully compared the trivial situation of a lovesick subject to "one of the most unimaginable insults of History" which was inflicted on the inmates of Dachau:

> The amorous catastrophe may be close to what has been called, in the psychotic domain, an *extreme situation*, "a situation experienced by the subject as irremediably bound to destroy him"; the image is drawn from what occurred at Dachau. Is it indecent to compare the situation of a love-sick subject to that of an inmate of Dachau? Can one of the most unimaginable insults of History be compared with a trivial, childish, sophisticated, obscure incident occurring to a comfortable subject who is merely the victim of his own Image-repertoire? Yet these two situations have this in common: they are, literally, panic situations: situations without remainder, without return: I have projected myself into the other with such power that when I am without the other I cannot recover myself, regain myself: I am lost, forever. [93]

The enormity experienced in both situations exceeds the measure of consciousness. For the one who is drowning in what *to her* is the bottomless pit, does it matter whether it is a pond or the Mariana Trench? "I am lost, forever." This irreversible point is the salient marker of the extreme situation. The quantitative difference beyond this point matters, perhaps, only to the objective bystanders, who calculate justice by matching retribution or compassion with the size of suffering. This is not to deny the justice of proper retribution; yet does not such a calculative attitude betray a certain indifference to the human face of pain, regardless of its color, age, or the cause of the suffering?

In Song 5:7, the suffering of the "I" is manifested in the active infliction of the other's non-responsiveness, which is dramatized through the masculine suffix -*w* that is the visual sign for "him/his" (5:6c–e) and "they" (5:7). Irony is found in the actions of both parties: her lover withdraws after having intrigued her; the watchmen of the walls afflict instead of guarding "the wall" (*haḥōmôt*; cf. 8:10). Rhetorically, the watchmen's assaults,[94] which her

---

93. Barthes, *A Lover's Discourse*, 48–49.

94. It is tempting to explain away and rationalize the violence that the watchmen do to the woman in social and cultural terms. For instance, Rudolph compares the female lover to a meddler whose feet cannot remain within her house (Prov 7:11; Rudolph, *Das Hohe Lied*, 157). Furthermore, through the lexical link of "one who rounds the city," the watchmen are said to have considered the female lover a prostitute (Isa 23:16; cf. Zakovitch, *Hohelied*, 218). Keel further contemplates an Assyrian influence on the beating and stripping of the woman, based on one stipulation in a Middle Assyrian law book from the twelfth century BCE:

lover's pounding voice and thrusting hand had insinuated, make tangible the ineffable infliction that the lover's withdrawal has passively dealt.

⁷ᵃmĕṣā'ûnî haššōmĕrîm	The watchmen find me,
ᵇhassōbĕbîm bā'îr	who make the rounds in the city.
ᶜhikkûnî pĕṣā'ûnî	They strike me, they wound me.
ᵈnāś'û 'et-rĕdîdî me'ālay	They lift up my mantle from me,
ᵉšōmĕrê haḥōmôt	those watchmen of the walls!

Formally, the repetitious, rhythmic itinerary of seeking and not finding turns into straightforward, fast-paced movements both in 3:4 and in 5:4b–c. However, critical differences are found in the two instances between the female lover and the watchmen. In the former, the two parties are united through the same actions of rounding the city (3:2, 3) and finding (3:1, 2, and 3). Though the watchmen find her, her immediate question to them maintains her active role, which climaxes in her act of taking her lover back to her house. Her seeking and finding move circularly from her bed to the city and back to the room. Thus, 3:1–5 completes a circle of desire, of finding the other, of the peace that ends one's insomnia.

It is not so in 5:7. While the first nighttime search may be said to have attested her soul's attachment to him with an assertive "yes!" the second search could be said to achieve the same goal through a sober "not, no." The set-up in 5:2–6b expects something coherent with the painful de-coring of her soul. The subject's passivity in the "I" lost to "me," which has been inaugurated in '*ānānî*, cuts ever deeper through the tripling of -*nî* in *mĕṣā'ûnî*, *hikkûnî* and *pĕṣā'ûnî*. Coherent with the flow of her feelings instead of the narrative plot, the watchmen's assaults give expression to her suffering, which is too passive for her to express and is more significant than the joy of being together. While a joyous rendezvous may be consumed as food or a game for-the-self, the wound of the other's withdrawal slits open the shell of *cogito* and exposes the-other-in-herself as already the soul of her soul.

After the watchmen reverse her seeking role, their role is further underscored (and later mirrored in 5:7e), while she completely disappears (5:7b). The emphasis on the watchmen as the subject, together with their beginning and ending actions (*mĕṣā'ûnî* and *nāśĕ'û*) allow lines 5:7a–b and 7d–e to frame the central line. Gravitating toward this center, the reader's

---

Anyone seeing a veiled prostitute should arrest her, gather witnesses, and bring her to the entrance of the palace. Her jewelry may not be taken, but the one who arrests her receives her clothing. She should be given 50 blows with a club and have asphalt poured on her head. (Riekele Borger et al. [eds.], *Rechts- und Wirtschaftsurkunden, historisch-chronologische Texte*, TUAT 1; Gütersloh: Mohn, 1982], 87–88; quoted from Keel, *Song of Songs*, 195)

However, any such attempt must answer to the different response in the sister scene (Song 3:1–5). I propose that the differences in emotions and themes between these two scenes better explain the different responses by the watchmen—that is, the violence in 5:7 is a dramatization of her traumatic experience.

attention is exposed to the subject's acute pain:⁹⁵ *hikkûnî pĕṣā'ûnî* ("they strike me, they wound me"). Violence, when reported without consequence, expresses not so much the desire for justice as the volume of the agony. The subjectivity of the "I" is deprived of its dominance and manifested in "a body suffering for another, the body as passivity and renouncement, a pure undergoing."⁹⁶ Through phonetic traces, her wounded state (*pṣ'*) resonates with her soul's going out (*yṣ'*) and her failed seeking (*mṣ'*), thereby illuminating the origin of her wound.

Rather than causing her suffering, the wounding of her body expresses it. "It was not the thorn bending to the honeysuckles, but the honeysuckles embracing the thorn."⁹⁷ The chasm between the *dôdî* who is assumed within the wall of her being and the *dôdî* who calls and disappears on the outside, and the panic situation in which his non-responsiveness has left her, constitute the original moment of her suffering. Whether the beating is reality, fantasy, or dream—given the fact that *she* has verbal control (even though not within the spoken situation) and allows it to appear in her words—it serves the purpose that she desires to achieve. Is it too far-fetched to look for similarity between this saying and posttraumatic responses such as "an eighteen-wheeler has run me over" or "I am being eaten alive"?

Though central to the expression of her pain, the wounding is not deep enough to measure her despair until the watchmen lift up her mantle from above her. In general ancient Near Eastern literature, stripping off someone's clothes as the ultimate exposure of vulnerability can also be found in the Sumerian myth *Inanna's Descent to the Netherworld*.⁹⁸ When the goddess passed through the seven gates to the underworld, the gatekeepers asked her at each gate to take off a piece of her attire that held her divine power. Consequently, her power and charm left her as her attire was stripped away: "She has been subjugated and her clothes stripped off."⁹⁹ Denuded, Inanna could not come back to life by her own power. In an analogous way, the forced exposure of the subject in Song 5:7d denudes and reveals a vulnerability inherent in the carnal body, which attire and consciousness conceal.

---

95. Used as a pair, *pĕṣā'ûnî* describes the state of wounding by *hikkûnî*; cf. 1 Kgs 20:37.
96. Levinas, *Otherwise than Being*, 79.
97. Brontë, *Wuthering Heights*, 71.
98. For a new edition and translation of this text, see Dina Katz, *The Image of the Netherworld in the Sumerian Sources* (Bethesda, MD: Capital Decisions, 2003), 251–87. Compare with Diane Wolkstein and Samuel Noah Kramer, *Inanna, Queen of Heaven and Earth: Her Stories and Hymns from Sumer* (New York: Harper & Row, 1983), 52–73; Thorkild Jacobsen, *The Harps That Once—: Sumerian Poetry in Translation* (New Haven, CT: Yale University Press, 1987), 205–32. The Babylonian myth "Ishtar's Descent to the Underworld," is a later, Akkadian version of this myth in which Ishtar replaces Inanna (Samuel Noah Kramer, *Sumerian Mythology; A Study of Spiritual and Literary Achievement in the Third Millennium B.C.* [New York: Harper, 1961], 84); see William W. Hallo and K. Lawson Younger (eds.), *The Context of Scripture* (Leiden: Brill, 1997), 1.108.
99. ID 122, 164 (Katz, *The Image of the Netherworld*, 259).

Her speaking of the exposure neither gives closure to nor sets the limit of the wound. Instead, the poetic language continues to destabilize. The last word, *meʿālay* ("from above me"), echoes the two prepositions (*min* and *ʿal*) that wrap around the stirring line *ûmēʿay hāmû ʿālāyw* (5:4b). The same preposition *ʿal* sets the different pronominal suffixes in contrast: the disappearance of "him" accentuates the desolation of "me." Furthermore, *rĕdîdî* ("my mantle") sonically plays up the traces of *rĕsîsê* ("my locks") in his speech and subtly contrasts her present desolation with the tresses that she could have touched. Finally, the reality of being stripped casts irony on her previous question: "I have taken off my robe; why should I put it on?"[100] In the foil of her tease that fed on his petition and desire, her current undergoing of exposure reveals an a priori vulnerability. Her pain—the feeling of an attack on her vulnerability—grows into an inextricable knot, because she has not done wrong but still finds herself guilty of being late.

Feeling the intensity of feelings, her speaking further exposes the separation between the "I" and its state: "the *I* grasps it and is overcome by it, as if encountering it in someone else."[101] When the intensity of her feeling overcomes her grasping and exposes the passivity upon which her self is grounded, when the ungraspable subjectivity reduces itself to pure vulnerability, the "I" that grasps and speaks of the grasping is lost in an enigmatic silence.

When what matters is that which transcends comprehension, the knowledge of the narrative loses its intrinsic value. The feelings of absurdity and pain and disorientation due to narrative incoherence befuddle the audience when one fails to make sense of the beating, because the subject provides no reason. Yet approached as poem, these reactions perform, without further description, the subject's feelings upon the audience's sensibility.

Knowledge transforms the strangeness of the lyric into the sameness of consciousness. If one seeks the poetic meaning by way of grasping knowledge, one will either be worn out in the struggle with the ungraspable or will recoil to a hermeneutic of violence that tunes deafness to the unthought.

In all types of artists, the psychoanalyst D. W. Winnicott observes "an inherent dilemma, which belongs to the co-existence of two trends, the urgent need to communicate and the still more urgent need not to be found."[102] The need to not be found has less to do with authorial intention

---

100. The indirect correspondence may confound readers who dwell on narrative coherence: "As the narrative stands, she would seem to have gone out naked; but later she has at least a veil (NRSV 'mantle') to be taken away" (Jenson, *Song of Songs*, 54).

101. Levinas, "The Other in Proust," 102.

102. D. W. Winnicott, "Communicating and Not Communicating Leading to a Study of Certain Opposites," in *The Maturational Processes and the Facilitating Environment: Studies in the Theory of Emotional Development* (New York: International Universities Press, 1965), 185. One should note, however, Winnicott's concept of "the True Self" that is not subject to external influence and thus warrants the right not to communicate shows the long-standing influence of the Platonic mind in Western cultural tradition.

than the exotic origin of artistic inspiration. This age-old inspiration that animates artistic work transcends consciousness and intentionality, so it cannot be assimilated into communicable signs and structures. "Artistic activity makes the artist aware that he is not the author of his works."[103] Hence, "far from elucidating the world," art "exposes the desolate, lightless substratum underlying it, and restores to our sojourn its exotic essence."[104] The "I"—poet, painter, musician—plays upon her or his sensibility esthetic notes and shades that resurrect how the "I" has been touched by alterity; and the time they need to feel the touch leaves them behind, too late to catch in time the intrigue of alterity. What can be communicated in the artistic work is within the said; what cannot be communicated is the saying that had inspired the said from without. The other remains on the outside, more radically than a postmodern refusal of a happy ending that remains within the plot of consciousness.

Song 5:2–7 aptly illustrates the nocturnal substratum underlying the light of the "I" that grasps. Like the lover's hand, the poem gives the sign while withholding its realization. The artistic way, with which the "I" grasps without assimilating her extreme state, emulates the way she experiences her lover's withdrawal. It further provokes in the audience a similar erotic desperation that cannot congeal into a consumable story. There is no recovery, no Hegelian synthesis, no closure of meaning in the said. The subject "does not succeed in working itself out into a story, but rather works itself up in its attempt to do so."[105] Narration re-presents the certitude of object and relation, however dynamic its movement may be, but poetry fundamentally thaws that factuality. Allusive, evocative, a poetic response to the original intrigue preserves more than any-*thing* the intrigue's almost-disappearance.

Provoked beyond grasping and unable to settle: this is also how I am subject to Béla Bartók's violin concerto no. 2. Even though it is composed with the standard three-movement "theme and variations," the way Bartók writes his music (that is, atonally) prevents me from remembering and representing it, from assimilating his music into the sameness of my representation, and thus losing its otherness. It neither lulls me into a rhythm that forgets nor solicits me to move into a fictional universe. Instead, it provokes me to sit on the edge with an expectation that is never met. It evokes sincerity at its initial moment and prolongs it, as the sound engages the mind-body without using it to think. I take home nothing but a sense of vivification, as after a sensual workout that targets the subtle muscles of feeling the felt. This concerto—and may I add, the present poem—sings an

---

103. Levinas, "The Servant and Her Master," 140.
104. Idem, "The Poet's Vision," *Proper Names*, 137.
105. Idem, "Exercises on 'The Madness of the Day,'" 169.

ode to what overflows being and entity to the interiority of the self that is primordially exposed to the other who remains on the outside.

Provoked but unable to complete a mental theme, only having sensibility awakened as pure undergoing for alterity: some mistake this experience—of Song 5:2–8 or Bartók's violin concerto no. 2—for a clear reflection of untranslatable irrational dream/fantacy pieces, but it is in fact the pre-rational appearing in the mental. The reception of the intrigue of alterity retains its integrity in the saying but must undergo negotiation when passing through the structures of language and culture. To maintain this integrity in the emerging said, the straightness of the words (or musical notes) defined by consciousness (which has always already been concretized by culture settings) is crooked.

Patience

Anyone who reads the poem in Song 5:2–8 with a narrative inclination will be surprised by the silence after 5:7. There is no report of consequences or a response to the atrocity in 5:7. The "I" who still speaks does not allow her (a voice in the situation) a say about the physical violence. Would she not be the first to speak out, if justice is what the subject has in mind?

The silence that has bespoken her passivity in the wounding now interrupts her linguistic control over her situation. Within the lyrical situation, she is exposed in pure vulnerability, being removed from the coincidence with herself and not yet touching the other. On the level of the lyrical body, the cessation of her verbal activity in speaking of the wounding manifests the insufficiency of rationality, "as if rationality . . . were still an intoxication," as if reason were "still insufficiently awakened."[106] The subject's verbal silence further attests her vulnerability, for "under the blow of affection" she cannot remain the same or return to her identity to sustain this discourse, for the "I" who speaks about her situation is lost.[107] Indeed, at this point, no heart is as whole as a broken heart, and no word is more fitting than no-word. Moreover, the silence about violence disorients the audience, whose feelings of provoked indignation are left abruptly hanging in poetic space. In this performed suffocation, one tastes the "without-response" that suffocates the subject's calling and seeking, and thereby reveals one's own vulnerability to the otherness of the poetry.

From this turbulent void, the poem suddenly moves up and away to a different level of discourse, where the "I" addresses the "you" (*'etkem*) who

---

106. Emmanuel Levinas, "From Consciousness to Wakefulness," in *Of God Who Comes to Mind*, trans. Bettina Bergo (Stanford, CA: Stanford University Press, 1998), 16.

107. Ibid. No matter how personal the source of lyrics is, the lyrical "I" is distanced from the writer through "a linguistic attitude" toward that source, says Vendler of Dickinson's lyrical "I" (Helen Vendler, *Dickinson: Selected Poems and Commentaries* [Cambridge: Harvard University Press, 2010], 8).

are the daughters of Jerusalem. Since the addressee is neither the male lover (5:3) nor the watchmen (cf. 3:3), the previous lines recede from the audience's present imagination into the content of her speech offered to the girls. There is a diachronic chasm between the lyrical happenings and the conclusive address in which the previousness of the lyrical happenings is absorbed into the subject's re-presentation to the third party.

⁸ᵃ*hišba'tî 'etkem*	I adjure you,
ᵇ*běnôt yěrûšālāim*	daughters of Jerusalem.
ᶜ*'im-timṣě'û 'et-dôdî*	If you find my lover,
ᵈ*mah-taggîdû lô*	what would you tell him?
ᵉ*šāḥôlat 'ahăbâ 'ănî*	—"Faint with love am I."

An invocation to the Jerusalem girls (5:8ab) has appeared twice in the refrain of the Song that concludes the lovers' joyous encounters (Song 2:7, 3:5). In its sameness, it accentuates not only the sharp contrast between her present desolation and their previous union but also the unique adjuration.[108] From the perspective of narrative conflict, the standard exhortation—"do not arouse and do not wake up love until it is ready" (Song 2:7; 3:5; 8:4)—would perfectly summarize 5:2–7 as a drama of "inopportune arousal."[109] This poem would then be conveniently concluded as a woman's lament about her lover's impatience, as in the case of Wylie's aforementioned poem. It would even serve as a fitting illustration of the thematic refrain at the heart of the poetic sequence. Yet, in spite of all these "benefits," the final note of the present poem falls sideways.

This is not to say that the typical adjuration has nothing to do with the present poem; rather, the echo is perceivable in the way that the two key words of the former adjuration, "arouse" and "love" (*'wr* and *'ahăbâ*), have demarcated the latter. In the beginning of the poem, the verb *'wr* provides a lexical tie between her wakeful heart and the previous enjoyment (4:16). From the joyous banquet of love to the lone night in bed, the lyric moves not so much by the unfolding of the story (e.g., the wedding day and night) as by the pendulum effect of lyrical emotions. After reaching the summit of being together, the lyrical movement swings toward the subject's anxiety of being together "but not yet."

Moreover, the wakefulness of her heart in 5:2 is already the result of love's intoxication. The delight of desire being met (4:16–5:1) holds the subject in hostage, similar to the way that her olfactory sense refuses to delight in any other scent but that of her lover. Delightful memories and

---

108. In the MT, Vulg., and Syr., the introduction in 5:8 differs from other occurrences by omitting the phrase "by the gazelles or by the hinds of the field." The addition of this phrase in the OG is very likely due to assimilation with the other occurrences of the refrain (2:7; 3:5; 8:4).

109. Cf. Barbara Wordsworth, *Jacob's Ladder*, with musical illustrations by Arthur Henry Brown (London: Wyman, 1880), 160.

unsettled desires colonize her heart in (spite of) her lover's absence. His absence in the quietness of the night allows her to internalize the enchanting image of her lover for herself. Unlike knowing, this interiorization does not result in digestion and nourishment; instead, the-other-in-oneself sweetens and hollows her heart with an agonizing bliss. Through the backdoor of the diachronic bodily memories, this thread of feeling the-other-in-oneself as the-absent-and-obsessively-present-other extends out of her being toward her lover.

At the end of the poem, the subject's confession, "faint with love am I" (ḥôlat ʾahăbâ ʾănî), recalls its appearance in 2:5. There, in the standard staging that subtends the refrain, the lovers happily embody love for the daughters of Jerusalem (2:7; also in 3:1–5 and 8:1–4). Here, however, in her speech the staging is reshuffled as *the girls* are poised to look for *the man*, while *she* is alone and faint with *love*. The central word, ʾahăbâ, magnifies the lingering *a* of ḥôlat with its tripling of *a* vowels; through alliteration, it also attracts ʾănî to itself. It reveals that, with love, the "I" experiences its pre-original vulnerability.

However, through the lens of the traumatic happening in 5:6–7 and in the context of her speech to the girls, this message reveals more than a self-diagnosis of her vulnerability exposed in her radical separation from her lover. Indirectly, the subject utters the abated response to her wounding. Not anger, not accusation, not even disappointment, the saying that sustains her self-exposure of vulnerability is patience. As pure bearing and obsession, patience does not wait for a time in the future to satisfy her desire but a response from the other. Here, her message to him, her exposed vulnerability without defense or covering, demonstrates that "the passivity of the wound *received*" could not turn back into "assumption, synthesis, and thus into a synoptic simultaneity of presence."[110] It is with a love given without being able to hold back that the subject realizes her unicity as an "I."

After having been absent in the traumatic time between 5:6c–7e, the last ʾănî reappears along with the sixth appearance of dôdî. In fact, the "I" and its other (ʾănî and dôdî) have been loosely tied together throughout the poem. Such linking marks the emotional ups and downs by the appearance and absence of this couple. Aside from the pairs used at the beginning and the end of the poem (5:2ab, 8c, e), four out of six ocurrences of dôdî and two out of four ocurrences of ʾănî appear in her positive response in 5:4a–6b. Yet none is found in the alienating dialogue (5:2c–3d) and the anti-climactic climax (5:6c–7e). This pattern invites one to postulate that it accentuates the dependence of the "I" on the other (2:16; 6:3; 7:11).

It should also be noted that in 5:8 the appearance of dôdî is sustained not so much by the female lover's words as by the love of the Jerusalem

---

110. Levinas, "From Consciousness to Wakefulness," 16; emphasis added.

girls (cf. 1:3, 4; 3:10). The role of the girls in this case is not the audience who takes advice about love but the subject's helper in finding her lover.[111] As best supporting actresses, they constitute a reposing point that sustains her in her lovesickness with their words (in place of raisin cakes and apples in 2:5) and facilitates the movement of her speeches (5:9; 6:1). Her conversation with the girls enables her to cross the barrier of the watchmen, who dramatized his withdrawal, on an overpass of sororal support that feeds on their shared love for him.[112]

The supporting role of the girls is also testified in the seventh appearance of *dôdî* in the larger unit. This key word appears six times in the present poem, befitting the unsuccessful rendezvous. It is on the platform of the dialogue between the subject and the girls that she finally speaks of the seventh *dôdî* in 5:10, which begins her only *waṣf* in the Song. The unsettling perception of his hand through the hole is settled in her head-to-toe vision of him. His presence in her words (5:10–16) is an answer not only to the girls' inquiry regarding his whereabouts (5:9) but also to her seeking, the futility of which had burned the flame of desire into ashes of patience. Therefore, unlike on the other three occasions, the subject's adjuration does not move away and summarize the immediate lyrical unit. Rather, it bespeaks her patience in finding him who gives her soul rest.

Subjectivity, awakened by the other's approach, is provoked to respond to, and seek rest in, the responsiveness of the other, short of which subjectivity is imploded as insomnia and denuded into vulnerability. The oneself-

---

111. The two actions that link the daughters of Jerusalem to the male lover (5:8c, d) are mostly applied to the subject when she looks for her lover (*mṣ'* [3:1–4; 5:6–8; 8:1, 10] and *ngd* [1:7]). By lexical links and by her plea, the girls are invited to continue her seeking (*timṣĕ'û* [5:8; cf. 5:6, 7, 9; 6:1]). However, the role of the Jerusalem girls will be revealed as less than her helper and messenger in the following poems. They do not know and are not invited to step onto her track (6:2; cf. 1:7) or to be with her lover (6:3). After the girls having become intrigued by her adoring portrait of him (5:9–16), and after the lovers' sudden meeting that allows no third party (6:2–3), the presence of the girls is no longer needed and their provoked desire is silenced as the lyrics move on with the lovers' mutual devotion (6:3). This weightless silence begs an answer to the question: does the third party and the justice that they call forth lose their voice in the songs of love? Stella Sandford questions the justice of an erotic relationship when the third party enters: "The love of love . . . would be the exclusivity of romantic or erotic love, ultimately not just privileging the beloved above all others, but also privileging the self—self-indulgent" (*The Metaphysics of Love: Gender and Transcendence in Levinas* [London: Athlone, 2000], 91). Admittedly, there are occasions when erotic love recoils back into self-indulgence and egoistic complacence, but that does not mean that this is all that an erotic relation is capable of. Further, the entrance of the third party does inaugurate the paradigm of justice, but it does not nullify the ethical significance of one's subjectivity and responsibility wakened by and devoted to the beloved other. Moreover, lyrical poetry makes use of voices instead of full-fledged characters, making it less appropriate to evaluate ethical relationships among *persons or characters*. Given the private nature of lyrical poetry, it is most felicitous in an exploration of the ethical significance of the I-You relationship.

112. Jacques Cazeaux, *Le cantique des cantiques: Des pourpres de Salomon à l'anémone des champs* (Paris: Cerf, 2008), 163.

as-for-the-other "who is exposed to another without defense or covering, in an incessant dis-quietude of not being open, and in the disquietude of knotting oneself up within oneself, is an opening of self."[113] Not only does the obstinate Same rend itself solely in substitution for the other, but also the unicity of the "I" verily lies in its humanness, instead of its essence and interiority. Any difference in form of being and essence can be categorized and thus replaced and, in the final analysis, is non-different.

In contrast, provoked by and for the other, one's irreplaceable breathing attests to one's unique responsibility. Hence, in one and the same passage Levinas writes, "the *for* of the 'for-the-other' of my responsibility for another is not the *for* of finality."[114] The human subject is not consumed by finality—be it spiritual elevation that consolidates the self's interiority or ultramateriality that does not move beyond the attributes that clothe oneself. The devotion to the extent of obsession embedded in the *for* of *for-the-other* reveals how the "I" transcends the horizon of the world. The transcendental does not refer to a being in a supreme sphere or as the center of the perceived world. "The transcendental *I* in its nakedness comes from the awakening by and for the other,"[115] that is, a wakefulness that precedes and inspires consciousness. This *for* (*lĕ*), marking the human and the transcendental, is highlighted and celebrated at the end of the larger poetic unit (5:2–6:3) to which the present poem belongs: *'ănî lĕdôdî wĕdôdî lî* ("I am of/for my lover and my lover is of/for me").

Looking back again at the poem—the initial insomnia, the intriguing sign of his hand that unites her fissured self, the withdrawal that removes the core from her soul of souls, his non-responsiveness that exposes her vulnerability, and the undying patience—one realizes that the poem that begins and ends with an "I" is deeply shaped by an anterior vulnerability to the other. Her mental and linguistic control of her situation could not break open the wall of her room; without reaching him, she remains in the seamless world of her being, no matter how far she goes out. This extreme madness of her unextinguishable, unachievable desire is expressed in the extreme wounding of her body and in her confessed vulnerability. In the end, the poem that grasps her grasping of her lover (in vain) exposes an exposedness of her self to the other—that is, "an 'unlimited' responsibility that exceeds and precedes my freedom, that of an 'unconditional yes.'"[116] Conceived in warring tension, this poem produces profound peace, a peace that rests on the subject's patience. With this realization, the last *'ănî* seals the poem.

---

113. Emmanuel Levinas, "Ideology and Idealism," *Of God Who Comes to Mind*, 12; emphasis original.
114. Ibid.; emphasis original.
115. Idem, "The Proximity of the Other," 98.
116. Derrida, "Adieu," 3.

In Other Words, or Words of the Other

The "I" of this poem reveals itself as otherwise than the essence and identity with which the "I" marks its place in the world for itself. Pascal has written in his *Pensées*: "'That is my place in the sun.' That is how the usurpation of the whole world began."[117] But is it not a just demand that I should preserve myself under the sun? If I were no longer, who could carry out the ethical obligation for the other? Is not ethics (and law) about how I trim my desires and tame my behaviors so others can preserve their places in the sun as well? Is it wrong for me to sleep when it is time for my body to rest? These are not unjust demands for my well-being.

Yet importantly, the human self is neither self-generating nor fundamentally solitary; rather, a responsibility to alterity precedes, provokes, and sustains subjectivity. The "I" appears in the subject's delayed response to the human intrigue and is always "accused of having delayed."[118] When the "I" forgets or suppresses the trace of the other that had already destabilized "me," the "I" cannot find peace. Importantly, peace should not be confused with the inertia of being. I eat, I sleep, I keep myself alive, I courageously face the possibility of death, alone: these are the characteristics of a being. Without the disturbance of an other, being falls into the slumber, the inertia, the animalistic gravity. But the human intrigue destabilizes and wakes up the subject, who becomes "sick" gauged by the law of being.

> Inertia is certainly the great law of being; but the human looms up in it and can disturb it. For a long time? For a moment? The human is a scandal in being, a 'sickness' of being for the realists, but not evil.[119]

In the present poem, the poetic subject wakes the sleeping self at the beginning to reckon with the sickness that reveals her humanness.

When the "I" anesthetizes the feeling of vulnerability that is pre-originally exposed to the other, the ontological privilege of "the right to exist" is capable of leading down the slippery slope to genocide.[120] That is to say, the "I" without being awakened to its origin, to the soul of its soul, is "how the usurpation of the whole world began":

> My ethical relation of love for the other stems from the fact that the self cannot survive by itself alone, cannot find meaning within its own being-in-the-world, within the ontology of sameness. That is why I prefaced *Otherwise than Being or Beyond Essence* with Pascal's phrase, "'That

---

117. Blaise Pascal, *Pensées: The Provincial Letters*, trans. W. F. Trotter and Thomas M'Crie (New York: Modern Library, 1941), 112.
118. Levinas, *Otherwise than Being*, 88–89.
119. Idem, "Philosophy, Justice, and Love," *Entre Nous*, 115.
120. Anesthetization in the case of genocide involves that of a social group who occludes vulnerability to certain others who are marked by their racial identity. On racial anesthetization, see Mab Segrest, "The Souls of White Folks," in *The Making and Unmaking of Whiteness* (Durham, NC: Duke University Press, 2001), 43.

is my place in the sun.' That is how the usurpation of the whole world began."[121]

The human appears when one rises up in a difficult freedom against the usurpation of ego, which manifests itself in the incessant murmuring of the WIIFM—"What's In It For Me?" When I follow the insomnia that preemptively destabilizes the sovereignty of the "I," I will find that, as the subject, I am already constituted with the wound of love, bearing the burden of loving the other before I could make the decision to do so. The relation between the other and me is not the being-with-the-other-person (*Miteinandersein*) that defines myself by our reaching out hands toward the same thing (*zu-handkeit*), nor a reciprocity that can be reduced to a principle of equality, which would still recoil back to inter-*ested*-ness. It is asymmetrical: the other had always already assigned me to responsibility before I designated him in my consciousness. It is "an inversion of intentionality"[122]—and responsibility—as a conscious commitment.

Does ethics begin from the self or the other? Perhaps the answer is neither, or both, for the self is already for-the-other, and the other is already one's soul of the soul. "I am defined as a subjectivity, as a singular person, as an 'I', precisely because I am exposed to the other. It is my inescapable and incontrovertible answerability to the other that first provokes me to be an individual 'I.'"[123] The "I" is found and exposed in the poem that cannot find and expose the "I" entirely, for the "I" is by love already for-the-other, and is thus a self-destabilization underneath my active effort to assume my place under the sun.

This is also to say, in the spirit of extreme skepticism, that the other cannot be revealed in my words, for how can my words tear open the assimilation of the other that characterizes *I think*? "How can transcendence withdraw from *esse* while being signaled in it?"[124] Unthinkable maybe, but it is not impossible. The ethical writing so desired does not go by the route of pure epistemology, which, motivated by curiosity and control, propels forward by projecting light into the unknown. "Writing the other is impossible if the focus or point of departure is an ego or consciousness."[125] The ego or consciousness functions within its constituted situation. Emitting the light of reason, it forgets the origin that had aroused it and the responsibility that has provoked its initiatives. Forgetting, it speaks of the other by assimilating the other into the same, into the closed language

---

121. Emanuel Levinas and Richard Kearney, "Dialogue with Emmanuel Levinas," in *Face to Face with Levinas*, ed. Richard A. Cohen (Albany: State University of New York Press, 1986), 24.
122. Levinas, *Otherwise than Being*, 47.
123. Levinas and Kearney, "Dialogue with Emmanuel Levinas," 26–27.
124. Levinas, *Otherwise than Being*, 10.
125. Gabriel Riera, *Intrigues: From Being to the Other* (New York: Fordham University Press, 2006), 85.

and thinking of the "I." The physical features, the social locations, the personal histories—these can be reduced to "things" that exclude the appearance of "you," while the irreducible that inspires the inertia of things remains withdrawn from knowledge's seeking. This kind of unknown is not one that can be grasped with better method, stronger will, or more resources. It is that which cannot be thought. To thinking, the vigilance for the other—insomnia, enucleation, vulnerability, patience—is already and again a dream; and to this responsive vigilance, thinking is a lucidity insufficiently awakened. Is not the inadequacy of an epistemic approach to the other that of explaining the flower by the fertilizer?[126]

Imposing and solving questions, consciousness moves on like a cat chasing its tail, because the language of stabilization cannot write what remains on the outside. The end of philosophy that Hegel pronounces ends totalizing language and solicits a continuation that writes differently. Indebted to the unthought, this writing ruins philosophy as it has been traditionally conceived and opens up a space that maintains a face-to-face contact. An ethical writing of the other is to be in contact with what lies beneath— beneath thematization, beneath identity, even beneath the consciousness of consciousness.[127]

Since I cannot cross or cross out the radical separation between the poem and myself, which is more radical than any spatial or temporal gap, I cannot reflect on and write the other directly except by writing the other's trace. The materiality of the other's inspiration is conveyed in poetic language "as the underside of categories."[128] My response to Song 5:2–8, intermeshed with selections of Levinas's writings, therefore, does not aim at elucidating this opaque poem or faithfully applying Levinasian philosophy to it; rather, it is a testimony to the consanguinity of their inspiration felt in my sensibility.

Sensibility, or the saying that lies beneath and does not consolidate into assumptions is the site of proximity to the other, which in fact "is not a state, a repose, but a restlessness, null site, outside of the place of rest."[129] Unable to be stabilized as a cultural, ideological, or geographical configuration, it remains as vigilance. Always on this side of the interruption, it realizes my responsibility to the other in a refraction of reality.

---

126. This paraphrases Gaston Bachelard's critique of psychoanalysis as he turned away from his epistemological approach to the world ("The Poetics of Space," in *Literary Debate: Text and Contexts*, ed. Denis Hollier and Jeffrey Mehlman, Postwar French Thought 2 [New York: New Press, 1990], 356).
127. Levinas, *Otherwise than Being*, 80.
128. Riera, *Intrigues*, 157.
129. Levinas, *Otherwise than Being*, 82.

Appendix

Song of Songs 5:2–8

²ᵃ*ʾănî yĕšēnā wĕlibbî ʿēr*	I am asleep, but my heart is awake....
ᵇ*qôl dôdî dôpēq*	The voice of my lover—he is pounding!
ᶜ*pithî-lî ʾăḥōtî raʿyātî*	"Open for me, my sister, my dear,
ᵈ*yônātî tammātî*	my dove, my perfect one!
ᵉ*šerrōʾšî nimlāʾ-ṭāl*	For my head is drenched with dew,
ᶠ*qĕwwuṣṣôtay rĕsîsê lāylâ*	my locks, the drops of the night!"
³ᵃ*pāšaṭṭî ʾet-kuttontî*	"I have taken off my robe,
ᵇ*ʾêkākâ ʾelbāšennâ*	how could I put it on?
ᶜ*rāḥastî ʾet-raglay*	I have washed my feet,
ᵈ*ʾêkākâ ʾăṭannĕpēm*	how could I soil them?"
⁴ᵃ*dôdî šālaḥ yādô min-haḥōr*	My lover extends his hand through the hole;
ᵇ*ûmēʿay hāmû ʿālāyw*	and my vitals are churning 'cause of him.
⁵ᵃ*qamtî ʾănî liptōăḥ lĕdôdî*	I rise to open for my lover,
ᵇ*wĕyāday nāṭpû-môr*	while my hands drip myrrh,
ᶜ*wĕʾeṣbĕʾōtay môr ʿōber*	and my fingers, flowing myrrh
ᵈ*ʿal kappôt hammanʿûl*	upon the handles of the bolt.
⁶ᵃ*pātaḥtî ʾănî lĕdôdî*	I open for my lover;
ᵇ*wĕdôdî ḥāmaq ʾābar*	but my lover has turned away and gone.
ᶜ*napšî yāṣʾâ bĕdabbĕrô*	My soul goes out because of his departure.
ᵈ*biqqaštîhû wĕlōʾ mĕṣāʾtîhû*	I seek him but do not find him,
ᵉ*qĕrāʾtîw wĕlōʾ ʿānānî*	I call him but he doesn't respond to me.
⁷ᵃ*mĕṣāʾūnî haššōmĕrîm*	The watchmen find me,
ᵇ*hassōbĕbîm bāʿîr*	who make the rounds in the city.
ᶜ*hikkûnî pĕṣāʿûnî*	They strike me, they wound me.
ᵈ*nāśʾû ʾet-rĕdîdî mēʿālay*	They lift up my mantle from me,
ᵉ*šōmĕrê haḥōmôt*	those watchmen of the walls!
⁸ᵃ*hišbaʿtî ʾetkem*	I adjure you,
ᵇ*bĕnôt yĕrûšālāim*	daughters of Jerusalem.
ᶜ*ʾim-timṣĕʾû ʾet-dôdî*	If you find my lover,
ᵈ*mah-taggîdû lô*	what would you tell him?
ᵉ*šāḥôlat ʾahăbâ ʾănî*	—"Faint with love am I."

Chapter 4
"The Human Form Divine"

> It is a movement toward the other that does not come back to its point of origin the way diversion comes back, incapable as it is of transcendence—a movement beyond anxiety and stronger than death.[1]

> The enigma of a God speaking in man and of man not counting on any god?[2]

To solicit meaningfulness from the Song of Songs that is appropriate to its canonical context, one cannot circumvent the turn from eros to a love without eros. The well-trodden path of allegory has mapped this turn by deciphering a literal *this* as a historical, moral, or teleological *that*. However, in order to allow for close contact between the reader and lyric, and in consideration of the changed hermeneutical climate, I will suspend the allegorical turn for fear that, while one is seeking what is right, the meaningful is lost.

It is not that the treasures of the Judeo-Christian allegorical readings should be forever buried in the shadow of history, since postmodern readers no longer live in the cultural environment that gave birth to them. More precisely, the integrity of reception vitally depends on whether a reader has instilled the assumed cultural and religious preconditions of the interpreters. As Levinas explains, "What matters is to know *in what spirit something is borrowed.*"[3] For contemporary readers who remain committed to the requisite preconditions, allegorical interpretations can indeed retain lively flames of love because of the shared subtending spirit. My essential

---

Author's note: The title is a quotation from William Blake, "The Divine Image," *Poems of William Blake* (Raleigh, NC: Hayes Barton, 1964), 18.

1. Emmanuel Levinas, "The Temptation of Temptation," in *Nine Talmudic Readings*, trans. Annette Aronowicz; Bloomington: Indiana University Press, 1990), 48.

2. Emmanuel Levinas, *Otherwise than Being: or, Beyond Essence*, trans. Alphonso Lingis; Pittsburgh: Duquesne University Press, 1998), 154. I shall add that, in the context of Song 8:6 it sould be "woman" instead of "man."

3. Emmanuel Levinas, "'As Old As the World?,'" in *Nine Talmudic Readings*, 75; emphasis original.

contention with an allegorical approach is not the borrowing of an external referential system to give meaning to the ambiguous lyrical text but the way this is done. Traditional allegorical interpretations typically reduce the lyrical experience to deciphering by a codebook. Such a turn also problematically assumes that eros is either too primitive or downright impure for religious consumption, so much so that the Song is denied at its core.

When allegorical transcription is set aside, the *-yh* at the end of *šalhebetyāh* (8:6) seems to offer the only desirable turning point from these erotic lyrics to a theology of love. For instance, reading it as a shortened form of YHWH (Yah), Richard Hess summarizes the moment when the love of a higher order transcends eros.

> [T]he absence of any direct reference to God, except at this point, suggests that here the erotic love of the Song reaches a level of love that transcends all and through which God is known. Thus God is love (1 John 4:8, 16), and those who would know and worship him must know that love.[4]

While I concur with this observation that, at the summit of erotic love, one may catch a glimpse of the divine, I would like to caution against the transcendental turn by way of emotional refinement and spiritual elevation. Both claim success by first dichotomizing *'ahăbâ* into agape as spiritually refined benevolence and eros as carnal sublunary desire.[5] The "without eros" would then become agape's negation of eros. However, as Hegel has

---

4. Richard S. Hess, *The Song of Songs* (Grand Rapids, MI: Baker, 2005), 240. See also Tremper Longman III, *The Song of Songs* (Grand Rapids, MI: Eerdmans, 2001), 212–13; Barry Webb, "The Song of Songs: A Love Poem and as Holy Scripture," *RTR* 49 (1990): 98; Christian D. Ginsburg, *The Song of Songs and Coheleth (Commonly Called the Book of Ecclesiastes)* (New York: Ktav, 1970), 188; Leo Krinetzki, "Die Macht der Liebe," *MTZ* 13 (1962): 256–79. Not all theologically inclined interpreters, however, agree with the necessity of this spiritual elevation. While using allegory to solicit a theological message from the Song, Robert W. Jenson nevertheless rebuts the idea that the love in the Song ought to be purified of its desire:

> ... if we must indeed distinguish between *agape*, self-giving love, and *eros*, desire, allegory solicited by the Song does not suppose that *agape* is the only sanctioned love between God and his people. In this poem, Israel *desires* the Lord, her love is precisely erotic; and later in the Song we will see that the Lord desires Israel. (Robert W. Jenson, *Song of Songs*, IBC [Louisville: John Knox, 2005], 17)

In fact, Hess also note that, as shown in historical interpretations and extrabibilical inscriptions, YHWH was once worshiped with a consort (Hess, *Song of Songs*, 240).

5. The application of agape and eros as a Greek guide to *'ahăbâ* stratifies the latter against its holistic grain (see *HALOT* 1.18), which includes "caress" (Prov 5:19), "feeling of love, passion" (2 Sam 13:15), that "of friends and individuals in general" (Ps 109:4), and "God's love for his own people" (Deut 7:8). Catherine Keller calls theologians to pay attention to "a multiplicity of loves" that compete as well as cooperate, that command an attentive reticence, as Jean-Luc Nancy recommends ("Afterword: A Theology of Eros, after Transfiguring Passion," in *Toward a Theology of Eros: Transfiguring Passion at the Limits of Discipline*, ed. Virginia Burrus and Catherine Keller [New York: Fordham University Press, 2006], 366–67). It is worth adding that this "attentive reticence" or reticent generosity differs from a politically correct "openness," which oftentimes is in danger of being deflated

observed, negation always contains in itself the existence of the negated and anticipates a synthesis that welcomes it back; thus eros never leaves the scene. Utilizing René Char's formulation ("The poem is the fulfilled love of desire remaining desire"), Jean-Luc Nancy aptly describes the dialectic of love as follows: "the contradiction (desire) opposed to the noncontradiction (love) and reconciled with it ("remaining desire")."[6] With a slight twist, one may say that the conversion of the erotic Song to a set of spiritual testimonies of divine love would have the negated desire remain desiring. Needless to say, suppression makes the sumptuous eros all the more tempting, like the forbidden fruit in Eve's eyes. Indeed, humans are embodied beings, and desire is enmeshed in the elements of the bodily existence. Self-castration practiced in early Christianity (due to a literal reading of Matt 19:12)[7] might have realized the physical negation of "remaining desire," but could the castrated be considered a human in its created wholeness?

Inspired by Levinas's marvel at the Song that such an erotic text should bear austere meaning,[8] as well as his fine elaboration on "the wisdom of desire,"[9] I propose an ethical turn from the erotic to the non-erotic that does not negate the erotic, and that purposelessly aims at the encounter with the transcendent through that of an inter-human love. Retaining the flesh and flame of eros while differentiating it from ultramateriality, this ethical turn hinges on eros's opening to the transcendent inside its movement. Instead of pegging down Y$_{HWH}$ in -yh, I hope to show that the trace of God is already revealed in a love strong as death (Song 8:6), for the other. Then, what the blinking light of -yh offers, instead, is for human subjectivity to face responsively, in a passing moment, the ambiguity capable of an enigmatic alternative—compared with the immobilized sense that "sticks to the phenomena, to the said."[10] Acknowledgment of this lyrical ambiguity is the ethical prerequisite for an encounter with God in and through words.

As is the case with any literary ambiguity,[11] not all of my readings that follow are derived from the lyrics exclusively, as an expansion that can seamlessly recoil back into the text. I take delight in allowing a breathing space between the text and my response, a necessary difference grown out

---

into an "easy generosity" (Jean-Luc Nancy, *A Finite Thinking*, ed. Simon Sparks; Stanford, CA: Stanford University Press, 2003], 7).

6. Idem, "Shattered Love," *The Inoperative Community* (Minneapolis: University of Minnesota Press, 1991), 87–88.

7. On the practice of self-castration in early Christianity, see Daniel F. Caner, "The Practice and Prohibition of Self-Castration in Early Christianity," in *Vigiliae Christianae* 51 (1997): 396–415.

8. Levinas, "As Old as the World?" 77.

9. Idem, *Otherwise than Being*, 153–62.

10. Ibid., 154.

11. William Empson offers a classic description to literary ambiguity: "[A]ny verbal nuance, however slight, which gives room for alternative reactions to the same piece of language" (*Seven Types of Ambiguity* [New York: New Directions, 1947]), 1.

of my responsiveness/responsibility to the text.[12] Following Levinas in the way he reads the sages' words with a lively difference, or in the manner that Dame Myra Hess transcribes J. S. Bach's "Jesu, Joy of Man's Desiring" for piano, I regard lyrical words as embers awaiting one's breath for an ardent transcription in prose—

> [T]hey become inflamed when one breathes on them. Ardor and light are here a matter of breath![13]

The Trace of God

In poetry, a close reading often begins with an attention to sound. "It is by their syllables that words juxtapose in beauty," Charles Olson observes, "by these particles of sound as clearly as by the sense of the words which they compose."[14] The phonemes provide not only the salient markers of semantic sense but also sonic effects that play along or against the semantic threads. This entwinement of sonic and semantic elements is palpable in Song 8:1–4, which is the first of the three lyrical units that build up to the climactic confession of love in the Song (8:6–7). There, first a thin thread of *i/e* vowels woven into the wish formula *mî yitten-* swoons into a desirous opening in the central *a* vowels, which help to salve the gliding of *-kā* ("you") across the slight caesura to *-āḥ* ("brother"), then a closing *i* vowel winds the wonder and wondering of the wish back to "me": *mî yittenkā kĕʾāḥ lî*. The particle *kĕ-* attracts the preceding pronoun *-kā* to *kĕʾāḥ* through the repeated consonant *kāp*, thus reinforcing the theme of her ardent wish—"you *as* my brother. . . ." Meanwhile, the grammatical function of the comparative particle and its placement between "you" and "my brother" underline what is contrary to the theme. That is, what is *like*, cannot *be*. While vocally conjuring up the intimacy that the wished fusion

---

12. In Levinas's commentary on Blanchot's "Madness of the Day," he embraces and practices this difference ("Exercises on 'The Madness of the Day,'" in idem, *Proper Names*; trans. Michael B. Smith [London: Athlone, 1996] 158).

13. In reference to an expression of the rabbis, Levinas write: "The words of the rabbinical doctors are compared to red hot embers (*Wisdom of the Fathers*, II, 15); they become inflamed when one breathes on them. Ardor and light are here a matter of breath!" (idem, "The Will of God and the Power of Humanity," *New Talmudic Readings*, trans. Richard A. Cohen [Pittsburgh: Duquesne University Press, 1999], 48). This is a refraction of the original words in *Wisdom of the Fathers*: "Warm yourself by the fire of the sages, but be aware of their glowing coals lest you be burnt—for their bite is the bite of a fox, their sting is the sting of a scorpion, their hiss is the hiss of a serpent, and all their words are like fiery coals" (Levinas, "The Will of God and the Power of Humanity," 48 n. 3). The observable thematic difference shows how Levinas's breath unabashedly inflames a new flame from the embers of the sages.

14. Charles Olson, "Projective Verse," in *Selected Writings*, ed. Robert Creeley (New York: New Directions, 1966), 17–18. Helen Vendler also cautions against (sometimes necessary) reductive interpretations of the poem, "which is restored only by a return to the shaped words and sounds of the poem" (Helen Vendler, *Dickinson: Selected Poems and Commentaries* [Cambridge: Harvard University Press, 2010], 10).

would generate, the particle *kĕ-* in fact prevents a direct fusion of "you" and "my brother." In other words, the rhetorical force of this wish derives precisely from the subject's pensiveness at its practical impossibility, from her bearing the burning that has driven her to a knot without denouement.

| ᵃ*mî yittenkā kĕʾāḥ lî* | If only you were like a brother of mine, |
| ᵇ*yônēq šĕdê ʾimmî* | a suckling of my mother's breasts. |

While the mundane imagery of breast-feeding[15] may slyly feed the erotic flame in the current setting, the intimacy so evoked (and preemptively bracketed by the aforementioned metaphorical formula) is directed to warrant the following series of acts:

ᶜʾ*emṣāʾăkā baḥûṣ ʾešāqĕkā*	I would find you outside, I would kiss you,
ᵈ*gam lōʾ-yābûzû lî:*	and no one would ridicule me.
²ᵃʾ*enhāgăkā ʾăbîʾăkā*	I would lead you, I would bring you
ᵇʾ*el-bêt ʾimmî tĕlammĕdēnî*	to the house of my mother who's taught me.
ᶜʾ*ašqĕkā mîayin hāreqaḥ*	I would let you drink of the spiced wine—
ᵈ*mēʿăsîs rimmōnî:*	the juice of my pomegranate.

"Find," "kiss," and then "lead," "bring in," "let you drink (or French kiss)": this chain of actions in two installments is so smoothly choreographed that it betrays her delicious premeditation. Reminiscent of the languishing desire in the opening scene of the book—"may he kiss me with the kisses of his lips,"[16] the two stages of her present wish both end with her taking the initiative to kiss him, with the second round sinking deeper and sweeter than the first. This set of her imagined busyness further expounds on the exuberance of her wish that is inflamed by his inaccessibility: if only so, then I would, I would, I would, O I would, I would. In the sustained syntactic pattern, the prefixed ʾ- ("I") directs the semantic force of these verbs toward the objective pronoun *-kā* ("you"). That is, the "I" lets its active power run over "you" but consciously limits this dominancy by her wish, the boundary of which is informed by a cultural sensibility of shame (8:1d). A similar awareness of social boundary is spelled out in the following Egyptian love song:[17]

---

15. The image of breastfeeding is also used to express how the suckling would share the status of the ones who give milk (Isa 60:16; 49:23). For a detailed study on the use of "breast milk" in the Scriptures, see Cynthia R. Chapman, "'Oh that you were like a brother to me, one who had nursed at my mother's breasts': Breast Milk as a Kinship-Forging Substance," in *Perspectives on Hebrew Scriptures IX: Comprising the Contents of Journal of Hebrew Scriptures, Vol. 12*, ed. Ehud Ben Zvi and Christophe Nihan (Piscataway, NJ: Gorgias, 2014), 125–68.

16. The locale of *baḥûṣ* also invokes the imagery (and the accompanied feelings) of her search through the streets and the squares (Song 3:2), as well as the searching-but-finding-not in Song 5:6.

17. Bill T. Arnold and Bryan Beyer, *Readings from the Ancient Near East: Primary Sources for Old Testament Study* (Grand Rapids, MI: Baker, 2002), 192.

My brother stirs up my heart with his voices,
making me take ill.
Although he is among the neighbors of my mother's house,
I cannot go to him.
Mother is right to command me thus:
Avoid seeing him!

This sense of boundary and the differentiating aspect of *kĕ-* fold open the the lusciously said wish, exposing the underlying saying as the subject's bearing of the unbearable separation between "you" and "me."

As common sense has it, the most erotic expanse in the space-time continuum is the "already, but not yet." This is the site from which the Song springs and gives life to its everlasting charm. Take the girl's voice, for example: I am always already with you through love in my soul (1:7; 3:1, 2, 3, 4; 5:4b) and in my wishful mind (1:1; 8:1–2); but your lips (1:1), your heart (8:6), your arms (8:6; cf. 2:6; 8:3) and your very self (5:6) are for my inquiring (1:7), finding (3:1, 2, 3; 5:6, 7; 8:1), seeking (3:1, 2; 5:6; 6:1), and hopefully keeping forever (8:6). The simultaneity of the subject's state of being taken hostage by love that drives her toward the erotic union with the beloved other, and the separation between "you" and "me" are at the root of her delicious pain. Or in Anne Carson's words, it is "eros the bitter sweet."[18]

This separation, which fuels the lovers' desire to be together, can be covered (partially) like geographical distance, as the young man leaping over the hills toward the woman's window (2:8–9), or it can be closed in by a chance meeting at night (5:1–4). But the Song remains sensitive to the radical separation between one and the other. Though it may be shown in poetic imagery as a social, cultural, or geographical gap, none of the phenomenological aspects can exhaust this radical separation. The man may go so far as to the wall/lattice (2:9) or the entrance (5:2) of the woman's world. But he could not force his way in (5:4); rather, even at the moment of the lovers eye-to-eye or ear-to-ear meeting, there is an insistence that eros be nurtured till it is ready (2:10–13; 5:2–6). The erotic consummation, in other words, is not to be achieved through the ego's expansion or consumption but through a mutual approach across the critical separation toward a ripen encounter. This actually is no news to the readers of the Song, because the thematic refrains (2:7; 3:5; 8:4) reiterate the idea.

It should be noted that the salient moment of eros—the separation between one and the other bridged by their mutual attraction—is more radical than "a relationship of dependence between independent beings."[19]

---

18. Anne Carson, *Eros the Bittersweet* (Normal, IL: Dalkey Archive, 1998), 26, 63; see also Richard Jackson, "Eros and the Erotics of Writing," in *Radiant Lyre: Essays on Lyric Poetry*, ed. David Baker and Ann Townsend (Saint Paul, MN: Graywolf, 2007), 72.

19. This is Simon Critchley's paraphrase of the Hegelian idea of love (Simon Critchley, *How to Stop Living and Start Worrying* [Cambridge: Polity, 2010], 63).

With eros comes passion, which, before appearing as a domineering emotional and physical discharge, is first and foremost a bearing of the inalienable and uncontrollable other "whom my soul loves."[20] Neither fight nor flight, in face of the other one subjected to love is exposed to a prior passivity inherent in subjectivity, and urged to act responsively. This erotic pain of forebearance is vividly conveyed in the second night scene: the beloved other had already awakened the subject's heart (5:2), while the "I" who is subjected to this past perfect condition cannot but play catch-up (5:6). Through love, the other had taken me hostage by enchanting my heart with his trace, yet the precarious other has an oblique side beyond my reach. In Song 5:6 one reads,

| pātaḥtî ʾănî lĕdôdî | I open for my lover, |
| wĕdôdî ḥāmaq ʿābār | but my lover has turned away and is gone. |

At the center of this couplet, the *dôdî* that attracts me to him through his trace in me (5:4) is contrasted to the *dôdî* who has abruptly turned away. The contrast is all the more pronounced across the *waw* and the line break, which visually dramatize the dislocation between the beloved who is ineffably deep in me and infinitely far beyond my control. This displaced identification on the subject's sensibility reduces her to a primordial state of vulnerability: "I am faint with love" (5:8). The modality of love exposes "you" as irresistible and "me" as inextricably subjected to "you." Such a condition exposes the subject's root of selfhood in vulnerability, in being called to respond to "you."

With this contextual background in mind, we may now catch up with the subject in Song 8:6. Out of her experience that knows the bearing of the otherness of the beloved, and settled in the ideal setting of his embrace,[21] the subject calls to the girls through the refrain formula one last time.

³ᵃšĕmōʾlô taḥat rōʾšî	his left one is under my head,
ᵇwîmînô tĕḥabbĕqēnî:	and his right enwraps me;
⁴ᵃhišbaʿtî ʾetkem	I adjure you,
bĕnôt yĕrûšālāim	O daughters of Jerusalem:
ᵇma-tāʿîrû ûma-tĕʿōrĕrû	do not wake or stir up
ᶜʾet-hāʾahăbā ʿad šetteḥpāṣ:	love, till it is ready.

Between the adjuration in Song 8:4 and the change of speaker in 8:8, Song 8:5–7 seems to be a random collage of three small units (5ab, 5c–e, and 6–7) without discernible formal or thematic ties. Clues of connectivity, however, can be discerned upon a close reading.

---

20. If one thinks one can completely control the other, eros by definition is lost in the certainty.

21. This couplet precedes the refrain in Song 2:7 as well (with the minor variation of the omission of the preposition *lĕ-* before *rōʾšî*). The implied embrace may serve as a formulaic setting for her speech that follows.

"*The Human Form Divine*" 115

To begin with, the lines in 8:5 are joined (indirectly through their internal feedback to other parts of the Song) to set the stage for the most powerful confession of love in the Song, which is about to unfold. The verbatim repetition of 3:6 in 8:5a recasts the consummate "day of bliss" (*yôm śimaḥat*) in 3:6–11 as the background for the emerging girl, who, after the previous wanting-but-having-not (8:1–3), finally has her desired lover by her side. Then her present leaning *upon* (*ʿal*) her lover (8:5) anticipates her request to remain *upon* (*ʿal*) his heart and arms (8:6ab). After much turning and returning in the previous lyrics and befitting the excitement of this climactic encounter, in the next montaged scene the emergence of the pair is immediately followed by the long-bated realization of the thematic wakening (*ʿrr*). The intermediate time is counted as if nothing, or at best an insubstantial blur—this, lovers of all ages know.

The central place of wakening/arousing in Song 8:5 is also shown in the three sonic clusters that group the five lines: *mem* marks the first couplet, *taw* sets off the third and the single line, and *šin* leads the last couplet.

⁵ᵃ*mî zōʾt ʿōlâ min-hammidbār*	Who is she that comes up from the desert,
ᵇ*mitrappeqet ʿal-dôdāh*	leaning upon her lover?
ᶜ*taḥat hattappûaḥ ʿôrartîkā*	Under the apricot tree I awaken you—
ᵈ*šāmmâ ḥibbĕlatkā ʾimmeka*	there your mother conceived you,
ᵉ*šāmmâ ḥibbĕlâ yĕlādatka*	there she who bore you conceived you.

In the central line, the perfect tense of the verb *ʿôrartîkā* suggests that the wakening, which has been repeatedly suppressed in the refrains,²² is finally seen happening, intriguingly nestled between the evoked day of bliss and the genealogy of love.²³

Here, I advise the reader not to fill up this enticing gap between wakening and begetting out of reason's penchant for totality, which risks reducing lyric to narrative, or worse, to a manual of operation. Though the group appearance of birth-related verbs²⁴ here imparts a physical tone, it falls beside the expected love-play under the tree. It is physical but is beside the point, like a teasing tap near the itchy spot: "I know it is *there*, but see, I am not touching it." This is a prime example of the way the Song masterfully feeds the erotic flame without having it consumed in sex (cf. 8:1b). At the point where a direct reference to sexual union is most likely to appear in the Song, the lyric decisively keeps at its erotic indecisiveness. In so doing, the poem remains anchored in the emotive aspect of eros, which graciously denies any reduction to an objective report on "sexual union"²⁵ and its resulting regeneration. In short, focused on an uncurbed flowering

---

22. Compare with the imperfect tense of the verb in Song 2:7, 3:5, 8:4.
23. The reference to "your mother" (8:5d) echoes "my mother" nearby (8:1, 2) and "his mother" more distantly (3:11); thus it literally resounds in the genealogy of love.
24. In this six-word couplet, *hbl* (2×) and *yld* (1×) appear with heightened frequency.
25. J. Cheryl Exum, *Song of Songs: A Commentary* (OTL; Louisville: Westminster John Knox, 2005), 250.

of joy—having been deliciously denied the possibility of "waking up" until now, even with the rustling hope for the future that the fruitful past portends[26]—she sets the tone for the confession that follows.

As I have noted, the underlying problem in Song 8:1–3 is the girl's separation from her lover, which drastically enhances her hard-earned joy at finally having him in 8:5. That is, what would someone who has long been famished and is able to take a bite of a loaf of freshly baked bread want next? What would a riverbed that has long been thirsty and finally flows with abundant water desire next? What else would the girl who has pined for the consummation of their love, which is happening, want next? Is it not that this abundance, this jubilation, will continue forever? This, I suggest, is the emotional timbre wherein the keyword *qin'â* in Song 8:6 is born.

If read independently, the pair *'ahăbâ* and *qin'â* in Song 8:6 could be understood as "love" and its biting edge, "jealousy." J. Cheryl Exum has offered a concise definition for the latter: "*Qin'â* is a violent emotion, usually aroused when a rival, specific or nebulous, is felt to threaten an exclusive relationship."[27] Though this statement summarizes jealousy well, the cause of *qin'â* so understood sits uneasily in the above-mentioned context. First, in the preceding lyrical units, one finds no third party that could provoke the girl's jealousy. Second, in the Song at large, when the girls are reported to love the King/lover, it serves but to testify to his charm (1:3; 3:10). When the girls do get enticed to voice their interest in seeking him *with her* (6:1), they are immediately fenced off by the declaration of the lovers' exclusive and mutual devotion (6:2–3). Moreover, when other women are compared with the girl, they are but a foil that sets her apart: "the most beautiful among women" (1:8, 5:9, 6:1), "the lily among the thorns" (2:3), and "the only one" of the queens, concubines, and damsels (6:8–9). In short, while the third party is evoked strategically to make the lovers appear attractive and to spice things up, the Song clearly does not allow other women to challenge the girl's relationship with her lover.[28]

Aware of the impotent threat of a real third party in the Song, Exum points out that the girl is here only speaking of jealousy in general and not her own.[29] Although this may be a reasonable option, I respectfully disagree. In my view, despite all the benefits of pushing to translate *qin'â* as jealousy here, it would fail to pay adequate attention to the fact that the

---

26. That is, the previous love-play under the tree had resulted in a male heir, "you." The Syriac reads the personal suffix in 8:5 as second-person feminine singular, but this correction is not well supported (ibid., 249–50).

27. Ibid., 251.

28. Certain ambiguous texts such as Song 2:15 may be taken as a reference to the third party that messes up the relationship between the man and the woman. I have elsewhere argued that the little ditty in 2:15 serves as the girl's indirect response to her lover's two invitations in 2:10–13 and 14 (see my "Imagery, Slippage and Proximity: Circling around Song 2:10–13," a paper presented at the annual meeting of the SBL in 2015).

29. Exum, *Song of Songs*, 252–53.

intensity of the girl's tone in Song 8:6–7 is born out of the preceding lines and should be explained in light of them.

Jealousy as commonly understood might surface, when distance dominates the erotic sphere and makes the entry of a third party possible, but not at a time when the lovers cannot have enough of each other. When the lovers are enamored with each other after a long wait, as in Song 8:5, the rest of the world (including a third party of any possible shade) is but a blurry background to their love play. In the erotic dance of separation and encounter, the distance between one and the other is here covered by the two en route to becoming "one flesh" (borrowing the language of Gen 2:24). I contend that, given the immediate and the broader context, the word *qin'â* as the girl voices it in Song 8:6 derives, not from anxiety over a third party, but from the subject's justifiable apprehension that the separation between one and the other would consume their attention again (cf. 1:1; 3:1; 5:2–8; 8:1–3). The threat to their erotic union is not so much a third party as the essential separation between one and the other.

Furthermore, it is worth noting that such a separation differs from any perceivable distance. Physical distance between the lovers can be temporarily removed, but the underlying separation remains. The subject bears the separation from her beloved in tension with love's irresistible attraction. This impossible tension urges her to appeal to her beloved for a permanent proximity, especially at the heightened moment when the two are united as though one. With the exuberant language of metaphor and a wish that is a continuation of 8:1–4, she asks him to set *her* as a seal on his heart and arm.[30] Submitting herself as the keeper of the other, she testifies to a proximity that reaches across distance but regards the immovable difference. Instead of vainly consuming erotic heat in one's sexual discharge, instead of fancying the elimination of separation through spiritual fusion, this request for proximity answers to erotic tension by seeking to restore shalom between the one and the other (cf. Song 8:10).

Now when readers come to the first line of Song 8:6, they hear again the voice that has sustained love's tension in 8:1–4 and 5. More specifically, the intense tone of v. 6 is born of, and will not easily let go of the intimacy that was erotically gapped in v. 5. But 8:5 differs from 8:1–4 in that, now emboldened by their bliss in v. 5, the subject makes a direct request to her beloved instead of making a wish upon a star.

| 6a*śîmēnî kaḥôtām ʿal-libbekā* | Set me as a seal[31] on your heart, |
| b*kaḥôtām ʿal-zĕrôʿekā* | as a seal on your arm! |

---

30. And by the reference to his heart within and arms without, the whole of her beloved is in view.

31. After the preposition *kĕ-*, the definite article on the compared is often used generically, hence the translation "a seal" (*GHB* §137i).

With the imperative *śîmēnî*, the subject makes a demand; but the active voice is instantly curtailed, because she who demands also offers herself as the accusative, "me."[32] Moreover, it is the passivity embedded in the accusative that will be picked up in the next couplet, where instead of summoning the power of love to achieve her rhetoric goal, the subject gives reason to her request by relating herself to love through her bearing of it. Her climactic confession gushes out of her unbearable bearing, in an upstream movement similar to the urgency of those who, having found meaningfulness in a pluperfect past, "beat on, boats against the current, borne back ceaselessly into the past."[33]

Carried by love's crushing force toward and against the otherness of the other, in Song 8:6 the subject pleads with an exposed urgency and vulnerability for the peace-giving proximity between oneself and the other. This proximity bears the erotic urgency as perceived by her sensibility and the nonerotic vulnerability as the ethical condition of perceiving the other. The constituting ethical condition is here constituted in her single-minded repetition of their verbal togetherness through the central simile *kaḥôtām*.[34]

As with the garment simile found in the Egyptian love song "Seven Wishes," the seal worn next to the beloved's chest accentuates the subject's desire for the physical proximity of her beloved. For, indirect and feeble as it might be, the intimacy could "strengthen" the subject in bearing the flame of eros (cf. Song 2:5).

> If only I were the laundryman
> of my sister's linen garment
> (even) for one month!
> I would be strengthened

---

32. André Robert and Raymond Jacques Tournay note the subject's active role, categorizing this demand as hortatory and accrediting the subject the initiative to evoke the force of love (André Robert and Raymond Jacques Tournay, *Le Cantique des Cantiques* [Paris: Gabalda, 1963], 299). In this thematic abstraction, however, the passivity of the accusative is ignored.

33. F. Scott Fitzgerald, *The Great Gatsby* (New York: Scribner, 1925), 180.

34. Seals were made of stone or metal, engraved with words and/or images, and worn around the neck with a cord or as a signet ring on the finger. They functioned as a sign of identity (Gen 38:18), used to mark security (1 Kgs 21:8) or ownership—for example, the eighth-century BCE seal bearing the word *l'ḥz* (Graham Davies, *Ancient Hebrew Inscriptions: Corpus and Concordance* [Cambridge: Cambridge University Press, 2004], 101.363). Additional studies on seals can be found in the following literature: Robert Deutsch and André Lemaire, *Biblical Period Personal Seals in the Shlomo Moussaieff Collection* (Tel Aviv–Jaffa: Archaeological Center, 2000); Nahman Avigad and Benjamin Sass, *Corpus of West Semitic Stamp Seals* (Jerusalem: Israel Exploration Society, 1997); Patricia. J. Berlyn, "Engraved with the Names," *JBQ* 21 (1993): 143–52; Nahman Avigad, "The Contribution of Hebrew Seals to an Understanding of Ancient Israelite Religion and Society," in *Ancient Israelite Religion: Essays in Honor of Frank Moore Cross*, ed. Patrick D. Miller et al. (Philadelphia: Fortress, 1987), 195–208; A. Reifenberg, *Ancient Hebrew Seals* (London: East and West Library, 1950).

by grasping [the clothes] that touch her body.³⁵

In comparison with the image of the clothes of the beloved, the imagery of a seal in Song 8:6 gives more emphasis to the subject's insistence on proximity. The image of a seal worn over one's chest simultaneously denotes identity, ownership, security, and intimacy (cf. Deut 11:18; Prov 3:3; 7:3; 6:21ff.).³⁶ Furthermore, because the specific reference to "heart" evokes more than what "chest" (the physical location of the worn seal) signifies,³⁷ physical intimacy alone cannot exhaust the significance of the simile "as a seal." Used metaphorically, the noun *ḥôtām* marks the protection of something precious or secret. It is found parallel to "guard" or "lock" (Sir 22:27, 42:6; see also Job 41:7). The scintillation of signifyingness along with the incomplete syntax attract the reader to continue reading to the line-end, where the consonant *kap* encircles the last two phrases, *kaḥôtām ʿal-libbekā*. By enshrining a tactile togetherness between me-as-the-seal and you-through-your-heart, the line-end at the sound of *-kā* reinforces the proximity that her request seeks. By turning *herself* into his seal, not only will she always be with him, but also his seal will convey her will,³⁸ which

---

35. Michael V. Fox, *The Song of Songs and the Ancient Egyptian Love Songs* (Madison: University of Wisconsin Press, 1985), 37. See also the third wish of the Egyptian love song "Seven Wishes" (ibid.):

If only I were her little seal-ring,
the keeper of her finger!
I would see her love
each and every day. . . .

36. Though the general use of seals as identification is fully recognized, interpreters opt for different shades of its meaning in this context: (1) marking ownership over the bearer (Duane A. Garrett, *Song of Songs*, WBC 23B [Nashville: Thomas Nelson, 2004], 254; Franz Delitzsch, *Das Hohe Lied untersucht und ausgelegt* [Leipzig, 1851], 67); (2) identification with the bearer (Hess, *Song of Songs*, 238; Roland E. Murphy, *The Song of Songs. A Commentary on the Book of Canticles or the Song of Songs* [Minneapolis: Fortress, 1990], 191 n. 6; Dianne Bergant, *The Song of Songs*, Berit Olam [Collegeville, MN: Liturgical Press, 2001], 97; Leo Krinetzki, *Das Hohe Lied: Kommentar zu Gestalt und Kerygma eines alttestamentlichen Liebesliedes*, KBANT [Düsseldorf: Patmos, 1964], 241); (3) constant closeness (Yair Zakovitch, *Das Hohelied*, HThKAT [Freiburg im Breisgau: Herder, 2004], 269–70; Fox, *Song of Songs*, 169; Robert Gordis, *The Song of Songs: A Study, Modern Translation, and Commentary* [New York: Jewish Theological Seminary, 1954], 96). Exum fuses these together, reading the seal as "a mark of ownership and sign of intimate identification (*Song of Songs*, 5, 250). On a more personal note, one day when I was in a Barnes and Noble café, the name "Daisy" was called to pick up her ordered coffee. A tall old man stood up to receive the coffee on behalf of his temporarily absent lady. I imagine this is how one carries the beloved "as a seal" in a nonexotic yet equally loving way.

37. In CTA 6 (62) I 4–6 (= 5 [67] VI 20–21), *drʿh* ("her forearms") is paired with *ap lb* ("the chest"; Yitshak Avishur, *Stylistic Studies of Word-Pairs in Biblical and Ancient Semitic Literatures*, AOAT 210 [Kevelaer: Butzon & Bercker; Neukirchen-Vluyn: Neukirchener Verlag, 1984], 378).

38. Robert and Tournay, *Le Cantique des Cantiques*, 300. One should not conflate wearing the seal with the stamping of it on the owned object (Garrett, *Song of Songs*, 254). The

is to be with him like this forever. As only she-the-seal-over-his-heart can denote, she expresses her desire to own the seat of his love and guard it out of "passion" (8:6d), which is comparable to separation anxiety.

It should be noticed that the subject's claim is unlike that of colonization, which subdues the other for one's own interest. Through *sîmēnî*, the subject's territorial claim is made with submission and substitution, with a giving of herself as the other's keeper. Her boldness in asserting her desire does not rise out of raw ultramateriality in the mode of converting another human into the object of one's consumption. Rather, the straightforwardness of her desire is braided together with the humble-ness of a human subject in proximity to an other. Without reducing to a kinesthetic "reciprocity of the sensuous,"[39] her giving-as-taking may be analogized in the ambiguity of embrace—the one embracing is embraced; the embraced also is embracing.

The thematic and verbal proximity is further enhanced in the next line. With the gapping of *sîmēnî* and the altered location in the second line, the persistence of *kaḥôtām ʿal-* in this couplet grips the audience as a breath refusing to be let go, until it rounds back again to *-kā*, "you."

Besides being worn on a necklace, a seal could be worn as a seal ring on a right-hand finger.[40] However, in 8:6b the noun being paralleled with *libbekā* is *zĕrôʿekā*, "your arm," and not the more frequently attested references, such as "finger" or "hand."[41] Again, I recommend that readers curb any social or historical curiosity[42] to make room for lyrical effect. Following the pulse of the latter, *zĕrôʿekā* first prevents an unnecessary sexual innuendo of hand and fingers here (cf. 5:4–5). Second, it builds on the latent

---

conflation causes Longman to read the girl's imperative as wishing him "to willingly give himself to her" (*Song of Songs*, 210).

39. David Abram, *The Spell of the Sensuous: Perception and Language in a More-Than-Human World* (New York: Pantheon, 1996), 68–69. A cautionary note should be added to the mutuality of touch. The touch of the other at its realization does enshrine mutuality, an ambiguity of touching and being touched, and therefore seems to entail intersubjectivity at the origin of the self. Yet the subject's desire for the touch assumes a prior ethical passivity, for one's obsession with the other entails and is embedded in the touch. Consider the opening words of the Song: "Oh that he may kiss me with the kisses of his lips" (Song 1:1).

40. Jer 22:24, Sir 49:11, Hag 2:23, Deut 6:8.

41. Donald Phillip Roberts, *Let Me See Your Form: Seeking Poetic Structure in the Song of Songs*, Studies in Judaism (Lanham, MD: University Press of America, 2007), 324 n. 25.

42. Just to name a few of the sought-after explanations: (1) Render *zĕrôaʿ* as "wrist" and envisioning that the seal was worn as a bracelet (cf. 2 Sam 1:10; Paul Joüon, *Le cantique des cantiques: Commentaire philologique et exégétique* [Paris: Beauchesne, 1909], 314). But this is not attested in archaeological finds and still begs the question why the subject avoids the more common option "hand." (2) Reconstruct the second *kaḥôtām* as *kaṣṣāmîd* ("as a bracelet"; Karl Budde, *Das Hohelied*, in *Die fünf Megillot: Das Hohelied, das Buch Ruth, die Klagelieder, der Prediger, das Buch Esther*, KHC 17 [Freiburg: Mohr, 1898], 44). However, the inscriptional similarity between *kaḥôtām* and *kaṣṣāmîd* is not evident. (3) Besides the possibility of wearing the seal higher up as an armlet, Fox suggests taking *zĕrôaʿ* as a reference to the whole arm, "including the finger" (Fox, *Song of Songs*, 169). While this plausibly explains why *zĕrôaʿ* can be used here, it still does not answer why it *must* be used.

evocation of her lover's embrace, which is achieved in the previous line through sound play (compare 8:3a and 8:6a). While the substantival uses of "his left one" and "his right one" in 8:3 focus on the completeness of her lover's embrace, the naming of his "arm" in 8:6b shifts the audience's attention to his physical presence and action, in contrast to his heart, which denotes his emotion and will.[43]

6a*śîmēnî kaḥôtām ʿal-libbekā*	Set me as a seal on your heart,
b*kaḥôtām ʿal-zĕrôʿekā*	as a seal on your arm!
c*kî-ʿazzâ kammāwet ʾahăbâ*	For[44] strong as death is love,
d*qāšâ kišəʾôl qinʾâ*	fierce as Sheol is passion.

At the beginning of v. 6c, the consonant *kap* continues the opening emphatic sound of 6b but then introduces a "shrill" *i*, enabling a "cutting-penetration"[45] to glide over the weak radical *ʿayin* to a sonorous *a-a* melody in *ʿazzâ*. Together, *kî-ʿazzâ* partially revert to (and invert) the consonantal sequence of *zĕrôʿekā* across the line-break: from *z-(r)-ʿ-k* to *k-ʿ-z-(h)*.[46] As noted above, the causal clauses in 8:6cd pick up the passive aspect of the accusative in *śîmēnî* and flesh out the propelling force behind her request. Thus the sonic linking, penetration, and reversal that the second couplet effects is set in harmony with its syntactic function.

Taking these two couplets as a whole, the length of the first (10-8 syllables) is tightened slightly and proportionally into that of the second (9-7 syllables), thus vocalically signaling her intensifying voice.[47] A few other syntactic and stylistic characteristics also help to knit the two couplets together: (1) the syntactic tie between the main and relative clauses, (2) the ellipse of the initial word of the second line (*śîmēnî* and *kî*, respectively), and (3) the similes at the center.

---

43. The chosen image of "arm" constitutes a fitting parallel with "heart" through the denoted pair of action and will. Hence, Fox explains that this parallelism "expresses the Shulammite's hope to be bound to her lover in all his thoughts and actions" (ibid.).

44. After the urgent imperative, *kî* introduces the reason (Gordis, *Song of Songs*, 74; Hess, *Song of Songs*, 238; Krinetzki, *Hohe Lied*, 240). However, Murphy reads this particle as asseverative (*Song of Songs*, 191; cf. *GHB* §164b). Zakovitch allows for both translations: "Denn/fürwahr" (*Das Hohelied*, 270). T. A. Perry also offers two alternative translations of Song 8:6c in his study of the particle *kî* ("The Coordination of *ky* / *ʿl kn* in Cant. I 1–3 and Related Texts," *VT* 55 [2005]: 528). In fact, all five occurrences of *kî* in the Song appear after volitional clauses (1:2; 2:5, 11, 14; 8:6) and supply reasons for the requests.

45. Krinetzki also notes these two sonic attributes (*Das Hohe Lied*, 242).

46. Scott B. Noegel and Gary Rendsburg group similar lyrical phenomena through the idea of alliteration and provide more examples from the Song (*Solomon's Vineyard: Literary and Linguistic Studies in the Song of Songs* [Atlanta: Society of Biblical Literature, 2009], 63–106). But this instance is not included in their examples.

47. The two couplets also feature different sonic markers: in the first couplet, the salient sonic marker is the consonant *kap*, which enwraps the words or phrases of comparison; in the second, it shifts to the rhyming *-â*, which ends the four words that form the two pairs of predications.

Though the convergence of syntactic, stylistic, and sonic patterns creates an organic unity between the first and second couplets, the lyrical flow is far from being idyllic. Before digesting the semantic sense, and while hearing the poetic lines, the audience may already sense an undercurrent of constricted passion that roars but cannot be freed. The repetition of *k/q/ḥ/z* generates hard vocal edges and so congruently performs the semantic ideas of "strong" and "fierce." With the speaker's giving voice to these words, the audience is getting worked up toward the intended level of emotional intensity. At the same time, the vocal provocation is salved through the very repetition of these phonemes as well as through the interspersed weak or smooth consonants and melodic vowel patterns.[48] Take 8:6c–d, for example: *kî-ʿazzâ kammāwet ʾahăbâ // qāšâ kišěʾôl qinʾâ*. In 6c, the initial syllables of the four words alternate as *k-ʿ-k-ʾ*. Then in 6d, the initial consonants (*q-, k-, q-*), are interspersed with the repeated *š* in the second syllables of the first and second words (*qš-* and *kš-*). The play of the *i/e* vowels and the *a/o* vowels in 6a also takes a new spin in 6c: the *i-a-a* melody in *kî-ʿazzâ* reverses into that of *a-a-e* in *kammāwet*, while the doubling of *a-a* in these two words (framed by *i/e* vowels) expands to the *a-a-a* pattern in the last word, *ʾahăbâ*. Finally, the decorous synonymous parallelism regulates the reader's semantic configuration and breath, achieving a rhythmic exuberance. In short, the lyric rides a bumpy current that nevertheless flows vigorously.

As "the living part of the poem,"[49] the sound of sense works up the audience by altering its breath, and by its altered breath, the mapping of its feelings and emotions.[50] This simplest element of poetic experience—my breath altered by the poem—modulates the very signifyingness of language, the saying beneath the said. Levinas writes, "[I]n reducing the said to the saying, philosophical language reduces the said to breathing opening to the other and signifying to the other its very signifyingness."[51] Seen from this ethical perspective, poetry is first to be experienced as a reduction and unsaying of the said in accordance with the affectivity of sensibility. In an antecedence that is not necessarily logical or temporal, the audience of Song 8:6 feels its breath altered by the subject's vehement and firmly sustained voice, being taken hostage, as the subject is, by love. Thus the au-

---

48. Tod Linafelt notices that the hardness of *k* in 8:6c–d gives way to the dancing sparkles of *r/s, š/ś* in 6e, which in turn grow into "an all-consuming blaze" (Tod Linafelt, "Biblical Love Poetry . . . [and God]," *JAAR* [2002]: 331).

49. This is a saying of Robert Frost quoted by John Felsteiner, in *Can Poetry Save the Earth? A Field Guide to Nature Poems* (New Haven, CT: Yale University Press, 2009), 119.

50. Cf. Paul Celan, "The Meridian," *Paul Celan: Selections*, ed. Pierre Joris, trans. Rosmarie Waldrop (Berkeley: University of California Press, 2005), 162; Les A. Murray, "Embodiment and Incarnation," *The Paperbark Tree: Selected Prose* (Manchester: Carcanet, 1992), 259.

51. Levinas, *Otherwise than Being*, 181.

dience is invited to participate in, and not just analyze, the lyrical subject's gripping passion.

The voice of passion in Song 8:6a–d is also expressed through the center that de-centers. A visual perception of the lineated text readily reveals that, vertically binding and horizontally occupying the central stage of the four lines are four words led by the comparative particle *kĕ-* (*kaḥôtām* [2×], *kammāwet*, *kišĕʾôl*). It sets off a series of metaphorical detours that interrupt the otherwise straightforward syntactic flow. The insertion of metaphors suspends and adds volume to the straight line between the subject and the predicate.[52] This sort of insertion is regularly seen in biblical poetry, mostly in one line,[53] or less frequently and with greater rhetorical impact, in a couplet as in Ps 78:27.[54] But rarely does it go through the course of two couplets, as in Song 8:6a–d (with an eclipse in 6b). It is as though the passion that drives the imperative finds a felicitous rhythm to incarnate itself in words: the centrality[55] and plain repetition of *kaḥôtām* crinkles the tissue of each line with an almost painful withholding that curbs and enriches the subject's eruptive passion. However, the first couplet is too short, keenly but insufficiently conveying what propels it. Hence, carrying and carried by the same breath, this syntactic pattern homogenizes the following couplet to allow for a fuller embodiment of the lyrical energy.

I am tempted to say that the sonic and syntactic staccato in these four lines mimics the trembling of a vehement desire that knows its limit. It is not out of a celebratory voice extolling the power of love but the voice of her bearing of love's burn—trembling, and bearing still. The felt power of love that mobilizes these lines lies not in one's ability to conquer the other through love but in the inability to stop this love that has taken one hostage.[56] It resides in the bountiful underlying, where the daylight of rational exposition cannot penetrate, "where everything shines as it disappears."[57] This wordless aura, wherein words arise and dissolve, absorbs the sound, sight, and syntax of the lyrics and saturates the otherwise indifferent site

---

52. This is in contrast to other more straightforward options, in which the metaphor led by *kĕ-* is placed before the subject and predication, e.g., *kīllînû šānênû kĕmô-hegeh* ("like a sigh we spent our years" [Ps 90:9]); or after them, e.g., *wayyilbaš ṣĕddāqâ kašširyān* ("he put on righteousness like a breastplate" [Isa 59:17a]).

53. E.g., *tĕšîtēmô kĕtannûr ʾēš* ("You set them like a furnace on fire"; Ps 21:10a); See also Ps 22:17c; Isa 1:25b; 5:24d, 25d; Ps 22:16, 17b; 31:13; 33:7; 37:6; 78:15, 52; etc.

54. For instance, see Ps 72:6; Job 15:33; and Prov 6:5. Sometimes the second line repeats the comparative phrase but changes the syntactic pattern (Ps 72:6; Amos 5:24; Job 27:16, 18; 41:23).

55. Though in Song 8:6b *kaḥôtām* is literally at the beginning of the line, the eclipsed *śîmēnî* extends its governing force to this line.

56. And if it were stopped, it would sink deeper away from consciousness as an incurable and hardly reachable wound.

57. Rainer Maria Rilke, "Sonnets to Orpheus," part 2/12, in *A Year with Rilke: Daily Readings from the Best of Rainer Maria Rilke*, ed. Anita Barrows and Joanna Macy (New York: HarperCollins, 2009).

of reading with the subject's fearfully wonderful feeling of the inability not to love the other. To be in love is to bear it without denouement or substitution.

At the urgency of full carnality, the subject of love is denuded to an originary vulnerability induced by the otherness of the beloved. In spite of their present intimacy, his inaccessibility haunts her with a desire that cannot entirely be met. Against the extended history of presence-as-absence, wanting-but-having-not, seeking-but-not-responded-to, the sweet taste of their current togetherness makes separation in the future so much more unbearable.

⁶ᵃśîmēnî kaḥôtām ʿal-libbekā	Set me as a seal on your heart,
ᵇkaḥôtām ʿal-zĕrôʿekā	as a seal on your arm!
ᶜkî-ʿazzâ kammāwet ʾahăbâ	For strong as Death is love,
ᵈqāšâ kišěʾôl qinʾâ	fierce as Sheol is passion.
ᵉrěšāpeyhā rišpê ʾēš	Its flashes are flashes of fire,
ᶠšalhebetyāh	a flame of Yah.

One notices on the syntactic and stylistic fronts how the organic extension from 6cd to 6ef [58] also unfolds with a new twist. Though similes continue in 8:6e, the comparative particle kĕ- and the point-of-contact (e.g., ʿazzâ and qāšâ) are omitted. The intensity of love that is strong as death is no longer expressed in positive statements as the rationale (6cd) behind the request (6ab) but is now embodied in passion's flame, which engulfs the audience's perception. The central detour of similes in the previous lines breaks free into a permeating fire through 8:6e (and beyond).[59]

---

58. Consider the first word, rěšāpeyhā, for example. Sonically through the rhyming a, the pronominal suffix -hā highlights the thematic statements marked by a string of feminine nouns and adjectives in 6cd: ʿazzâ . . . ʾahăbâ, qāšâ . . . qinʾâ. Then, with the suffix -hā syntactically recuperating its immediate antecedent, qinʾâ (and by way of synonymous parallelism, it also absorbs the compound force of qinʾâ and ʾahăbâ), it channels the semantic intensity penned up in the doubling of ʿazzâ and qāšâ to fume the blazing flashes that it modifies: rěšāpeyhā. Furthermore, after the elapse of the couplet, the suffix -hā will soon be matched through an aural and syntactical echo with -yāh in šalhebetyāh, forming a teasing inclusio of sorts around this couplet. The reading περίπτερα αὐτῆς . . . φλόγες αὐτῆς ("its flashes . . . its flames") in the OG draws the outline of the flames even more emphatically with the semantic sameness of αὐτῆς. Other sonic links include and are not limited to the following: the permeating š in 6ef picks up from 6d this repeated phoneme (qāšâ kišěʾôl); and through the sibling semblance of š/ś, it also echoes to the beginning imperative śîmēnî.

59. Besides the payoff of preventing stylistic monotony, this altered formula focuses lyrical energy on the repetition of rešep and melts the boundary between the near and the far, the real and the metaphorical, the erotic and the non-erotic in the flames that burn through both camps. Note also the subtle instability in the foregrounding of the flames. In the initial reading, the repetition of rešep in this line does foreground the image of fiery flames. But precisely because of its repetition, it also recedes as a blazing background—with all the intensity that it induces nevertheless—as the varied constituents ("it" and "fire") give saliency to the predication. In what follows, the plurality and double-reference

The sheer volume of the blinding fire does not stop at providing an image for reason to process. Having exhausted consciousness's imagination[60] and still begging for more, it occasions an opening for the saying that is sustained as a pure bearing (in line with the accusative "me" in śîmēnî). Fierce and strong as passion is, she bears it nevertheless, and lets the bearing tremble her voice. At the very edge of her patience, which is "exceeded by a demented suffering,"[61] emerges her urgent and vulnerable voice pleading for the proximity with her beloved, out of which she speaks. The subject's awe-struck testimony to passion through the image of fire finds a mighty echo in Rilke's poem "To the Beloved,"[62] which erupts as a torrent of elaborations set in a modern tempo.

> Extinguish my eyes, I'll go on seeing you.
> Seal my ears, I'll go on hearing you.
> And without feet I can make my way to you,
> without a mouth I can swear your name.
>
> Break off my arms, I'll take hold of you
> with my heart as with a hand.
> Stop my heart, and my brain will start to beat.
> And if you consume my brain with fire,
> I'll feel you burn in every drop of my blood.

By a similar bearing of flame as the ultimate sign of undergoing, of love's burning beyond death's crashing force, Rilke's poem sounds differently the same testimony to love thoroughly loved: reducing to the last bit of me, it is my feeling of you, burning that last bit of me.

This is not the voice of a conquering ego who possesses you, the *beloved*, but a witness to how the grand "I am" is already a hostage, passive with no way out except responding to "you." In this lyrical testimony, the way one seals the other as the beloved is not through imposing the power of love on the other, who passively receives, but through bearing for the other who had already defined the "I."[63] Passion (or passivity), as the double for love, is therefore at the very heart of oneself and "stronger than death."[64]

---

of *rešep* (see note below on *rešep*) are emblazoned into one consuming fire, *šalhebet*, while the modifying -*hā* and *'ēš* in this line are single-handedly matched by the mysterious -*yāh*.

60. That is, the lurking imageries of death (Mot, Sheol, and Reshep) may be superceded by a reference to Yah.

61. "To not be reabsorbed into meaning, the patience of passivity must be always at the limit, exceeded by a demented suffering" (Levinas, *Otherwise than Being*, 153). The idea of "a demented suffering" refers to one's bearing of the unbearable, without being able to stop, and "for nothing," because suffering for the other begins before "I am."

62. Rilke, *A Year with Rilke*.

63. The "I" as defined in "you burn in every drop of my blood" or "the one my soul loves" (Song 1:7; 3:1, 2, 3, 4).

64. Emmanuel Levinas, "The Temptation of Temptation," *Nine Talmudic Readings*, trans. Annette Aronowicz (Bloomington: Indiana University Press, 1990), 48.

With her double expression of urgency and vulnerability, the subject enacts an encounter with the other in which the trace of God, the ultimate Other, becomes tangible. This encounter reveals not so much what one may know or possess of the other/Other as what kind of passivity and responsibility one bears in facing the other. As one integrally lives out this modality of love in responding to the other (lover or neighbor), God's trace passes by in this subjectivity and humanness, whether consciousness captures it or not. Briefly, as Levinas states, the trace of God "is inscribed . . . in the encounter with the Other; a double expression of weakness and strict, urgent requirement."[65]

With the figures of Mot, Sheol,[66] and Reshep[67] piled up, death looms as an impressive foil to love, because both come upon and render powerless the human subjects. However, the shadow of death will disappear in the all-consuming flame befitting a divine origin as the lyric intensifies into

---

65. Idem, *Ethics and Infinity* (Pittsburgh: Duquesne University Press, 1985), 86.

66. Personified Sheol and Death are paired in poetry by their insatiable appetite for and seemingly irresistible claim to human life (2 Sam 22:6; Hab 2:5; Ps 89:48; 116:3). But their powers are not taken as absolute: people have the illusion that they can make a covenant with them (Isa 28:15, 18), but only God can trump them (Hos 13:14).

67. The noun *rešep* is employed here with the semantic sense of "flash, flame" (Ps 76:4; Job 5:7), which is attested in a group of synonyms shown in ancient translations: περίπτερα (OG, "the ones flying around," i.e., "sparks"), λαμπάδες (α', "torches"), σπίνθρακες (θ', "sparks"), ὁρμαὶ πυρινοί (σ', "fiery flashes"), *lampades* (Vulg., "torches"); the Syr. also translates it "flames of fire" (Maciej M. Münnich, *The God Resheph in the Ancient Near East*, ORA 11 [Tübingen: Mohr Siebeck, 2013], 233). In other biblical contexts, it also refers to "pestilence, plague" (Deut 32:24; Hab 3:5), and "lightening bolt" (Ps 78:48). The etymology of *rešep* is rather uncertain: it may have the sense of "the one who burns" (Hartmut Gese, Maria Höfner, and Kurt Rudolph, *Die Religionen Altsyriens, Altarabiens und der Mandäer* [Stuttgart: Kohlhammer, 1970], 142) or may be associated with the Akkadian verb *rašābu(m)*, "to be awe-inspiring" (Hans-Peter Müller, "Religions-geschichtliche Beobachtungen in den Texten von Ebla," *ZDPV* 96 [1980]: 10). Münnich traces it to "the reconstructed Semitic root **ršp*, which would mean 'to blaze, burn, light'" (*The God Resheph*, 8). The deity Rešep was worshiped throughout the ancient Near East, and his trace can be recovered in literary and archaeological materials that span 3,000 years (Edward Lipiński, *Resheph: A Syro-Canaanite Deity* [Leuven: Peeters, 2009]; Walter Burkert, *Rešep—Figuren, Apollon von Amyklai und die "Erfindung" des Opfers auf Cypern: Zur Religionsgeschichte der "Dunklen Jahrhunderte"* [Amsterdam: Rodopi, 1975]). Rešep has also been identified with Nergal, Babylonian god of the underworld, plagues, and war (James B. Pritchard, *The Ancient Near East in Pictures* [Princeton, NJ: Princeton University Press, 1954], 476). In his study of Ugaritic personal names, Frauke Gröndahl finds that the characteristics of Rešep include both death and fertility (*Die Personennamen der Texte aus Ugarit* [Rome: Pontifical Biblical Institut, 1967], 181; see also D. Conrad, "Der Gott Reschef," *ZAW* 83 [1971]: 179). Given the previous references to Death and Sheol, the demythologized noun may indirectly evoke the deity Rešep (Münnich, *The God Resheph*, 234; William Fulco, *The Canaanite God Rešep*, AOS 8 [New Heaven, CT: American Oriental Society, 1976], 60). Some scholars even push for a foregrounded image of the deity in Song 8:6 (W. F. Albright, "Archaic Survivals in the Text of Canticles," in *Hebrew and Semitic Studies*, ed. G. R. Driver [London: Clarendon, 1963], 7; Longman, *Song of Songs*, 212; Exum, *Song of Songs*, 253–54). The potential mythological connotations of *rešep* would enhance the interpretation of -*yāh* as Yah (Exum, *Song of Songs*, 253; Müller, *Hohelied*, 85).

šalhebetyāh (when read as "a flame of Yah"). Rumi's lines from "The Battle of Love" help to unpack the contest between death's grip and love's flame:

> But Hell is extinguished by Love's burning.
> Hell says to the sincere lover, "Go quickly,
> or my fire will be destroyed by your flames."[68]

Given its height and density, the final punch through *šalhebetyāh* temporarily halts the lyrical progression, for it cannot go any higher in the positive direction. Facilitated by the word pair fire and water,[69] the lyric pendulum swings from the passionate fire to the engulfing water in Song 8:7a–c, elaborating on the impossibility of the negative to again affirm the positive.

⁷ᵃ*mayim rabbîm lōʾ yûkĕlû*	Mighty waters cannot
ᵇ*lĕkabbôt ʾet-hāʾahăbâ*	quench love,
ᶜ*ûnĕhārôt lōʾ yišṭĕpûhā*	nor can rivers drown it.
ᵈ*ʾim-yittēn ʾîš*	If a man offered
ᵉ*ʾet-kol-hôn bêtô bāʾahăbâ*	all the wealth of his house for love,
ᶠ*bôz yābûzû lô*	he would be utterly ridiculed.

With the emphasized verbal construct *bôz yābûzû* ringing back to the main verb in 8:1 (*yābûzû*), this set of the girl's lyrics comes to a completion (8:1–7). In the second triplet of 8:7, the lighthearted *i* vowels that chain together in *ʾim-yittēn ʾîš* morphs into a series of gloating *o* vowels in the direct object (*ʾet-kol-hôn bêtô*) and further envelops the main clause (*bôz yābûzû lô*). These sonic perceptions anticipate the thematic message:[70] while voicing them, the reader performs the moral contempt before making a conscious

---

68. Rumi, "The Battle of Love," *Love's Ripening: Rumi on the Heart's Journey*, trans. Kavir Helminski and Ahmad Rezwani (Boston: Shambhala, 2010), 149.

69. The word pair fire/water is taken as a symbol for the extremities of life (cf. Ps 66:12). Moreover, in contrast to the way the decorous parallelism intensifies into one all-consuming flame in 8:6, the running lyric in 8:7 mimics the movement of water that rolls in, trickles down, and then is decisively dammed.

70. Vocal attributes in this lyrical unit interact with other lyrical aspects such as themes, imageries, lineation, and grammatical structures. Here are a few examples: (1) in 8:7a, the *mem* rounds off *mayim rabbîm*, mimicking the waves crashing onto the shore and retreating into themselves; (2) the consonant *lamed* frames the next two words; together with the emphatic use of *ykl*, it grinds out a firm "CANNOT"; (3) in the way that water cascades down and meanders over, the consonants *lamed*, *waw*, and *kap*, which are key sonic components of the first line, flow into the first word of the next line (*lōʾ yûkĕlû/lĕkabbôt*); (4) the direct object marker gives weight to "love" in 7b as if marking out an unshakable mountain that stands against and stops the crushing waves of "many waters"; the clause consisting of the first two lines is then succinctly paralleled in the last line of the triplet (in the formation of "a + b // c"); (5) beginning the next clause, the *ʾalep* that has discreetly followed the loud *lamed* in the emphasized *lōʾ* moves to the front. It opens and closes the conditional clause (*ʾim, ʾîš*), as well as connecting the subject and the direct object across the line break (*ʾîš* and *ʾet*). With its light vocal texture, it helps the switch from the intense declaration in the first triplet to the gloating dismissal in the second.

judgment. The second double-negative scenario (wealth) sets the ultramaterial mentality of reducing love to merchandise as a laughable foil to the love embodied herein. As waters to the fire, riches are no match for love (cf. Zeph 1:18). With the double-negative imageries in 8:7 reinforcing the positive request for proximity (8:6), the lyric flows to a natural stop: love cannot be suppressed or substituted; it can only be borne by "me" (8:6a). Love unbearable and inextinguishable is borne without substitute, so be mine as I am already, always yours (2:16; 6:3; 8:6ab).

My concluding note on proximity (or peace), which the one in love desires, branches forth from my experience of another artwork—Johannes Brahms's Piano Concerto no. 1. Underneath every human triumph, is there not always an unutterable restlessness, arising as if from nowhere, from a null-site? Just as one begins to wave hands exuberantly when the triumphant theme rings out at the beginning of this piano concerto, it thins into a tenderness, as if just now, finally, and only through the musical medium, is the musical subject able to face an inspiring, un-representable, and haunting wound that had cut through his soul anterior to the rise of his will. Instead of a sharp sense of being at a loss when having it all, this restlessness bespeaks a profound yearning for the proximity of the other. It exposes the frailty and inalienability of subjectivity, incessantly waiting to respond, and unable to transgress. And even though the subject does not cross to the other side, the beloved other has already colonized the subject's soul through his vast and extremely tender feelings aroused by and for her. All these, of course, "make sense" when one is given the knowledge of Brahms's respectful infatuation of Clara Schumann that inspired this brilliant piece—and immediately risks the danger of letting it be petrified as another instance of "I love you, you don't love me, boo boo."[71] Such immobilizing categorization understands only the least of the musical significance: at the end, the reconciled triumph is realized, not in overcoming its antithesis, but (with sincerity) in proximity that is never too close and can never be closer.

Detour on Human Finitude

Following the direction of the central metaphorical detour and pushing it even further, I will temporarily shift the focus from text to meaning, especially that of death and love. In terms of meaning, for the poet beyond the voice of the subject, the essential question is not how to homogenize the material in service to a theme, but to look or not to look at the original intrigue directly. Phrasing it in the language of the Greek myth of Orpheus,

---

71. John O'Hara summarizes all love poetry in the formula "I need you, you need me, yum yum" (Helen Vendler, *The Art of Shakespeare's Sonnets* [Cambridge, MA: Belknap, 1997], 14). Linafelt suggests the alternative, in his colleague Darlene Weaver's phrase, "I need you, you don't need me, boo boo" (Linafelt, "Biblical Love Poetry," 330 n. 6).

Blanchot keenly captures the poet's original dilemma in a paragraph worthy of full quotation:

> The Greek myth says: a work can be produced only if the measureless experience of the deep—which the Greeks recognized as necessary to the work and where the work endures its measurelessness—is not pursued for its own sake. The deep does not reveal itself directly; it is only disclosed hidden in the work. This is an essential, an inexorable answer. But the myth shows nonetheless that Orpheus's destiny is not to submit to this ultimate law. And, of course, by turning toward Eurydice, Orpheus ruins the work, which is immediately undone, and Eurydice returns among the shades. When he looks back, the essence of the night is revealed as the inessential. Thus he betrays the work, and Eurydice, and the night. But not to turn toward Eurydice would be no less untrue. Not to look would be infidelity to the measureless, imprudent force of his movement, which does not want Eurydice in her daytime truth and her everyday appeal, but wants her in her nocturnal obscurity, in her distance, with her closed body and sealed face—wants to see her not when she is visible, but when she is invisible, and not as the intimacy of a family life, but as the foreignness of what excludes all intimacy, and wants, not to make her live, but to have living in her the plentitude of her death.[72]

Orpheus's passion for Eurydice generates and ruins both his work and Eurydice's return to the living, for he turned to her without thinking to help her on the last steep steps. To look to her, his work is forever undone, or not to look, his work is forever insufficient. That is not the question. If one hangs onto the said, the apophansis, both tracks will fail "to have living in her the plentitude of her death."[73] Sure, death can be measured by the annihilation of a being, but the plentitude of death overflows it to an enigmatic dilemma: a desiring of that which forever escapes my power but eternally holds me hostage, a deadly intrigue that death cannot undo. Death appears here, not as a formidable force that defies the subject's feeble power, but as an extremity that undoes the *I* of work, identity, and history to its primordial passivity, which is pregnant with an inalienable responsibility, a bearing of the unbearable, tempted by a desire to kill what cannot be killed.

The passion in Song 8:6, also, was not that the strong force of love overpowered the subject's perception and self-assemblage but that her unstoppable desire could never be met. She desires him whom she could not find (3:1; 5:2, 6), or found but could not kiss (1:2; 8:1–3), or whom she has had all the way but not every living minute thereafter (8:5–6). It is the otherness of the other that keeps her desire ablaze. "That is Eros in all its ontological purity . . . direct relationship with what gives itself in withholding

---

72. Maurice Blanchot, *The Space of Literature*, trans. with an introduction by Ann Smock (Lincoln: University of Nebraska Press, 1989), 171–72.
73. Ibid., 172.

itself, with the other *qua* other, with mystery."[74] The sincerity of eros is kept, not by an impossible fusion of two beings in their embedded times and places, but by the remainder that this fusion has made agonizingly impossible. In erotic love, the self is incessantly lured toward the outside of her being, toward the Infinite that passes by in the otherness of the other.

His foreignness—that which remains inaccessible even at the moment of physical intimacy—when approached through her love for him, denudes her to a passive bearing in which she tastes the plentitude of death. Love comes upon the subject like death, in which *I am* is "no longer able to be able."[75] Death dissolves all activities that *I* am capable of initiating and reveals the essential *me* that incessantly bears. "Instead of power, to the subject, love is compared to death through inescapability."[76] In other words, love strong as death awakens oneself to the *me* before the conscious *I*. The effort of sustaining oneself in love, at the end, exposes the lateral extremity of one's being, wherein the touch of the other who had intrigued *me* is needed to make happen the significance of the *I*. In other words, the meaning of one's being is found not so much in the assumed dead end of one's interiority that is extinguished at death, but in the opening at one's innermost toward the outside, where a voice awakens and summons the subject. The one who has tasted such death in love fulfills its significance as for-the-other.

Yet passion, bearing or saying, is too passive to enter the active work of writing. It is always discussed too much and insufficiently,[77] with participants hanging too much on the said. As a conscious effort, a poetic work is inspired by the desire for that which is beyond consciousness and work. That is to say, pursuing with full force across the distance that cannot be covered by force is the poet's calling and integrity. In seizing the inspiration with words, the inspired poet writes of an exit from the endless englobing of daytime, from the constant recoiling back into theme, in an uttermost closeness that reveals a still farther away.

Poetic writing may, as Blanchot's essay demonstrates, meticulously exemplify the language of clarity and consciousness, but it reveals the latter's insubstantiality by kindling a desire for that which is beyond the said. Inspired by an authenticity that does not abide in the faceless truth, by the restlessness of the mental that cannot close on itself, Blanchot's reader

---

74. Emmanuel Levinas, "The Other in Proust," *Proper Names*, trans. Michael B. Smith (London: Athlone, 1996), 103.

75. Emmanuel Levinas, *Totality and Infinity: An Essay on Exteriority*, trans. Alphonso Lingis (Pittsburgh: Duquesne University Press, 1969), 234; Richard A. Cohen, "Thinking Least about Death—Contra Heidegger," *Levinasian Meditations: Ethics, Philosophy, and Religion* (Pittsburgh: Duquesne University Press, 2010), 68.

76. Cohen, "Thinking Least about Death," 65.

77. Jean-Luc Nancy observes writings on love in similar language: "They have never said it enough, having always discoursed it too much, declared it too much" ("Shattered Love," 105).

encounters the exit from the world of being to the unknowable outside.[78] It should be noted that the outside is not any super-world outside our perceptible horizons. Instead of conjuring up the invisible as being devoid of all visibility, the outside reveals, rather, "how invisible the invisibility of the visible is."[79] Instead of a gap that may or may not be filled by knowledge—be it a scientific not-yet about the Higgs Boson or a phenomenological never-ever about the-Thing-Itself—"the invisibility of the visible" testifies against one's despondence about the other, in reducing the other to a construed image outlined by the rational light of daytime, about a familiar hand without exoticism and inspiration. Similar to how the saying and the said are used to turn readerly attention to the significance of human speech, this oxymoronic phrase gestures toward the ethical turn of non-indifference in writing and reading. For example, there are a million different ways to say "I love you"; one just has to pay attention.

Desiring the plentitude of death through poetic words is more than desiring the first night in which everything disappears, more than even desiring the other night in which "everything disappears" appears.[80] More than a patient bearing of impatience for the unsaying, of going through myriads of self-knowledge contextualized in language for the essentially unconditioned, a poetic saying breathes its first breath as exhalation, obliged by an unrepresentable inhalation. Orpheus's songs are all the more authentic because of his unstoppable longing for his irretrievable Eurydice, because of the infinite abyss in the synthesis of desire and its negation. An echoing erotic irreconcilablity is heard in the alteration between the two occurences of *dôdî* across the *waw* in Song 5:6: even though the lyric presents them side by side, the other as the core of my soul differs decisively from the other on the outside.

In Song 8:6, the subject of love comes (again) to the end of her being as she presses herself upon her lover's heart. There, it is not of her own death that she has a foretaste, but of the finitude of her being that comes like, but is otherwise than, death. At the summit of the erotic encounter, on the one hand, appears a revelation that inspires genuine religious and ethical life: the human subject is defined—that is, demarcated as finitude—not by one's linear end in death but by one's radical difference from the other. On the other hand, as the other had taken me hostage through my unstoppable longing for him, I am already non-indifferent to him, to the point

---

78. Levinas, "The Poet's Vision," *Proper Names*, 135. One is also reminded of the words that Blanchot puts on the lips of Thomas the Obscure: "I think, therefore I am not" (Blanchot, *Thomas the Obscure*, trans. Robert Lamberton (New York: Lewis, 1973], 99).

79. Michel Foucault so describes the importance of space in Blanchot's novels and short writings ("La Pensée du dehors," *Critique* 229 [1966]: 529; quoted from Steven Ungar, "Night Moves: Spatial Perception and the Place of Blanchot's Early Fiction," *Yale French Studies* [1979]: 124). See also Kas Saghafi, "The 'Passion for the Outside': Foucault, Blanchot, and Exteriority," *International Studies in Philosophy* 28 (1996): 79–92.

80. Blanchot, *The Space of Literature*, 163.

that I subject myself to his taking—as a seal that reserves his love and touch for me—now and till eternity.

Taking the plenitude of death as "the ceaseless repetition of what cannot be grasped,"[81] one may even say that the significance of death for the human subject is grasped not so much in the fear of one's own deceasing as in one's suppressible but incessant mourning for the departed other (through death or dejection).[82] Death as the possibility of the impossible is not primarily experienced as the vast emptiness of "there is" after taking all lives out of existence. That would deprecate the significance of death. It is the death of the dearly beloved that shakes the identity of the "I" to the core, as mourning exposes the insufficiently examined constitution of the "I" by the other. In Simon Critchley's preface to the second edition of his book *Very Little . . . Almost Nothing*, which grew out of his mourning for his father, he wrote: "As my father, I have already died."[83] The "I" of this book lives the plenitude of death in that the mourning, growing ever deeper and so appearing fainter to the consciousness, has no finish to the "I" who says, ". . . I have already died." It is in the repeated death of this "I" through the ceaseless bearing of the unbearable—which is all that is left in the denuded reality—that love is strong as death, and the human measures up to the finitude of being and overflows it.

The human has a meaning beyond what he or she can *be* and *show* as oneself,[84] such as personal histories, family heritages, social functions, various ambitions, or idiosyncratic tastes. Certainly this meaning does not appear as a separate and graspable category; rather, it is always embodied in the graspable, which betrays it if attention is hung on the graspable. Memory and mourning of "you" who are no longer here with me, neither for the sake of knowing history nor for positive reconstruction of identity, is before all psychoanalytical mapping an undying responsibility for the other, who has given rise to and furnished my self. Waiting and forgetting, one protects oneself from overbearing and accuses oneself for not bearing enough. The fear of *the other's* death, the trauma of the other's despondence, the suffering at the foreignness of the other, whose trace is always within my heart—these are the symptoms of bearing the lateral extremity of human life.

---

81. Levinas, "The Poet's Vision," 132.

82. "I think that *the Human* consists precisely in opening oneself to the death of the other, in being preoccupied with his or her death" (Emmanuel Levinas, *Alterity and Transcendence*, trans. Michael B. Smith (New York: Columbia University Press, 1999], 157–58).

83. Simon Critchley, *Very Little, Almost Nothing: Death, Philosophy and Literature* (London: Routledge, 2004), xv. Given the limited scope of this book (in the relation between one and the other before the entrance of the third and the social), I will leave the question of why one grieves for some and not others to other scholars' investigation. For instance, see Judith Butler, *Frames of War: When Is Life Grievable?* (London: Verso, 2009).

84. Emmanuel Levinas, "Notes on Meaning," *Of God Who Comes to Mind*, trans. Bettina Bergo (Stanford, CA: Stanford University Press, 1998), 167.

The otherness of the other is not solely experienced in the beloved who can be grasped for awhile (Song 3:4; 8:6) and yet decisively remains on the outside of one's world of sameness (Song 5:6). In every stranger that crosses my path is shown the otherness of the face that "puts me in question" and imposes responsibility upon me.

> Is it certain that man might not have a meaning precisely beyond that which man can *be*, beyond that which he can *show himself*? Does this meaning not reside precisely in his face as the first-come and in his foreignness (or, might we say, his alienness) as an other [*autrui*]? Does this meaning not reside in his face to the degree that it is precisely to this foreignness that his call to me, or his imposition on my responsibility, is attached? Is not this imposition on me—this devolving-upon-me of the stranger—the way by which there "arrives on the scene" or comes to mind a god who loves the stranger who puts me in question by his demand and to which my "here I am" bears witness?[85]

Yes. So much so that on his deathbed Markel tenderly utters: "Everyone of us has sinned against all men, and I more than any."[86] The "I" is summoned into its unicity through the responsibility for an other—any other who comes "as the first-come"—before the degrees of strangeness are discerned consciously. Every human that appears to me in his or her foreignness reveals the trace of God through the face that embodies the divine command. Through my assuming responsibility for the other, God invisible but tangible has arrived on the scene, as in one's poetic resuscitation of Song 8:6a–d.

To briefly reprise what has been expounded, love for the other and death of oneself show the lateral and linear ends, respectively, of a human being (that is, one's being of being in the human world). Both exceed the work of consciousness, and neither is susceptible to reason.[87] Since the tool of intelligence and knowledge cannot be applied as adequate means to what is beyond their scope, the pair of love and death is best made into antithesis through one's living of life, either as for-the-other or as toward-my-death. This antithesis can be expressed in the contrasted concepts of Heidegger's Dasein and Levinas's subjectivity. To begin with, one should note that Heidegger and Levinas overlap in the anteriority of subjectivity/Dasein, as well as in the radical difference between one and the other, but their overall trajectories are utterly different.

In Heidegger's phenomenological-ontological reduction, worldly relations and their derived dramas are but insubstantial dreams (the state

---

85. Ibid.
86. Fyodor Dostoyevsky, *The Brothers Karamazov*, trans. Constance Garnett (London: Dent; New York: Dutton, 1927), 742.
87. "For love is not a knowledge, is not susceptible to reason more than death is" (Ira F. Stone, *Reading Levinas/Reading Talmud: An Introduction* [Philadelphia: Jewish Publication Society, 1998], 12).

of *Verfalien*) to be awakened by the authentic state of being—the anxiety about one's own death. The meaning of being is revealed in Dasein's courageous mastering of the anxiety over its own death. "For Dasein, the end is not the final point of a being but a way of assuming or taking on the end in one's very being."[88] Others relate to me only through work, through the *zu-handkeit* of things. That is, the other human beings are the ones who stretch out their hands for the same piece of bread, to the last bottle of water, to the coveted land and its resources. One's relation to the other is ultimately defined by the "struggle for existence," which is motivated by the inalienable fear of one's extinguishment. In this light, Heidegger's Dasein and Darwinian *Kampf ums Dasein*, which spills into the social realm as social Darwinism, can be seen as kindred spirits.[89]

Targeting the Heideggerian death complex, Levinas adopts the formula "Love, strong as death" to compare two understandings of human subjectivity. Instead of taking power or force as the point of comparison, as an objective observer of Song 8:6 would do, love is compared to death through one's bearing at the approach of the inescapable. Levinas then advances to where Heideggerian death marks finitude for human beings and argues for the excess of love over death in a phenomenological-ethical account.[90] In Richard A. Cohen's reflection, Levinas's account is superior by virtue of a deeper origin than ideological categories and ontological self-understanding:

> It [Levinas's phenomenological-ethical account of death] begins more deeply, in subjectivity conceived in the self-sensing of sensibility, thus in suffering, rather than in a subject first defined by the worldly (instrumentality) and social ("the they") distractions that are overturned in anxiety and the resolute self-understanding of one's ownmost nonrelational being-toward-death.[91]

Heidegger claims that Dasein lives to its full potential when it confronts its death as the "possibility of the absolute impossibility of Dasein."[92] If this merely speaks of being completely absorbed in its being, to Levinas, the red flag flies in the following sentence: "When it stands before itself in this way, all its relations to any other Dasein have been undone."[93] For Heidegger, being as a non-relational entity is in essence not answerable to goodness.

---

88. Emmanuel Levinas, "The Death and Totality of Dasein," *God, Death, and Time*, trans. Bettina Bergo (Stanford, CA: Stanford University Press, 2000), 40.

89. Robert Bernasconi, "Levinas and the Struggle for Existence," in *Addressing Levinas*, ed. Eric Sean Nelson, Antje Kapust, and Kent Still (Evanston, IL: Northwestern University Press, 2005), 171.

90. For a concise survey, see Cohen, "Thinking Least about Death," 59–79.

91. Cohen, "Thinking Least about Death," 78.

92. Martin Heidegger, *Being and Time*, trans. John Macquarrie and Edward Robinson (Oxford: Blackwell, 1978), 592.

93. Ibid.; Emmanuel Levinas, "Dying for . . . ," *Entre nous: Thinking-of-the-Other*, trans. Michael B. Smith (London: Continuum, 2006), 214.

Levinas takes Heidegger's above assertion as a reverberation of Cain's answer after the first murder of humankind: "Am I my brother's keeper?" (Gen 4:9). He further writes on this assumed independence from and irresponsibility for the other: "Cain's answer is sincere. Ethics is the only thing lacking in his answer; there is only ontology: I am I, and he is he. We are separate ontological beings."[94] Levinas pushes the critique further in his 1990 introduction to "Reflections on the Philosophy of Hitlerism": "[T]he essential possibility of *elemental Evil* . . . is inscribed within the ontology of being concerned with being."[95] The totalitarian bubble in which being is demarcated from the center of its anxiety over its own death leaves no ground for a genuine human relation, or for that matter, a human-divine relation, for the humanness of human that bears the divine image is stripped away.

However, Cain succumbed to the temptation of murder, not merely in the modality of being's survival instincts applied against other beings while competing for limited resources (e.g., God's favor). Behind the thematizable clash of wills and interests, the face of the other provokes in one the realization of being's lateral end. What agitates the "I" to the point of killing is not only an element in the drama but also the otherness of the other, the face that cannot be mine, the transcendent incarnated in the neighbor. "One can only want to kill that which cannot be killed,"[96] for it is out of *my* control. To make murder more tempting, the agitation is accompanied by the reckoning of the other's vulnerability. Seeing the fraility of the face of the other, one realizes that there is "always the death of the other and thus, in some way, an incitement to murder, the temptation to go to the extreme, to completely neglect the other."[97] Resolutely transcendent and utterly vulnerable, "[t]he face is exposed, menaced, as if inviting us to an act of violence."[98] Now, murder is the token, the extreme example, of a category of violent acts expressing one's uncurbed desire to de-face the other. They may be seen in a voyeuristic glance at an other, a tendency to take advantage of the simple, an indifference to immigrants in crisis, and many, many more instances.

Precisely with this carnal ambiguity on the face of the other enters a divine epiphany that commands: "Thou shalt not kill." It grips one at the moment of one's full carnality and desire and thus takes hostage the subject's will, strength, and mind, which come afterward. Antecedent to the subject's consciousness, therefore, is the coming-into-being of human

---

94. Idem, "Philosophy, Justice, and Love," in ibid., 110.
95. Idem, "Reflections on the Philosophy of Hitlerism," *Critical Inquiry* 17 [1990]: 63; see also Bernasconi, "Levinas and the Struggle for Existence," 174.
96. François Raffoul, *The Origins of Responsibility* (Bloomington: Indiana University Press, 2010), 188.
97. Levinas, "Philosophy, Justice, and Love," 104; idem, "The Proximity of the Other," *Alterity and Transcendence*, 105.
98. Idem, "Philosophy, Justice, and Love," 108.

subjectivity inscribed with the very impossibility of saying no, to cease responsibility for the other. In its provocative fullness, the vulnerability of the other incites murder (or its like) and calls for its suspension: "the temptation and impossibility of murder."[99] This vulnerable urgency—rising toward but impossible to infuse, inescapable and without denouement—which is characteristic of one's encounter with the other, is finely textured in the subject's imperative to her beloved along with her submission of herself in Song 8:6ab. In the ethical excess of "you" over "mine" or "it," the subject encounters the lateral end of her being, which is not a line between two independent beings, but the responsibility for the other that is inscribed in her subjectivity as passivity.

Now if I may paraphrase the aforementioned philosophical proposition by impersonating and modernizing the first-person voice of Song 8:6 in an extremely simplified binary alternative, the sobering up through the intoxication of love may be said as follows: I desire you, to the point that only consuming you entirely could satisfy the incessant flame within me. But that I cannot do, for when the consumption was finished, I would return to my place under the sun where nothing was new, where the flame of life ignited by love was smoldered or extinguished, as I cooled down, congealed back into a set of identities in the social web for my own survival. That cold confinement, life-as-being-toward-death, tastes worse than death itself, after the flame of love has attached me to you. Therefore, I cannot reduce you to a thing so as to possess you and suck out nutrients or pleasure; in the love made possible through you, I desire first and foremost my proximity to you (and would not all other delights follow?). Just be with me, only me, always. Indeed, "Set me as a seal on your heart, yea, as a seal on your arm!"

No matter how perfectly I handle my being, it responds neither to the first and most original evil of humankind nor to the word from the Most High. A significance that grows out of the concern for—and recoils back into—oneself is of the modality of interestedness rather than goodness. Even if one remains in an authentic state of being, it is always short of true humanness. "The perfect is not perfect because it suffices for itself."[100] Hence, instead of the Heideggerian non-relational death, Levinas looks for the significance of death in the death of the other experienced in oneself[101] and ultimately locates it in my dying for the other. That is, the human is

---

99. Idem, "Is Ontology Fundamental?" *Entre Nous*, 11.

100. Gabriel Marcel, *Metaphorical Journal*, trans. Bernard Wall (Chicago: Regnery, 1952), 210–11; quoted from Levinas, "A New Rationality: On Gabriel Marcel," *Entre Nous*, 62.

101. Simon Critchley paraphrases how Levinas inverts the Heideggerian account of death in the following: "He [Levinas] says: Heidegger is exactly wrong; actually, my relationship to death does not come into the world through my relationship to my death, but through my relationship to the other's death. It is through the other's death—my

not the one who masters the fear of one's own death but the one who fears the death of the other.[102]

> Thinking least about Heideggerian ownmost death, Levinas nevertheless thinks most about the death of the other person. Indeed, it is precisely when and only when thinking least about one's own death and most about the other's death, precisely when care for the other's death takes precedence over care for one's own—all the way to the extreme point of "dying for" the other—that the human subject achieves its true humanity, and hence the proper height of a morally and socially responsible selfhood.[103]

Obsessed with that which is beyond essence, the human subject encounters the other in an erotic, enigmatic, and traumatic knot without denouement. In humanness *qua* subjectivity, "where the substantiality of 'supporting oneself' is desubstantified in a 'supporting the other,'"[104] oneself-as-for-the-other replaces one's courageous control of the anxiety over one's own death as the originary site of the human. Being taken as a hostage of love—not against but before one's will—the subject of Song 8:6 exemplarily manifests the primordial knot between one and the other. Bearing love strong as death, she gives herself as a seal over his heart, as a keeper of her beloved, not for self-interest but out of the proximity that defines her humanness.

Levinas's rewriting of the significance of death is matched in brilliance by his observation of love. Just as he prompts the readers to rethink the significance of death, he also remaps love ethically. Instead of "a relationship of dependence between independent beings"[105] or an intense discharge of physical desire,[106] Levinas speaks of love as more excessive and transgressive, that which gives rise to (*donner lieu*) the human subject against the pull of the gravity of my-living-toward-death.

Given its unrelenting materiality, erotic love grounds one in the here-and-now of carnal existence; and through its being brought to the edge for

---

bereavement, grief, mourning—that finitude gets a grip" (*How to Stop Living and Start Worrying*, 39–40).

102. Levinas, "From the One to the Other," *Entre Nous*, 146.
103. Cohen, "Think Least about Death," 62–63.
104. Levinas, *Otherwise than Being*, 153.
105. Critchley, *How to Stop Living and Start Worrying*, 63.
106. The lines from *Gilgamesh* 10.7.11–12 are quoted to explain the pairing of love and death in Song 8:6 (W. G. E. Watson, "Love and Death Once More (Song of Songs VIII 6)," *VT* 47 (1997): 386; Longman, *Song of Songs*, 238), as the experience of erotic summit overpowers the intense grip of death:

The fine young man, the beautiful girl,
when making love, together they confront death.

However, desire is not love, for desire is an extending of itself to its end, but love does not extend to an end in oneself (cf. Nancy, "Shattered Love," 98).

the beloved other, it reveals, without stripping away its flesh and blood, the non-erotic love that precedes all genuine human relationships. In this spirit, Levinas writes: "The real dynamism of love leads it beyond the present instant and even beyond the person loved. This end does not appear to a vision outside the love, which would then integrate it into the place of creation; it lies in the love itself."[107] The non-erotic inspires and enfolds in the erotic, while love here-and-now is also love infinite through its sincerity of oneself-as-for-the-other. The turn from the erotic to the non-erotic lies in the inherent movement of love, which does not abandon itself for a promised future or retract into its being. Instead, it goes through an upstream and sobering movement, passing the suppression of desire, passing even the rise of desire, toward the pre-originary goodness that obliges one to the other, or the hospitality that is the center of Levinas's ethical thought according to Derrida's *Adieu à Emmanuel Lévinas*, or the charity of which Levinas himself sometimes speaks:[108]

> Perhaps the spiritual bond resides in the non-in-difference of persons toward one another, which is also called love, but which does not dissipate the difference of strangeness and is possible only on the basis of a word [*parole*] or an order coming, via the human face, from most high outside the world.[109]

The difference between one and the other, which is more radical than the non-relational essence of being, is bridged through an ethical non-in-difference toward the other, which is found upon an order from God, the original otherwise than being, through the words "Thou shall not kill."

Returning to the comparison of love as death in Song 8:6, I suggest that one follows the said intensity (ʿazzâ and qāšâ), not to the realm of power[110] but to the voice that trembles at bearing this intensity. Love is not to be examined through an indifferent spectator's lenses as a mystical power or a biochemical reaction that subdues the subject's free will, causes her to fall, to lose her mind, or to annihilate herself, "for better or for worse." And one may or may not encounter it in one's lifetime. Rather, is it not first an awakening woken *by and for the other* under the fruit-bearing tree? Short of this, would not love be just sexual drive expressive of ultramateriality, and the beloved would be an inconveniently replaceable object, as lamented in "My Darling Clementine"?

How I missed her!
How I missed her,

---

107. Levinas, "Judaism and the Feminine," *Difficult Freedom: Essays on Judaism* (Baltimore: Johns Hopkins University Press, 1990), 36.
108. Idem, "Philosophy, Justice, Love," 108.
109. Idem, "Two Texts on *Merleau-Ponty* by Emmanuel Levinas: Sensibility," in *Ontology and Alterity in Merleau-Ponty*, trans. Michael B. Smith, ed. Galen A. Johnson and Michael B. Smith (Evanston, IL: Northwestern University Press, 1991), 60.
110. Exum reads Song 8:5c–7 as "a paean to the power of love" (*Song of Songs*, 249).

> How I missed my Clementine,
> But I kissed her little sister,
> I forgot my Clementine.[111]

If Song 8:6 is read as an expression of love's power, and the beloved other is but an accidental vassal that occasions one's praise of this force, it will remain inconsequential to the remnant that lament how blood was poured like water around Jerusalem (Ps 79:3), to the survivors of the Holocaust who have but a difficult love for God, or to the remembrance of the children who never came home after the Newtown shooting. Rather, love is non-in-difference, the proximity to the other, and the very significance of finite human life.

The reality of human life is that one cannot help but be in lovesickness for an other. In spite of its initiatives, the "I" is always already a bearing, a pure undergoing; its initiatives are therefore always the provoked initiatives. In other words, for humankind, free will is a narrative illusion: either slavery to Pharaoh or servitude to God, bound to sin or joined to God, caged inside the drive for biological preservation toward one's solitary death or having given oneself already for the other. In reality, there is only one human freedom; of course, it is not a more efficient effort at self-preservation and complacency. A difficult freedom is given in the very humanness of the human, proximity before solitude, responsibility before will, as the meaning of life is fulfilled in carrying out the demand of the face of the other.

It is worthwhile reiterating that this moral imperative is born out of and demands the response of love, which precedes desire and will. Intentional abjuration of eros does not yield agape but negativity, as Blake protests in "The Garden of Love": [112]

> I went to the Garden of Love,
> And saw what I never had seen:
> A Chapel was built in the midst,
> Where I used to play on the green.
> And the gates of this Chapel were shut,
> And 'Thou shalt not' writ over the door;
> So I turn'd to the Garden of Love,
> That so many sweet flowers bore.
> And I saw it was filled with graves,
> And tomb–stones where flowers should be:
> And Priests in black gowns, were walking their rounds,
> And binding with briars, my joys & desires.

---

111. Percy Montrose, "Clementine," in *500 Best-Loved Song Lyrics*, ed. Ronald Herder (Mineola: Courier Dover, 1998), 66.
112. William Blake, *Songs of Innocence and of Experience*, ed. Andrew Lincoln (Princeton, NJ: Princeton University Press, 1994), 191.

Asceticism and altruistic benevolence may be admired as ideal expressions of agape, the work of which can be carried out according to the law or the commandments. But even Kant could not agree that this is love's manifestation, for "what is done from constraint is not done from love."[113] He further explains, "Love is a matter of feeling, not of will or volition, and I cannot love because I ought (I cannot be necessitated to love); hence there is no such thing as a duty to love."[114] Only when one is denuded to the anterior sincerity and passivity as through bearing the flame of eros, then can the totalitarian grip, the kinesthetic being-toward-death, be shaken off. Then eros is recognized as the maternal body of agape. "Indeed, the Bible knows that true *erōs* is *agapē*,"[115] Samuel Terrien thus boldly claims.

It should also be noted that being, ontology, and knowledge come in after ethics and responsibility and when justice is at issue. Recently, one finds critics phrasing their response to Levinas's philosophy in terms of a perceived absolute alternative between "being and the other."[116] This very notion shows that the critics in question have not left the realm of consciousness and ontology and have already reduced the other, "otherwise than being," into an entity, a being, a noema. It continues the a-ethical tradition of philosophy as the love of wisdom, instead of responding to ethics as the first philosophy, as the wisdom of love. The accompanying cynical annoyance at Levinas's critique of Heidegger, the suspicion that Levinas has compromised his philosophical objectivity because of personal experience, exposes a certain indifference to Levinas's criticism of philosophy due to one's preconditioned love of wisdom and knowledge that strives for an unalterable perfection. In Levinas's defense, he has always readily admitted the brilliance of Heidegger's philosophy and its impact on his think-

---

113. Immanuel Kant, "On Love of Men," *Metaphysical Elements of Ethics*, trans. Thomas K. Abbott (London: Forgotten Books, 2008), 37.

114. Ibid.

115. Samuel Terrien, *Till the Heart Sings: A Biblical Theology of Manhood and Womanhood* (Grand Rapids, MI: Eerdmans; Dearborn, IL: Dove, 2004), 29.

116. Françoise Dastur, "The Call of Conscience: The Most Intimate Alterity," in *Heidegger and Practical Philosophy*, ed. Françoise Raffoul and David Pettigrew (Albany, NY: SUNY Press, 2002); Raffoul, *The Origins of Responsibility*, 205; Jeffrey L. Kosky, "Love Strong as Death: Levinas and Heidegger," in *The Exorbitant: Emmanuel Levinas between Jews and Christians*, ed. Kevin Hart and Michael Alan Signer (New York: Fordham University Press, 2010), 120–22. On a nonacademic level, I find it unsettling to read of a third party's "correct" analysis of how Levinas's writing bears the marks and traces of Heideggerian philosophy in order to disabuse Levinas's criticism of Heidegger. It is not a matter of right or wrong but of whether one would do that to Levinas's face? Job's three friends speak convincingly on the theological interpretation of suffering, too. A triumph of the love of truth over that of goodness. I am not saying that one cannot possibly speak about the similarity between the philosophies of Heidegger and Levinas but that the saying of proximity and charity is wanting, and the said so presented has already lost the very spirit of Levinas's writings and thus injustice follows. There is something more important than getting it right. If one does not know it, one never "gets" Levinas.

ing, in spite of his unapologetic rejection of Heidegger's association with the Nazis. Moreover, in terms of phenomenological progression, Levinas's challenge of Heidegger's propositions conforms to the "self-correcting" principle of phenomenology: "[A]ll of its results are subject to and demand confirmation or disconfirmation. Superficial or incorrect analyses are replaced with deeper or more correct ones."[117] It is not that one competes with another for the only throne called Truth but that one observation, informed by the other, reveals what the other does not see. Finally, it would be so much easier to appreciate an ethics nestled in Heideggerian ontology if the philosopher had not so relentlessly persisted in his attachment to the Third Reich, which murdered millions of "others."

To conclude, as Jeffrey L. Kosky points out, there is a certain similarity between Levinas and Heidegger in terms of how the subject is already obliged to the previous, being unable to constitute itself and appearing after that which gives birth to it.[118] Yet, however similar, a system that is built upon being, which is in essence a tensing upon oneself, a necessary survival instinct, does not reach the site where ethical encounter happens. It is in the subject's denuded bearing of love strong as death, which is manifested in her vulnerable and urgent request in Song 8:6, that one witnesses and participates in an ethical encounter with the trace of God.

"The Question Mark in This Said"[119]

In the first section of this chapter, I mentioned in passing a possible reference to the divine name in *šalhebetyāh*. Quite a few interesting questions are persuant to this possibility: Do the fiery flames of passion break off from the sublunary to the Most High, or do they merely overflow the semantic substance to the rhetorical edge of the superlative? Does the reader stop at romanticizing the vehemence of love (via ardant passion) as a natural force[120] or go on to reckon that the flames "emanate from the Eternal"[121] and that their power comes from participating "in divine qualities"?[122] Or, is it really an ode to power, whether the power of romantic love or of God's agape? The response to these inquiries naturally depends on how one reads the *-yāh* at the end of *šalhebetyāh*. When uncertainty appears, the rational inclination is to analyze possible interpretations toward finding the one "right" reading. However, this monological tendency all too quickly bypasses the possibility opened up by poetic ambiguity. Instead of strictly

---

117. Cohen, "Thinking Least about Death," 62.
118. Kosky, "Love Strong as Death," 116.
119. Levinas, *Otherwise than Being*, 154.
120. Exum, *Song of Songs*, 249; Murphy, *Song of Songs*, 197; Marvin H. Pope, *The Song of Songs: A New Translation with Introduction and Commentary*, AB 7C (Garden City, NY: Doubleday, 1977), 667.
121. Ginsburg, *Song of Songs*, 188.
122. Krinetzki, *Das Hohe Lied*, 244.

arguing for one reading of the phrase, this section will highlight the moment before the rise of the desire for clarity, draw attention to the significance of poetic ambiguity, and underscore the fecund moment when one faces the possibility of alternatives.

Before diving into an examination of *šalhebetyāh*, I will briefly recapitulate the lyrical unit where this key word is situated (Song 8:6–7). Antecedent to 8:6f are two couplets of synonymous parallelism that readily transit through the syntactical tie of the main (6ab) and causal clauses (6cd). Taken together, the unit 8:6 offers a personal and positive testimony to one's bearing of the unbearable love, illustrated with an image of the most exuberant fire consuming the shadow of death from the bottom up (8:6f). After *šalhebetyāh* (6f), the lyric switches to a sequence of double-negative reaffirmations of this love: the love borne by the subject withstands the mighty waters gushing down from the top (8:7a–c), as well as the buying power of wealth, which is otherwise valued (8:7d–f). From this brief sketch, one can see that *šalhebetyāh* marks the turning point of this lyric unit, and it functions admirably well in this role.

For starters, given the semantic opacity of *šalhebetyāh*, the audience comes to a halt at the end of 8:6. The smooth transition in the previous two couplets has accelerated to a flashing momentum in Song 8:6e, thanks to the repeated *rešep* and the threading consonant *š*. However, with the rare *ša*-prefixed noun *šalhebet* (*lhb*)[123] and the mysterious suffix -*yāh*, *šalhebetyāh* dramatically slows down one's mental digestion. Indeed, the energy aroused for deciphering is a testimony to its vital importance.

Easily being the most complicated word in the Song, *šalhebetyāh* knots together strands of poetic, textual, inscriptional, idiomatic, and religious issues and triggers a thicket of speculations. I will begin with the issue of lineation. Traditionally, *šalhebetyāh* is written as a separate line in BHS as well as in many scholarly works.[124] However, this lineation is challenged on two grounds. First, theoretically a line in biblical Hebrew poetry has two to six stresses, with each stress typically corresponding to a word in Hebrew.[125]

---

123. Ezek 21:3, Job 15:30, Sir 51:4, 1QH 8:30 (*šlbth* scribal error for *šlhbt*), 1QM 6:3 (*šlhwbt*). For the latter two, see Karl Georg Kuhn, *Konkordanz zu den Qumrantexten* (Göttingen: Vanderhoeck & Ruprecht, 1960), 220. Alternatively, *šalhebet* is considered an Aramaism (Max Wagner, *Die lexikalischen und grammatikalischen Aramäismen im alttestamentlichen Hebräisch*, BZAW 96 [Berlin: Alfred Töpelmann, 1966], 305; Hans Bauer and Pontus Leander, *Historische Grammatik der hebräischen Sprache* [Hildesheim: Olms, 1962], 486k; Rudolf Meyer, *Hebräische Grammatik* [Berlin: de Gruyter, 1966–72], §40:6).

124. Exum, *Song of Songs*, 243; Hess, *Song of Songs*, 237; Longman, *Song of Songs*, 60; Murphy, *Song of Songs*, 191; Müller, *Das Hohelied*, 84; Krinetzki, *Das Hohe Lied*, 240; Robert and Tournay, *Le Cantique des Cantiques*, 301. Fox, *Song of Songs*, 167.

125. Stephen A. Geller summarizes that biblical Hebrew poetic lines usually have two to six stresses, which correspond to each "metric unit" (commonly taken as "a 'word' in the Masoretic graphemic system"), though long terms of five or more syllables may receive two stresses ("Hebrew Prosody and Poetics [I Biblical]," in *The New Princeton Encyclopedia of Poetry and Poetics*, ed. Alex Preminger and T. V. F. Brogan [Princeton, NJ: Princeton Univer-

Second, in practice a single-word line is nowhere attested in biblical poetry. It is therefore understandable that scholars have proposed other ways of lineation and/or emendation.

At the risk of spoiling the suspense, I quickly add that *šalhebetyāh* has two stresses according to the Masoretic notation, thus reading it as a separate line technically falls within the above-mentioned range. Moreover, if the textual decision concerning *-yh* is made in favor of "Yah" and against "its," one can find support for this lineation in the formulaic expression of *halĕlûyāh* in Psalms. In those instances, *halĕlûyāh* features the same use of *-yh* as a suffixed noun[126] and is typically performed/read separately from other lines. In brief, a single-word line may be rare, but it is not impossible, especially if it is a complex hapax legomenon that marks the end of a lyrical unit.

Yet, even if reading *šalhebetyāh* as one line is theoretically possible, is it necessary? I will address this issue through an analysis of the syntax. It is clear that *rĕšāpeyhā rišpê ʾēš* and *šalhebetyāh* (8:6ef) constitute an explanatory addendum that manifests the fierceness of *qinʾâ* (and through synonymous parallelism, *ʾahăbâ*). Yet their internal relation is not certain: 8:6f can be in apposition to or an ellipsis of 8:6e. As apposition, *šalhebetyāh* gives emphatic explanation to *rišpê ʾēš*: "Its flashes are flashes of fire / —indeed a flame of Yah!" This interpretation prompts some scholars to analyze *rĕšāpeyhā rišpê ʾēš šalhebetyāh* as one line, which then pulls down the previously perceived couplet (8:6cd) to form a triplet.[127]

kî-ʿazzâ kammāwet ʾahăbâ	For strong as death is love,
qāšâ kišĕʾôl qinʾâ	fierce as Sheol is jealousy;
rĕšāpeyhā rišpê ʾēš šalhebetyāh	its flashes are flashes of fire, a flame of Yah.

---

sity Press, 1993], 509–10). For additional theoretical references, see F. W. Dobbs-Allsopp, "Poetry, Hebrew," in *NIDB* 4.552; Michael Patrick O'Connor, *Hebrew Verse Structure* (Winona Lake, IN: Eisenbrauns, 1980), 87; Stephen A. Geller, *Parallelism in Early Biblical Poetry* (Missoula, MT: Scholars Press, 1979). Tod Linafelt and F. W. Dobbs-Allsopp apply the constraints to line formation in biblical Hebrew verse in their (re)construction of Qoh 3:1 ("Poetic Line Structure in Qoheleth 3:1," *VT* 60 [2010]: 253–54). In the following, I adopt a comprehensive, dynamic view of Hebrew lines in the spirit of Benjamin Hrushovski's "semantic-syntactic-accentual" system (Benjamin Hrushovski, "Prosody, Hebrew," *EncJud* 13 [1971]: 1200–1201.) Besides the three named aspects, I will also consider other lyrical threads (such as metaphors) when their impacts are felt in the reception of the lines.

126. It also takes two other forms in BHS: *halĕlû-yâh* or *halĕlû yāh*. That is, the verb and the object of praise may be linked with or without a *maqqēf*, or even written as two words. See Pss 105:45; 106:1; 106:48; 111:1; 112:1; 113:1; 115:18; 116:19; 117:2; 135:21; 146:1, 10; 147:1, 20; 148:1, 14; 149:1, 9; 150:1, 6.

127. Roberts, *Let Me See Your Form*, 327–28; Zakovitch, *Das Hohelied*, 270. Marvin H. Pope effectively reads a triplet by removing *šalhebetyâ* as a gloss to the previous flame imagery (Marvin H. Pope, *The Song of Songs: A New Translation with Introduction and Commentary* [Garden City, NY: Doubleday, 1977], 670–71); See also the lineation in BHQ.

In this proposed lineation, the last line wraps up the triplet with the confluence of line-end, semantics, and the perceived syntax. It even finds support in the lineated OG text:[128]

ὅτι κραταιὰ ὡς θάνατος ἀγάπη,
σκληρὸς ὡς ᾅδης ζῆλος·
περίπτερα αὐτῆς περίπτερα πυρός, φλόγες αὐτῆς·

It should be pointed out, however, that the OG has an important textual variation. By reading *-yh* as "its" (αὐτῆς), we round off the last word as a varied repetition of the first ("its flashes . . . its flame") in the long last line. Consequently, the semantic density of this line is significantly reduced through the repetition of both περίπτερα and αὐτῆς, and so is the tension due to fitting a long line into the end of this unit (8:6a–f). If the textual variation in the OG is not adopted, the burden of the evidence leans heavily toward the argument for a longer and more complex last line as ending a triplet.[129]

This commonsensical observation is supported by the normal formations of triplets in the Song, which I have outlined elsewhere.[130] It suffices to note that the long last line of the projected triplet in 8:6c–f appears to be overly cumbersome due to the joined force of the syllable count (9-7-11), the stress count (4/3/5), and the semantic complexity. Thus it pushes the envelope of the normal length of the line that ends a triplet in the Song to an uneasy and even artificial point. Essentially the same argument against reading 8:6f as one line—that is, its rarity—also applies to the solution of the proposed triplet (8:6c–f).

Parting ways with the first option (without eliminating the possibility of the relevant syntactical relationship), I will examine the second possibility regarding the syntactic tie of 8:6ef—that is, ellipsis. In this view, the first word of the second line is gapped, with the remainders of the first and second lines mirroring each other. These two lines thus form an incomplete

---

128. Jay Curry Treat, "Lost Keys: Text and Interpretation in Old Greek Song of Songs and Its Eearliest Manuscript Witnesses" (Ph.D. diss., University of Pennsylvania, 1996), 69.

129. This is far from saying that apocopation, or a shorter last line, is a dominant form of ending any lyrical unit, or that a longer and more complex last line is impossible. For one thing, in general, the end of a lyrical unit is marked by a dynamic combination of varied factors (semantics, syntax, stress, imagery, theme, etc.). For another, apocopation is meaningful when there is a preceding, established rhythm. Finally, a (slightly) longer and more complex last line is possible when qualified by other factors (e.g., Song 8:12c).

130. The most common formation of triplets in the Song (16 out of 29 triplets) is a "sandwich" shape, in which the first and the third lines have similar length and are in contrast to the middle line. Considering the syntactic relationship of 8:c–f, the projected triplet would fit better with a small group of triplets with a short-short-long pattern (1:3, 8:7a–c, and 8:12). However, the syllable variations among the lines in 1:3, 8:7, and 8:12 are more moderate and further balanced out by the stress counts to achieve a dynamic equilibrium, which the projected triplet lacks (Sarah Zhang, "Triplets in the Song of Songs," paper presented at the Society of Biblical Literature, 2014).

synonymous parallelism: "Its flashes are flashes of fire / [its flame] a flame of Yah!" With the assumption that parallelism is meant to be complete, some scholars treat the omission as haplography.[131] This view is especially attractive because of the established synonymous parallelism in the previous two couplets (8:6a–d), where the second lines parallel the first semantically and syntactically. Moreover, these two couplets are all made up of verbless clauses in which the subjects are adjoined to the predicates through similes led by *kî-*. Hence, given the syntactic pattern of *rĕšāpeyhā rišpê ʾēš*, would it be reasonable to emend the text to *šalhăbōt-yāh šalhăbōtêhā*,[132] *šalhăbōteyhā šalhăbōt yāh*, or *lahabōteyhā šalhăbōt yāh*?[133] A perfect parallelism may therefore be reconstructed: the masculine-plural noun (*rešep*) parallels the feminine-singular noun (*šalhebet*), while the general noun *ʾēš* is intensified through the specific reference to Yah. Neat as it appears, the proposed parallelism remains hypothetical, because the supporting textual evidences are wanting. Furthermore, if one reads with the MT tradition, the aforementioned emendations seem to create a "perfect" local parallelism at the price of the dynamic movement of the whole. In other words, could it be that such balancing reconfigurations *perform* the tripping effect of apocopation, a deliberately shortened last line?

From the vantage point of poetic closure, cutting off an established rhythm is an effective means of preparing for its ending.[134] The poetic phenomenon of apocopation at the end of an extended parallelism can be seen in biblical texts such as Ps 94:9–10 and Ruth 1:16d–17b.[135] For instance, the apocopated line in Ps 94:10b plays a Janus role by triggering the audience to catch a flashback view of the four lines as a whole (to see what is omitted) and welcome the bated naming of this Person (to see how it is compensated).

---

131. Robert and Tournay, *Le Cantique des Cantiques*, 302. Recently, Murphy and Exum also contemplate the possibility that a word may have fallen out of the original, which would be "its flames are flames of Yah" (Exum, *Song of Songs*, 254; Murphy, *Song of Songs*, 192).

132. Wilhelm Rudolph, *Das HoheLied*, KAT 17/2 (Gütersloh: Mohn, 1962), 179–80; Karl Budde, *Das Hohe Lied*, 45; Helmer Ringgren, *Das Hohe Lied*, in Helmer Ringgren and Otto Kaiser, *Das Hohe Lied: Klagelieder. Das Buch Esther* (Göttingen: Vandenhoeck & Ruprecht, 1981), 287.

133. See the survey in Robert and Tournay, *Le Cantique des Cantiques*, 302. Martti Nissinen's recent poetic analysis similarly reads it as "'*šalhăbōtêhā*' *šalhăbōt yāh*" (Nissinen, "Is God Mentioned in the Song of Songs?" 279).

134. The tendency toward apocopation at the end of a poem can be found in later poetic traditions such as medieval Arabic and Persian lyric poetry (Julie Meisami, *Structure and Meaning in Medieval Arabic and Persian Lyric Poetry: Orient Pearls* [Richmond: Curzon, 2003], n.p.). However, this chapter does not address the general issue of poetic ending. For discussions on that topic, see Barbara Herrnstein Smith, *Poetic Closure: A Study of How Poems End* (Chicago: University of Chicago Press, 1968).

135. Sarah Zhang, "Interrupting an Extended Parallelism," paper presented at the annual meeting of the Society of Biblical Literature, 2015.

⁹hănōṭaʿ ʾōzen hălōʾ yišmāʿ He who plants the ear, does he not hear?
ʾim-yōṣēr ʿayin hălōʾ yabbîṭ or he who forms the eye, does he not see?
¹⁰hăyōsēr gôyim hălōʾ yôk̲îaḥ He who disciplines the nations, does he not punish?
hamlammēd ʾādām dāʿat He who teaches knowledge to humankind—
¹¹yhwh yōdēaʿ maḥšûbôt ʾādām Yahweh knows human plans,
kî-hēmmâ hābel that they are vain.

With this interruption of the extended parallelism, the accumulated force of the rhetorical questions is channeled to the victorious declaration of God's omniscience and humanity's vanity. Similar to Ps 94:10b, Song 8:6f may have a retract-and-redirect function through apocopation. But it should be noted that the ellipsis in Song 8:6f is not a typical apocopation of the last line in that it follows the previous couplets by the use of gapping with its initial word. In other words, it is not in the sudden appearance of ellipsis but in pushing the same ellipsis toward the extreme that the gapping in Song 8:6f carries out the strategic function of apocopation at the end of the extended parallelism. In this light, Song 8:6 may be delineated as a series of incomplete synonymous parallel lines characterized by the ellipsis of *śîmēnî*, *kî*, and *šalhăbōtêhā*:

⁸ᵃ*śîmēnî kaḥôtām ʿal-libbekā*
ᵇ[*śîmēnî*] *kaḥôtām ʿal-zĕrôʿekā*
ᶜ*kî-ʿazzâ kammāwet ʾahăbâ*
ᵈ[*kî-*] *qāšâ kišěʾôl qinʾâ*
ᵉ*rěšāpeyhā rišpê ʾēš*
ᶠ[*šalhăbōtêhā*] *šalhebetyāh*

In fact, the structural sameness of the three couplets accentuates the sonic brevity of the last line. The contrast is especially stark when compared with the second lines: while the previous second lines (6b, 6d) have 7 syllables, the last one (6f) has only 4 syllables. Linafelt has helpfully described this "cutting-off" effect as follows:

> Given the equally weighted lines the [sic] precede it and the syntactical parallelism they manifest, this abbreviated final line pulls the reader up short, causing one to pause, to stumble, and thereby to dwell on the effect of that all-consuming blaze, love.[136]

To better appreciate his comment, I outline how Song 8:6 is intensified rhythmically:

Line	Stress	Syllable
6a	3	10
6b	2	8
6c	3	9
6d	3	7
6e	3	7
6f	**2**	**4**

---

136. Tod Linafelt, "Biblical Love Poetry . . . [and God]," 332.

As the lyric unit moves to the end, a vocal contraction happens in 6f. One may even fancy that the aural fluctuation in 8:6 emulates the visual image of fire, from its felt power (ab) to its all-comsuming body (cde) and down to its extraordinarily heated core (f).

Speaking of imagery, this rhythmic intensification is further enhanced by the figures to which the poem alludes. Were Mot, Sheol, and Reshep (8:6c–e) taken as allusions to mythological figures,[137] it would suit the Israelite ideology to have Yhwh superseding them and sitting at the pinnacle of the series of similes. At this point, when it cannot go any higher, the lyric shifts gears—thanks to the extra breathing room in 6f due to apocopation—to the gushing down of mighty waters in 8:7, which takes a semiprosaic rhythm that mimics the rapid movement of water. The juxtaposition of fire and water surrounding the divine presence in question further evokes the classic epiphany of Yhwh through fire (Exod 3:2, 13:21, 14:24, 19:18, 24:17, 40:38) and the tradition of Yhwh's victory over mighty waters (Exod 14:21; Josh 2:10, 3:13, 4:23, 5:1; 1 Kgs 18:38; 2 Kgs 2:14; Isa 44:24; Jer 51:55; Ezek 31:15; Ps 18:16, 93:4). With these subtle intertextual allusions, the audience is further persuaded of the superlative intensity of love.

To be brief, due to the different configurations of words—vowel length, syllable counts, the number of stresses, semantic complexities, context, metaphorical references, and allusions—words are not created equal. Though *šalhebetyāh* constitutes a rare single-word line, the rhythm, semantics, syntax, imagery, and line end of Song 8:6 work in concert to embody the idea of bearing love as bearing an inextinguishable fire. That being said, I will leave the lineation of *rĕšāpeyhā rišpê ʾēš šalhebetyāh* for the reader to decide, because my interpretive route makes turns to which not all agree. Meahwhile, I will heuristically follow the conventional lineation in the following pages.

The second question of *šalhebetyāh* concerns its meaning, which depends largely on the textual, idiomatic, and theological interpretations of -*yāh*. First, in the Hebrew Bible the shortened form of Yhwh (*yh*) is written together with, separately from, or connected by a *maqqēp* to the preceding word and always takes a *mappîq* in *h*. In the Ben Asher tradition, *yh* in *šalhebetyāh* is part of the word, and *h* is unmarked, so it may have been read as "*its flames*." In contrast, in the Ben Naphtali tradition the *h* in *šalhebetyāh* takes a *mappîq*, suggesting that it is read as the abbreviated divine name.[138] Indeed, the lack of *mappîq* in *h* in the Ben Asher tradition dissuades some commentators from reading *yh* as Yah. Gillis Gerleman, for instance, argues that *šalhebetyāh* is but an intensive form of *šalhebet*.[139]

---

137. See Nissinen's summary of possible allusions to West Semitic deities and mythological powers in Song 8:6–7a (Nissinen, "Is God Mentioned in the Song of Songs?" 282–83).

138. L. Lipschütz, "Kitāb al-Khilaf: The Book of the Ḥllufim," *Textus* 4 (1964): 16.

139. Roberts, *Song of Songs*, 302; Fox, *Song of Songs*, 170. Gillis Gerleman, *Ruth; Das Hohelied*, BKAT 18 (Neukirchen-Vluyn: Neukirchener Verlag, 1965), 216–17.

The ambiguity shrouding -*yh* can be traced to ancient versions: the LXX has φλόγες αὐτῆς ("its flames"), reading the affix as a third-person-feminine suffix; the Vulg. (*atque flammarum*, "and of flames") and Syr. (*wĕšalhēbītā*, "and of flames") both omit the affixed -*yh*.[140]

Second, even if the lexical form of Yah is accepted, it does not guarantee a freeway for theological explanations. Earlier on, Rudolph, Bauer, and Leander converted *šalhebetyāh* into an idiom for lightning.[141] Now more interpreters adopt the idea that this is an unusual superlative expression.[142] In general, this group of superlative expressions joins a word with a reference of God (*'el* or *'elohîm*), to convey the idea that God is the originator or owner of the object in question, or that it measures up to God's estimation (Gen 23:6; 1 Sam 14:15; Ps 36:7, 80, 11; Isa 51:3; Jonah 3:3). Commentators favoring this interpretation yield translations such as "the very hottest fire,"[143] which has no lexical reference to Yhwh. As Garrett surmises, "The ending here has virtually lost all theological significance."[144] Given that most examples of the divine superlative employ *'el* or *'elohîm*, Zakovitch even transcribes *šalhebetyāh* as "Gottesflamme."[145]

With the assumed equation between "the flame of Yah" and "the most powerful flame," the erotic love in Song 8:6 in effect does not elevate itself to the divine dimension. Like Sheol and Mot, Yah is considered an idiomatic reference to the extremity of human love. Moreover, by the vocalic interlocking of *š*/*ś* and the syntactic retraction, the subject's passion resubmits itself with all of its intensity to her initial imperative.[146] Hence, one may conclude that the subject matter of this lyrical unit remains human love and not that of God, as Exum argues:

> If the *hapax legomenon šalhebetyāh* in 8:6 refers to the "flame of Yah"—*yah* being a shortened form of the divine name—that no more makes Israel's god the subject of the poem than "strong as death [*māwet*]" or "flames [*rešep*] of fire" makes the Canaanite gods Mot or Resheph its subjects.[147]

---

140. For a more detailed and updated survey of the related textual issues, see Nissinen, "Is God Mentioned in the Song of Songs?" 276–78.

141. Bauer and Leander, *Historische Grammatik*, 503i; Rudolph, *Das Hohe Lied*, 179–80. Fox continues this tradition (*Song of Songs*, 167).

142. *IBHS* 14.5.b; *GHB* §141n; D. Winton Thomas, "A Consideration of Some Unusual Ways of Expressing the Superlative in Hebrew," *VT* 3 (1953): 209–24; P. P. Saydon, "Some Unusual Ways of Expressing the Superlative in Hebrew and Maltese," *VT* 4 (1954): 432–33; A. B. Thomas, "The Use of נצח as a Superlative in Hebrew," *JSS* 1 (1956): 106–9; idem, "Some Further Remarks on Unusual Ways of Expressing the Superlative in Hebrew," *VT* 18 (1968): 120–24.

143. For example, see Garrett, *Song of Songs*, 255; Murphy, *Song of Songs*, 191–92; Gordis, *Song of Songs*, 96; Robert and Tournay, *Le Cantique des Cantiques*, 302.

144. Garrett, *Song of Songs*, 98, 255.

145. Zakovitch, *Das Hohelied*, 270.

146. Exum also observes that "the climactic affirmation of love in 8:6–7 is grounded in the erotic imperative" (*Song of Songs*, 5).

147. Ibid., 64.

Certainly, metaphors cannot replace the subject matter. Yet one also needs to be cautious about going to the other extreme, whereby Yah is assimilated into human experience as a measurement to gauge degrees of power. Considering the fact that the superlative use of -*yāh* is not indisputably attested,[148] I suggest caution in eliminating the lexical form "Yah" and substituting it with a safe, banal expression. For metaphors take the reader away from the present and enrich it with a depth that the pedestrian could not hope to fill.

An idiomatic interpretation denies the entrance of theological explanations, while the lexical form -*yāh* remains suggestive of Yah. Commentators have drawn different conclusions from this ambiguity, depending on whether they see the glass as half empty or half full. While Murphy reckons that there is room for "theological evaluation,"[149] Fox rejects any effort to "hang too much theological weight" on this "uncertain reference" to God.[150] Alternatively, Martti Nissinen in his recent essay observes a growing unease among scholars "toward the strict division" between a spiritual and a sexual reading.[151]

I concur that the assumed binary frame should be questioned before one offers yet another opinion. From the perspective of lyrical experience, the ambiguity in question may be described as follows: the morpheme -*yāh* unsettles the reader's reception with possible interpretations (regardless of the reader's final choice) that are shaped by their referential systems. This passing moment of ambiguity before rational decisions cannot be fully represented in one's consciousness or discarded as irrelevant sensory data, for this raw encounter with an opening sealed by human intelligence, this seeing the back of God without knowing the face—is this not the closest the mind comes to beholding a divine epiphany? In fact, in the contemporary world—which extols human intelligence and power, which exchanges information on the verifiable plane, which reserves the word "God" for rhetoric, imagination, and belief—it serves readers better if -*yāh* is not read as a direct reference to Y$_{HWH}$ but as a blinking light that signals the possibility of alternatives.

This is to say: what is said to be *not* nevertheless haunts us with the enigmatic alternative "what if . . . ?" What a pinpointed definition of *šalhebetyāh* denies and poetic ambivalence evokes is a question mark in the said that refracts the ambivalence of intention and is *capable* of an enigmatic alternative, and thus it embodies "the very pivot of revelation":

---

148. Michael A. Fishbane suggests that *maʾpēlĕyâ* ("darkness") in Jer 2:31 shows a similar intensive use of the divine complement -*yāh* (*Song of Songs: The Traditional Hebrew Text with the New JPS Translation*, JPS Torah Commentary [Philadelphia: Jewish Publication Society, 2015], 209). But others read -*yāh* in *maʾpēlĕyâ* as marking the substantival use of the feminine adjective in -*î* (*HALOT* 541; cf. Bauer and Leander, *Historische Grammatik*, 502c).
149. Murphy, *Song of Songs*, 197.
150. Fox, *Song of Songs*, 171.
151. Nissinen, "Is God Mentioned in the Song of Songs?," 275.

But is not this dilemma rather an ambivalence, and the alternative an enigma? The enigma of a God speaking in man and of man not counting on any god? It is a dilemma or an alternative if one sticks to the phenomena, to the said, where one passes, successively, without being able to stop, from the affirmation of the Infinite to its negation in me. But the question mark in this said, which, contrary to the univocal logos of the theologians, is alternating, is the very pivot of revelation, of its blinking light.[152]

This light does not clarify perceptions with an intended focus, but calls for attentiveness to the Other who is neither present nor absent in human perception; for neither *cogito* nor language can contain God: "The presence of the present that Descartes discovered in the *cogito*, without suspecting the unconscious which was eating away at it, immediately shattered between his fingers with the idea of God that presence could not contain."[153] To human perception at its best, God is always coming (as through the question mark in the said) but never arrives on the scene (as adequately defined in the said).

What marks the moment when the word "God" is heard is not whether *-yāh* stands for YHWH but the excessive alertness awakened in (un)saying the said. The said, like the rays through the shutter, can be altered and even removed of its particular semantic configuration, yet what "prints" is forever the attentiveness to the Other who summons the self. Thus Henry David Thoreau writes:

> Much is published, but little printed. The rays which stream through the shutter will be no longer remembered when the shutter is wholly removed. No method nor discipline can supersede the necessity of being forever on the alert.[154]

The primary emphasis on the definitiveness of theme, immobilizing lyrical ambiguity in accordance with yet another frame of reference—sacred marriage, allegory, psychoanalysis, queer, ideologies, etc.—may create the perfect blinds to manipulate the rays by specifying a *this* as *that* and to enjoy the admiration for its intellectual finery, then suffer impotence when the reference it uses for deciphering becomes irrelevant to the reader. This does not mean that all of the above-mentioned approaches without exception fall into this track. Rather, I caution against the practice whereby attention to methodology or identity clouds the reader's mind so much that

---

152. Levinas, *Otherwise than Being*, 153–154. Of course, in identifying theologians with "the univocal logos" Levinas does not consider theologians who do not assume or argue for "the univocal logos"; cf. Mark L. Taylor, *The Theological and the Political: on the Weight of the World* (Minneapolis: Fortress, 2011), 1–24.

153. Emmanuel Levinas, "Wholly Otherwise," *Re-Reading Levinas*, trans. Simon Critchley (Bloomington: Indiana University Press, 1991), 7.

154. Henry David Thoreau, *Walden, Or Life in the Woods* (New York: Forgotten Books, 1927), 77.

one forgets the foundation of theories—the responsibility of the human subject to alterity. Poetic ambiguity calls for personal substitution before, and sometimes even instead of, decipherment. If one's writing becomes a manipulation of the rays for no more reason than to reassert the interests of an individual or a social group, it *may* never arrive at where Song 8:6 happens, and where God happens.

Of course, the reader's intentions or frames of reference are not in any way in competition with the ambiguity and responsibility that poetry insists on. Instead, the awakening of the subject as-for-the-other inaugurates the saying that authenticates one's utterances—be it poetic, ideological, or social. The lyrical is also deeply ethical in terms of the requisite patience and attention that uncertainty calls for in a human subject. Rowan Williams makes a similar observation in his book *Where God Happens*:[155]

> Unless we are capable of patience before each other, before the mysteriousness of each other, it's very unlikely that we will do God's will with any kind of fullness. Without a basic education in attention, no deeply ethical behavior is really going to be possible.

Lyrical ambivalence is not merely a polyvalence of sense or "a purely esthetic event";[156] it is that which generates meaning while rupturing closure. The dislocation of the assumed synchrony between words and worlds that is articulated in the difference between the said and the saying does not belong to the work of deconstruction, for deconstruction remains symbiotic with truth, though coming as a dismantling of it. In its place, the blinking light in poetry calls for the "here I am" that is antecedent to "I think" and enacts the diachrony of responsibility *qua* sensibility. Through the poet's breath altered by intrigue and altering the breath of the reader in the lyrical contact, poetry refracts and responds to alterity's summon without assimilating it, breaking the closure of language as a power game or a condemned immanence.

In other words, the site of poetic ambivalence is pre-originary, for it is beyond conscious re-presentation, but accessible by contact, such as the audience's breath when it is altered by the poetic rhythm, such as a trace that "refers to an absence that cannot be presented."[157] Unable to appear in the said that always goes through the representation of consciousness, the site of poetic significance shows itself as the saying embodied in the said, as the taste of the wine to be drunk. One imagines that the extra white space enshrining *šalhebetyāh* in Song 8:6f may be an entrance to this site, as it

---

155. Rowan Williams, *Where God Happens: Discovering Christ in One Another* (Boston: New Seeds, 2005), 84.
156. Levinas, "The Servant and Her Master," *Proper Names*, 185 n. 4.
157. Philippe Crignon, "Figuration: Emmanuel Levinas and the Image," in *Encounters with Levinas*, ed. Thomas Trezise, trans. Nicole Simek and Zahi Zalloua, Yale French Studies 104 (New Haven, CT: Yale University Press), 120.

invites one to pause and savor, to take the whole of "here I am" that has been bared of its passivity in the former lines (especially 8:6a) and make contact with the enigmatic alternative in the purposelessly purposive way that poetic language is famous for.

The amphibology of poetic language—proffering the said and relying keenly on the saying—most felicitously demonstrates that humans and God are not of essence but of responsibility, their relationship is not of theme but of contact. With God breathing life through in-spiration into the entities of molecules that all creatures share, humans recurrently become human because they receive and respond to this breath. (Humans short of humanness are not hard to find; in reality, don't we all need an alarm clock from time to time to jolt us back to alertness?) The inertia of things, of gravity's pull on beings to self-preserve until death, is overcome; love is expressed in an active carrying-out of knowledge and justice in accordance with the modality of oneself-as-for-the-other. In so doing, meaningfulness that overflows sense is enacted, and one is awakened to the full measure of the human, as earthenware is inflamed by divine fire.[158] Truly, as Yah overtakes all figures of death, love is performed as stronger than death.

I will conclude the queries regarding 8:6f by saying that poetry should not be examined on a one-dimensional platform consisting of true-or-false grids. Its ambiguity partakes of poetry's summon to a human subject by its unicity: "Poetry is not ordinary speech, it partakes of inspiration, vision, oracles, carrying us from humdrum *here* to a mythic *there*."[159] To write about the poetic encounter with authenticity, I aspire to an ethical, prosaic account that is both a blossoming of poetic elements in the air of subjectivity along the successive unfolding of poetic lines, and a countercurrent perseverance in remembrance of an immemorial intrigue. Ardor is resuscitated in this journey as an homage to alterity, testimony to in-spiration.

The Moment the Word "God" Is Heard

If not directly inside the lexical trace of *-yh*, how could one draw any theo-logy from Song 8:6? The answer, in my view, lies in the way that human subjectivity participates in the unfolding of the lyrics. Thanks to extreme skepticism, a postmodern intellectual[160] would more readily accept the notion that the word "God" is not a signifier in human consciousness

---

158. Krinetzki, *Das Hohe Lied*, 243.
159. Felstiner, *Can Poetry Save the Earth?* 105.
160. It should be acknowledged that the idea of "a postmodern intellectual" is itself in flux. Instead of referring to a set category of people, here I only wish to draw attention to the shared rejection of the univocal logos and to a direct correlation between language and reality. For another reference on postmodern approaches to the idea of God, see Mayra Rivera, *Touch of Transcendence: A Postcolonial Theology of God* (Louisville: Westminster John Knox, 2007); Burrus and Keller (eds.), *Toward a Theology of Eros*; Gary Ward (ed.), *The Postmodern God? A Theological Reader* (Oxford: Blackwell, 1997).

representing an objective entity on the outside, that its meaningfulness is inseparable from the embodied human experience, and that this word becomes meaningful in the fertile soil of subjectivity as sensibility and responsibility, in one's proximity to the transcendent.

Instead of offering an alternative methodology in the form of a set of terminologies and a way of writing, a Levinasian approach to theology as words of God cuts through a way of thinking about God to the very question of *thinking of* God. God is not to be subsumed under the structure of human thought—however brilliant the thinker is—or to be taken as a power agent promoting human prosperity, for God essentially is not a being.

The precondition of a genuine relation with God is for the human to first realize the radical difference between the "I" and the Other; and yet this realization is not to be thematized again as knowledge, as how God is presented as a *that* to the mind. God is not an entity, not a noema that is presented through noesis in human mental activities. The absoluteness of the difference cannot be pierced with epistemic light. The *I think* always already stands inside being and consciousness, incapable of grasping and presenting its originary moment through mental synchronization, in the thinking of thoughts. The otherness of the other is a past-perfect event through the duration of diachrony, which does not identify itself with memory or recapitulation that, being conscious activities, always move from the present toward the future. Therefore, constantly poised to move downstream in the temporal current, the thinking, belatedly awakened, does not encounter the already-passed Other. To think about God is always to re-present God, to reduce my experience of God to a datum in consciousness, meaningful by being a reference to my being. Rilke finely captures this orphic dilemma—

Piously we produce our images of you
till they stand around you like a thousand walls.
And when our hearts would simply open,
our fervent hands hide you.[161]

Every definition of God with the verb "to be," I venture to say, is provisional in essence, and is best to be taken in the likeness of metaphor. If it assumes an ontological ground—a world stabilized by the being of beings, a dwelling of the *cogito* among objectives—crouching indifference and arrogance will be ready to strike violence to meaning. For with the assumption of the direct correspondence between word and world that reason sustains, God would be reduced to an epistemic object awaiting human intention to bestow meaning and situated in the right place to serve the

---

161. Rainer Maria Rilke, *Rilke's Book of Hours: Love Poems to God*, trans. Anita Barrows and Joanna Macy (New York: Riverhead, 2005), 49.

human world. The pursuit of truth through reason alone accompanies the magnification of *cogito*, which gives order to the concepts in writing: tree, road, sun, or God. The pitfall of defining theology as a branch of knowledge is that, when God is defined in terms of the totality of being and the permeating light of logos, humankind, through reason that is believed to be a manifestation of logos, conducts "an idolatrous fusion with the Totality of being."[162] Writing in this vein is practiced as a power game, which remains as a struggle within ontology.

Atheists and posttraumatic religious survivors who cannot return to the Same share the rejection of such fusion. The former reject the existence of the supernatural, while the latter reject the fusion that is indifferent to human suffering. Some may take the historical happenings at Auschwitz as "food for thought," but for survivors like Levinas, the repulsion at "the assemblage of data into a meaningful whole"[163] that the suffering one suffers on top of physical or emotional pain, ruins not God but the thinking of God. "The disproportion between suffering and every theodicy was shown at Auschwitz with a glaring, obvious clarity."[164] This clear disproportion is unable to be thematized while retaining its significance, for suffering (not limited to that of Auschwitz)—pure undergoing, passive bearing—stretches into and makes contact with the unthinkable, the infinite.

Undergoing the wound of extreme affliction *and* divine silence afterwards, how could the remnants and survivors chant the Song and continue an idyllic love relation with God? While impersonating the canonizer of the Song, James Kugel proscribes meek resignation to the capriciousness of fate and a blind hope in chance: "[L]ove is so, so strong, though sometimes also so bitter; you always have to take a chance."[165] Love, and love for God—these are forces too strong for humans, so one can only take whatever is one's portion, hoping for good and being resigned to the bad if it so happens. In this bleak picture, the Song, for those who cannot—or cannot always—be lucky, appears to be but an empty luxury, a passing pleasure that betrays the impersonal meaninglessness of being—"vanity of vanities."

However, what if the problem and its solution are not of power, of struggle or adaptation? To Levinas, one's genuine approach to God in (and in spite of) suffering entails a necessary rejection of the God of power.[166]

---

162. Richard Kearney, "Returning to God after God: Levinas, Derrida, Ricoeur," *Research in Phenomenology* 39 (2009): 168; Levinas, *Totality and Infinity*, 58.

163. Levinas, "Useless Suffering," *Entre Nous*, 91, 97; idem, "The Will of God and the Power of Human," *New Talmudic Readings*, 48. On posttraumatic religious survivors, see Taylor, *The Theological and the Political*, 189–220; Dianna Ortiz and Patricia Davis, *The Blindfold's Eyes: My Journey from Torture to Truth* (Maryknoll, NY: Orbis, 2002).

164. Levinas, "Useless Suffering," 97.

165. James L. Kugel, "Sea of Love," in *The Great Poems of the Bible: A Reader's Companion with New Translations* (New York: Free Press, 1999), 277.

166. Levinas, "Useless Suffering," 97–100. See also Taylor, *The Theological and the Political*, 213–14.

The refusal to weigh God in terms of Being and power does not equal a rejection of God's authenticity after failing to solve the problem of theodicy. In fact, at the time when God hid God's face, for many Jews the love of God took the detour of "loving Torah more than God."[167] It persists in proximity to the hidden God—who does not appear on our terms—through carrying out one's responsibility to one's neighbor, which God has ordered in the Torah and which continues to furnish and revive the human subject. It is in the saying of proximity instead of the language of power that the talk of God—theology—becomes meaningful.

God is indomitable not really because God is more powerful but because where God appears is beyond the categorization of power. Richard Kearney pushes it even further, saying, "God cannot advene until we have resigned our attachment to divine omnipotence."[168] Or in Jeffrey Dudiak's exposition, the concept of God as a Supreme Being appearing in the world will result in the utter oppression of humanity, to the point of annihilation.

> For were God to appear on the scene directly, were to enter into evidence, were to enter directly into experience as a theme or as an interlocutor, overwhelming being with His Presence, humanity would be reduced to a mere functionary of this presence without freedom, without dignity—caught up in the most oppressive totality, so "oppressive" in fact that, there being no taking distance from it, there could be no semblance of oppression, for there would be no semblance of a freedom to be oppressed.[169]

God would be experienced as an oppressive sovereignty, if God were to enter the world as a being—the most powerful one at that. The Psalmist gives a poetic vision of how God the divine warrior would appear on stage: heavens would be bent, thick clouds and deep darkness surrounding him, hailstones and fiery coals shooting from him, arrows of lightning bolts be scattered, even the ocean bed would be exposed (Ps 18:10–16). Indeed no one stands a chance looking directly into God's face (Exod 33:20).

To understand these descriptions of theophany better, one ought to be mindful of the difference between the ancient and the contemporary referential frameworks. In many ways like the gods of the ancient Near Eastern myths, the "God of the Old Testament," as some Christians say, is not portrayed as a transcendent being according to Greek philosophy. Rather, God is often depicted through speeches and actions that are analogous to

---

167. Levinas, "Loving the Torah More Than God," *Difficult Freedom: Essays on Judaism* (Baltimore: Johns Hopkins University Press, 1990), 142; see also Michael L. Morgan, *Discovering Levinas* (New York: Cambridge University Press, 2007), 341–42, J. Aaron Simmons, *God and the Other: Ethics and Politics after the Theological Turn* (Bloomington: Indiana University Press, 2011), 70.
168. Kearney, "Returning to God after God," 168.
169. Jeffrey Dudiak, *The Intrigue of Ethics: A Reading of the Idea of Discourse in the Thought of Emmanuel Lévinas* (New York: Fordham University Press, 2001), 339.

those of a human.[170] This cultural practice underscores, not the rejection of the idea of the transcendent as infinity, but the analogy of human contact in approaching the Other. That is, God's transcendence is not experienced as a quality of being, as the invisibility behind the visible, but through human's proximity to the other, which is subtended by responsibility. Through one's proximity to the other—be it the idiomatic neighbor or the indomitable beloved—one's responsibility to the other is exposed as one's bearing of infinity in the finitude, as the detour to God in and through the human.

To look to God directly is to fail the work, as Orpheus does in bringing Eurydice in her nocturnal obscurity to the daylight; but not to look would be infidelity to God. Levinas helps us to work through this dilemma through the detour of the face of the other. Instead of an absolute invisibility, the divine transcendence shines forth as the invisibility of the visible in the face of the beloved or the neighbor or the stranger. It is encountered in the diachronic saying, the pre-original synthesis of "the affirmation of the Infinite" and "its negation in me"[171] as my unique responsibility to the other. Only *my* adoring eyes meet your beautiful glance in a way that does not fade into meaninglessness; only *my* hands touch your face in accordance with how it has become meaningful to me. (And how many glances have you and I cast and emptied into thin air because of despondency? And how it lights up our faces when someone from the sea of faces returns a smile to our greeting glance!) It is in this unique, inescapable responsibility that *I* am introduced into the plot of the Infinite, an anarchic birth (pre-original to consciousness) of *'ănî* ("I") from the passivity of the accusative *-î* ("me"). That is, before the original moment wherein *I am* a being, the other had devolved upon *me* the responsibility to care for the other, for his/her mortality—through a naked goodness (shalom, charity or love).

What is realized in the modern proclamation that "God is dead" is, for humanity, not an absolute freedom but a "faceless neuter" that dehumanizes the human psyche.[172] For the human, the power struggle begins with the assumption that a human subject is a being who is motivated by his or her existential and essential anxiety. The principle or theme of being—the fight against and because of anxiety over death—originates from the solitary awareness of the vast chilling substratum that manifests itself in its automatic homogenization of things into objects and the extradition of that which cannot be mine or for my interest. In the great *il y a*, there are winners and losers, fighters and flighters, but *there is* no place for humanity. All seem to be stuck in the power struggle—a societal version of the animal

---

170. Cf. Meir Steinberg, *The Poetics of Biblical Narrative: Ideological Literature and the Drama of Reading* (Bloomington: Indiana University Press, 1985), 153–63.

171. Levinas, *Otherwise than Being*, 154.

172. Idem, "The Poet's Vision," 128; cf. idem, "Jean Lacroix: Philosophy and Religion," *Proper Names*, 82.

instinct for survival—without a way out. Is the human therefore merely a better equipped animal? Where does the image of God appear?

Take writing, for example. Under the law of being, writing originates from a consciousness of the anxiety of finitude, of which one's own death is the consummate realization. It carves a place for the "I" in the epoch of the Book, lest my spark of life dies out and returns to the darkness in which all beings find themselves, without a name. It is a courageous fight against the essential fear of being as but a vain breath, of life as nothing but the listless drama of "vanity of vanities," of the totality that makes "nothing new under the sun."

Against this backdrop, writing is also an expression of an ideological contention that is based on a person or a group's concern for being-among-others. Cutting off the Absolute that used to anchor human discourse does not lead to a liberation of writing, for the writing born under the law of being could not *be* until finding another center of gravity. Henceforth, the adjectives become writing's point of departure for their wearers: the white, the black, the rich, the poor, the queer, the Latino, the African, and others according to the zeitgeist. The words of Zarathustra anticipate this development: "Once spirit was God, then it became man, and now it even becometh populace."[173] Of course, the reverse of the aforementioned proposition cannot be true: neither is diversity-speak itself incapable of genuine proximity to the other, nor should the subgroups so mentioned not stand up to defend themselves. Rather, I again draw attention to the underlying spirit that is all too quickly passed over in a direct gaze at the thematic. When attentiveness to the other—and the call for justice that follows the entrance of the third—is blurred in a clash of interests, there is neither truth nor goodness. One who is anesthetized to pre-originary attentiveness is closed off in the struggle for power. The success of a postmodern round-table discussion is abandoned to luck, dependent on the whim of the participants, their willingness to tolerate others. Under the guise of increased freedom and equality, power is substituted for the divine favor that the first murderer was reaching for.

When an objective approach to God (in the form of arguments for or against the divine being) is deconstructed, and no way out is opened by the politically correct openness to diversity that remains under the paradigm of power struggle, subjectivity begotten by the proximity to the other offers an alternative ground on which to begin the human witness to God, for it is subjectivity that realizes humanness, and humanness that refracts the image of God.

> The sole manner by which an otherwise than being could signify is in the relationship with the neighbor—which the human sciences reduce to

---

173. Friedrich Wilhelm Nietzsche, *Thus Spake Zarathustra*, trans. Thomas Common (Radford, VA: Wilder Publications, 2008), 40.

being. The search for a non-onto-theo-logical God does not come out of a thinking that is adequate to its object [*d'une pensée adéquate*]. This search must understand that it starts from a model without a world, and that the relationship with the other is a *contra-diction* [*contre-sens*].[174]

Levinasian ethics does not understand *human* as a noun that stands for an entity, or an adjective that surmises one's salient social position, or a verb that backs itself against the essential structure of being. The human appears in the concrete, urgent, vulnerable encounter with the other, who in the infinity of the face bears the image of God. It shines forth in a friendship that punches a hole in one's treasured religious tradition, or in a difficult freedom that loves Torah more than God. A genuine human life is signified in submitting oneself to be the keeper of the other, as opposed to Cain's answer, and following the subject's urgent request in Song 8:6ab. To love God through loving the other, therefore, is like drinking the wine already stored in the grapes of creation (cf. Gen 1:27).

Am I overstating the case, as critics have said of Levinas? Is it not against Nature, against instinct, or even against theology to say that being is ingrained with an evil undertone? Did not God create the world good? Is it not sickening and unnatural to risk my life for a total stranger? Yes, Levinas agrees, it is sickness to being; but it is not evil. Life in accordance with otherwise-than-being reveals a naked goodness that cannot be captured alive and contained in the said, in being's manifestation in and through a certain overlapping of cultural and ideological data. At the end of the human psyche's denuding of the insubstantial, the repeatable, and replaceable, lives not the nucleus of an ontological being that desires and suffices in its own perfection but this "here I am," to the point of laying down my life for you, that appears in response to the other's summon.

The combination of the skepticism of human intelligence, the phenomenological reduction of the psyche, the ethical turn to the immemorial past whose content can only be supplied by a religious breath—these converged mental strands not only anchor the human subject in the otherwise than being but also replace the traditional approach to God—a journey from one spot to another, a relation between two beings—with a new vision: for a human subject, God is first encountered through being responsible for the other, in whose imposition on me the trace of God is attested.[175]

The postmodern deconstruction of ontology, of egology, will not leave us in a primordial chaos of different entities competing for power and resources, subject to the mercy of the survival of the fittest. For this is what humans retain after being denuded of all that can be separated: "Resources

---

174. Emmanuel Levinas, "Sincerity of the Saying," *God, Death, and Time*, trans. Bettina Bergo (Stanford, CA: Stanford University Press, 2000), 194.

175. The trace of God is primarily described here in the situation of the face of the other, who appears as the first-come. Obviously, the trace is not limited to the I-You relationship that the text of Song 8:6 affords. The question how it is manifested in relation to the third deserves a separate monograph and cannot be addressed here.

of charity that have not disappeared beneath the political structure of institutions: a religious breath or a prophetic spirit in man."[176] The ethical turn that Levinas proposes captures the undying hope of the human: subjectivity breathed in by the other, by God, whose name is heard when one bears for the other, without promises and with dis-interestedness. "That goodness escapes all ideology."[177] It must be added that this escape is not that of a hermitic retreat, which removes one from embodied living in the world, from manifesting love in tending to the needs and interests of others (or allowing them to tend to themselves). It means that the underlying attentiveness born out of proximity to the other should antecede and condition its varied expressions of that same goodness in concrete social, ideological situations.

Love as goodness generated out of proximity entails that even a love for God is embodied, in the double sense that it is visible in how one carries out responsibility for the other and that it is inseparable from human subjectivity. In the lyrical situation of the Song, erotic love is shown to pulsate as flesh inspired by and for the other; and in its inalienable responsibility, it exercises a nonerotic significance that ripples toward ethics and theology.

Seeing the dynamic integrity of human love, Jenson asserts that "[a]ll religion is doubtless in some way lovesickness for the one God."[178] Of the whole Bible, it is the Song that lyrically embodies love, and mutual love at that; in turn, the lyrical ethical experience nourishes and conditions its reader's experience of love that is at the heart of the Torah, so much so that one can taste, feel, and be inspired to carry out the same sincerity and cornucopia of love in serving God and/through caring for others.

If so, one should take seriously Balthasar's admonishment—"Lovers are the ones who know the most about God; the theologian must listen to them."[179] Anterior to its first word and posterior to its last word, does not theology, a thematization of God, receive its meaningfulness from this love, this saying, and caress in response to having been caressed without knowing? This love—both human and divine—is testified in Song 8:6 and further echoed in Blake's lyrical expression, from which comes the title of this chapter:

For Mercy has a human heart,
Pity a human face,
And love, the human form divine.[180]

---

176. Emmanuel Levinas, "Dialogue on Thinking-of-the-Other," *Entre Nous*, 203. Given how the word "love" has been abused, Levinas often avoids using it. It should be noted that the term "charity" can also denote a problematic sense that is not intended in Levinas's formulation—i.e., the paternizing or maternalizing of one's "care for the other" as the major conduit of ethical action.
177. Idem, "The Proximity of the Other," 108.
178. Robert W. Jenson, *Song of Songs*, Interpretation (Louisville: John Knox, 2005), 54.
179. Hans Urs von Balthasar, *Love Alone Is Credible* (San Francisco: Ignatius, 2004), 12.
180. Blake, "The Divine Image," 18.

So to Speak

> God writes straight with
> crooked lines.[1]

Even if writers do not speak of it openly, they have implicit expectations of their readers: smartness with respect to conceptual interplay, rage fueled by power rhetoric, or hunger for sheer volume of knowledge.... They secretly desire ideal soil to receive and grow their seeds. I am not exempted from this urge. What I desire from my readers is patience—a bearing of unknowable passion, an insomniac heart that haunts the smooth cycle of sleep and wakefulness, a passion that cannot appear, for every active appearance is already a representation of consciousness. It is with this wakefulness and alertness—not of mental clarity but attentiveness to the otherness of the other—that I am able to greet my readers, even as I regard the hand stretched forth through the Song.

When one rises from the nocturnal to the daytime, the genuineness of the underlying distorts or fractures the orderliness of consciousness, in the likeness of irrationality and crookedness. But this diachronic imprint is different from irrationality, which remains one pole of reason. From an immemorial past, God inspires; and this in-spiration does not appear neatly in the said to be grasped by the *I think*. Yet it is unmistakably touchable through unsaying the ambiguous or crooked said. In this sense, "God writes straight with crooked lines" (cf. Qoh 1:15).

If so, would there be crookedness when a human writes in straight lines, of poetry and of God? The straight line—perspicuity, love of wisdom, intelligence—stabilizes ambiguous, chaotic incidentals into a secured map of the known, the named, or the same, in the light of consciousness that does not enlighten its origin. Indeed, we do need functional and precise language in communication: "Whatever is mentionable can be more manageable."[2] And yet, such language does not break the invisible case of consciousness, does not get at the exotic origin of in-spiration; therefore, it misses the meaningfulness fiercely embodied in materiality that reason alone cannot touch. Love seizes before "I know" (Song 6:12); hence, "I" have to go to the periphery of knowing to grope for the center of significance.

---

1. Paul Claudel uses this Portuguese proverb as the epigraph of his epic verse drama (*The Satin Slipper: Or, The Worst Is Not the Surest*, trans. John O'Connor [New Haven, CT: Yale University Press, 1931]), from which Levinas fondly quotes (*Otherwise than Being*, 147).

2. This quotation of Fred Rogers is used to promote the application "Mister Rogers Makes a Journal for Preschoolers" by PBS Kids, http://itunes.apple.com/us/app/mister-rogers–make–journal/id333177396?mt=8# [accessed March 31, 2011]). The idea is that, if preschoolers learn to use words to express their emotions, they will manage them better.

The unmentionable remains unmanageable; it is good to reckon that not all can be "managed," can be represented in my consciousness and according to my being of being. Where power stops, the "I" admits to its preoriginary passivity. There, *hinĕnî* precedes *il y a*, love proclaims itself as goodness anteceding creation.

When the straight and coherent arrives at the essence but misses out on significance, a certain perverseness saves human speaking from the unbearable lightness of banality. For example, Critchley considers his new book "perverse" for this very reason:

> *Very little . . . Almost Nothing* is a meditation on my father's death. But I couldn't do that directly, because what was I going to say except that I love him and I still miss him? It's banal. So I did that indirectly through a series of philosophical or conceptual structures, hundreds of pages.[3]

These hundreds of pages have inherent philosophical and conceptual values, as the Song has inherent values as love lyrics about human love. By focusing on rational structures and topics, indirectly Critchley was able to allow his love and mourning to breathe life into the said and its ingrained cultural and linguistic structures.

In a similar manner, the Song breathes a divine inspiration. The ineffability of spirit is akin to that of the saying, which cannot manifest and make itself into being. As smoke colors the waft of the wind, the sound of sense incarnates the saying. Through the in-spiration of the saying, lyrical words are threaded together and signify more than the lexical and semantic whole of the words. Thusly, poetry proffers the digestion of knowledge while embodying responsibility. By awakening attentiveness to the otherness of the other embodied here and now, the Song entreats its readers to be awakened to a poetic opening to the Other, a possibility of experiencing God through experiencing love. In this spirit, I concur with Rabbi Akiva in saying—

> All the ages are not worth the day on which the Song of Songs was given to Israel; for all the *Ketuvim* are holy, but the Song of Songs is the Holy of Holies. (*t. Sanhedrin* 12:10)

Translated into a modern setting: Williams envisions how attentiveness unveils the crooked as the authentic:

> [T]he truth is that we are looking or listening here for speech that can be playful and not just useful, for words that disturb and change us not because they threaten but because they "fit" a reality we are just beginning to discern. If communities of faith took language this seriously, they would be extraordinary signs of transformation.[4]

---

3. Simon Critchley, *How to Stop Living and Start Worrying* (Cambridge: Polity, 2010), 43.
4. Rowan Williams, *Where God Happens: Discovering Christ in One Another* (Boston: New Seeds, 2005), 81.

Instead of saying that a *this* of the Song is really a *that* of religious belief translated with intellectual suaveness, which often gains objectivity at the expense of the blood and flame of the embodied life,[5] I exhort with a lyrical and ethical way of speaking, crooked though it may be, so as to make necessary allowances for the possibility of the word "God" to inspire the reader.

> We spoke one day about the names of God as they are found in the Jewish tradition. He [Levinas] devoted a lesson to this theme, detailing each of them (Elohim, HaShem, El Shaddai . . .) with the proper signification attached to each one. There was one that he did not know, namely Kavyakhol, which I told him my father used sometimes—it was before I learned from Chaim Brézis, a mathematician and lover of biblical exegesis, that the word is found in rabbinic literature.
>
> Literally, it means: "Making necessary allowances." Or more simply, "So to speak."
>
> So to speak. Like an otherwise said. Or an otherwise than being. He liked the expression very much. He repeated Kavyakhol, Kavyakhol, Kavyakhol, like a candy melting in his mouth.[6]

And so I hear and write God's trace in the Song of Songs.

---

5. Cf. Nietzsche's words: "Of all that is written, I love only what a person hath written with his blood. Write with blood, and thou wilt find that blood is spirit" (*Thus Spake Zarathustra*, trans. Thomas Common (Radford, VA: Wilder Publications, 2008], 40).

6. Salomon Malka, *Emmanuel Levinas: His Life and Legacy* (Pittsburgh: Duquesne University Press, 2006), 186–87.

Bibliography

Abu-Lughod, Lila. *Veiled Sentiments: Honor and Poetry in a Bedouin Society*. Berkeley: University of California Press, 1986.
Alter, Robert. *The Art of Biblical Poetry*. New York: Basic Books, 1985.
Altieri, Charles F. "Lyrical Ethics and Literary Experience." *Style* 32 (1998): 272–97.
_____. "Taking Lyrics Literally: Teaching Poetry in a Prose Culture." *New Literary History* 32 (2001): 259–81.
Armstrong, Isobel. *The Radical Aesthetic*. Oxford: Blackwell, 2000.
Astell, Ann W. *The Song of Songs in the Middle Ages*. Ithaca, NY: Cornell University Press, 1990.
Avishur, Yitshak. *Stylistic Studies of Word-Pairs in Biblical and Ancient Semitic Literatures*. Alter Orient und Altes Testament 210. Kevelaer: Butzon & Bercker; Neukirchen-Vluyn: Neukirchener Verlag, 1984.
Baasten, M. F. J., and W. T. van Peursen. *Hamlet on a Hill: Semitic and Greek Studies Presented to Professor T. Muraoka on the Occasion of His Sixty-Fifth Birthday*. Orientalia Lovaniensia Analecta 118. Leuven: Peeters, 2003.
Baker, David, and Ann Townsend (eds.). *Radiant Lyre: Essays on Lyric Poetry*. Saint Paul, MN: Graywolf, 2007.
Bal, Mieke. *Lethal Love: Feminist Literary Readings of Biblical Love Stories*. Indiana Studies in Biblical Literature. Bloomington: Indiana University Press, 1987.
_____. "Poetics, Today." *Poetics Today* 21 (2000): 479–502.
Barthes, Roland. *A Lover's Discourse: Fragments*. New York: Hill & Wang, 1978.
_____. *The Pleasure of the Text*. Translated by Richard Miller. New York: Hill & Wang, 1975.
Bergant, Dianne. *The Song of Songs*. Berit Olam. Collegeville, MN: Liturgical Press, 2001.
Bernard, of Clairvaux, Saint. *On the Song of Songs*. 4 vols. Translated by Kilian Walsh. Introduction by M. Corneille Halfants. Cistercian Fathers 4, 7, 31, 40. Spencer, MA: Cistercian, 1971–80.
Bernasconi, Robert. "Levinas and the Struggle for Existence." Pages 170–84 in *Addressing Levinas*. Edited by Eric Sean Nelson, Antje Kapust, and Kent Still. Evanston, IL: Northwestern University Press, 2005.
Bernasconi, Robert, and Simon Critchley (eds.). *Re-reading Levinas*. Bloomington: Indiana University Press, 1991.
Berquist, Jon L. *Controlling Corporeality: The Body and the Household in Ancient Israel*. New Brunswick, NJ: Rutgers University Press, 2002.
Bettan, Israel. *The Five Scrolls: A Commentary on the Song of Songs, Ruth, Lamentations, Ecclesiastes and Esther*. Cincinnati: Union of American Hebrew Congregations, 1950.
Bevis, Kathryn. "'Better than Metaphors'? Dwelling and the Maternal Body in Emmanuel Levinas." *Literature and Theology* 21 (2007): 317–29.
Black, Fiona C. "Beauty or the Beast? The Grotesque Body in the Song of Songs." *Biblical Interpretation* 8 (2000): 302–23.

Blanchot, Maurice. *Awaiting Oblivion (L'Attente l'oubli)*. Translated by John Gregg. Lincoln: University of Nebraska Press, 1997.

_____. *The Space of Literature*. Translated with an introduction by Ann Smock. Lincoln: University of Nebraska Press, 1989.

Blasing, Mutlu Konuk. *Lyric Poetry: The Pain and the Pleasure of Words*. Princeton, NJ: Princeton University Press, 2007.

Bloom, Harold. *The Song of Songs: Modern Critical Interpretations*. New York: Chelsea, 1988.

Blumenthal, D. "Where God Is Not: The Book of Esther and Song of Songs." *Judaism* 44/1 (1995): 80–92.

Boer, Roland. "The Second Coming: Repetition and Insatiable Desire in the Song of Songs." *Biblical Interpretation* 8 (2000): 276–301.

Booth, Wayne C. *The Company We Keep: An Ethics of Fiction*. Berkeley: University of California Press, 1988.

Brenner, Athalya, and Carole R. Fontaine (eds.). *The Song of Songs: A Feminist Companion to the Bible*. Sheffield: Sheffield Academic Press, 2000.

Bruns, Gerald L. *The Material of Poetry: Sketches for a Philosophical Poetics*. Athens: University of Georgia Press, 2005.

_____. "Should Poetry Be Ethical or Otherwise?" *SubStance* 38/3 (2009): 72–91.

Budde, Karl, Alfred Bertholet, and G. Wildeboer. *Die fünf Megillot: Das Hohelied, das Buch Ruth, die Klagelieder, der Prediger, das Buch Esther*. Freiburg: Mohr, 1898.

Burrus, Virginia, and Catherine Keller (eds.). *Toward a Theology of Eros: Transfiguring Passion at the Limits of Discipline*. Transdisciplinary Theological Colloquia. New York: Fordham University Press, 2006.

Carr, David M. "Gender and the Shaping of Desire in the Song of Songs and Its Interpretations." *Journal of Biblical Literature* 119 (2000): 233–48.

_____. "The Song of Songs as a Microcosm of the Canonization and Decanonization Process." Pages 173–89 in *Canonization and Decanonization*. Edited by Arie van der Kooij and K. van der Toorn. Leiden: Brill, 1998.

Carson, Anne. *Eros the Bittersweet*. Normal, IL: Dalkey Archive, 1998.

Cazeaux, Jacques. *Le cantique des cantiques: Des pourpres de Salomon à l'anémone des champs*. Paris: Cerf, 2008.

Celan, Paul. *Collected Prose*. Edited by Rosemarie Waldrop. Manchester: Carcanet, 1986.

_____. *Paul Celan: Selections*. Edited by Pierre Joris. Translated by Rosemarie Waldrop. Berkeley: University of California Press.

Champagne, John. "Levinas and the Question of the Other." Pages 170–224 in *Ethics of Eros: Irigaray's Rewriting of the Philosophy*. Edited by Tina Chanter. New York: Routledge, 1995.

Cig, M., and S. N. Kramer. "The Ideal Mother: A Sumerian Portrait." *Belleten* 40 (1976): 413–21.

Ciocan, Cristian, and Georges Hansel. *Levinas Concordance*. Dordrecht: Springer, 2005.

Cohen, Richard A. *Elevations: The Height of the Good in Rosenzweig and Levinas*. Chicago Studies in the History of Judaism. Chicago: University of Chicago Press, 1994.

_____. *Ethics, Exegesis and Philosophy: Interpretation after Levinas* (Cambridge: Cambridge University Press, 2001.

_____. *Levinasian Meditations: Ethics, Philosophy, and Religion*. Pittsburgh: Duquesne University Press, 2010.
Cooper, Jerrold S. "Gendered Sexuality in Sumerian Love Poetry." Pages 85–97 in *Sumerian Gods and Their Representations*. Edited by Irving L. Finkel and Markham J. Geller. Cuneiform Monograph 7. Groningen: STYX, 1997.
Crignon, Philippe. "Figuration: Emmanuel Levinas and the Image." Translated by Nicole Simek and Zahi Zalloua. *Yale French Studies* 104 (2004): 100–125.
Critchley, Simon. *How to Stop Living and Start Worrying*. Cambridge: Polity, 2010.
_____. *Very Little, Almost Nothing: Death, Philosophy and Literature*. London: Routledge, 2004.
Culler, Jonathan. "Approaching the Lyric." Pages 31–37 in *Lyric Poetry: Beyond New Criticism*. Edited by Chaviva Hošek and Patricia Parker. Ithaca, NY: Cornell University Press, 1985.
Dahood, M. "Ugaritic-Hebrew Parallel Pairs." Pages 71–382 in *Ras Shamra Parallels: The Texts from Ugarit and the Hebrew Bible*. Edited by Loren R. Fisher, F. Brent Knutson, and Donn F. Morgan. Analecta orientalia 49. Rome: Pontifical Biblical Institute, 1972.
Damasio, Antonio R. *Looking for Spinoza: Joy, Sorrow, and the Feeling Brain*. Orlando, FL: Harcourt, 2003.
Davies, Paul. "The Face and the Caress: Levinas's Ethical Alterations of Sensibility." Pages 252–72 in *Modernity and the Hegemony of Vision*. Edited by David Michael Levin. Berkeley: University of California Press, 1993.
Delitzsch, Franz. *Proverbs, Ecclesiastes, Song of Solomon*. Translated by M. G. Easton. Volume 6 of *Commentary on the Old Testament in Ten Volumes*. Grand Rapids, MI: Eerdmans, 1975.
Dempsey, Carol. "Metaphorical Language and the Expression of Love." *The Bible Today* 36 (1998): 164–69.
Derrida, Jacques. *Adieu to Emmanuel Levinas*. Stanford, CA: Stanford University Press, 1999.
Dever, William G. "Archaeology and Ancient Israelite Iconography: Did Yahweh Have a Face?" Pages 461–75 in *"I Will Speak the Riddle of Ancient Times": Archaeological and Historical Studies in Honor of Amihai Mazar on the Occasion of His Sixtieth Birthday*. 2 vols. Edited by Aren M. Maeir and Pierre de Miroschedji. Winona Lake, IN: Eisenbrauns, 2006.
Dobbs-Allsopp, F. W. "I Am Black *and* Beautiful": The Song, Cixous, and Écriture Féminine." Pages 128–40 in *Engaging the Bible in a Gendered World: An Introduction to Feminist Biblical Interpretation in Honor of Katharine Doob Sakenfeld*. Edited by Linda Day and Carolyn Pressler. Louisville: Westminster John Knox, 2006.
_____. "Ingressive *qwm* in Biblical Hebrew." *Zeitschrift für Assyriologie* 8 (1995): 31–54.
_____. "Late Linguistic Features in Song of Songs." Pages 27–77 in *Perspectives on the Song of Songs*. Edited by Anselm C. Hagedorn. Berlin: de Gruyter, 2005.
Dove, Mary. *The Glossa Ordinaria on the Song of Songs*. Kalamazoo: Published for TEAMS by Medieval Institute Publications, Western Michigan University, 2004.
Drabinski, John E. *Sensibility and Singularity: The Problem of Phenomenology in Levinas*. SUNY Series in Contemporary Continental Philosophy. Albany: State University of New York Press, 2001.

Eaglestone, Robert. *Ethical Criticism: Reading after Levinas.* Edinburgh: Edinburgh University Press, 1997.

———. "Flaws: James, Nussbaum, Miller, Levinas." Pages 77–87 in *Critical Ethics.* Edited by Dominic Rainsford and Tim Woods. London: Macmillan, 1999.

———. "One and the Same? Ethics, Aesthetics, and Truth." *Poetics Today* 25 (2004): 595–608.

Elliott, M. Timothea. *The Literary Unity of the Canticle.* Europäische Hochschulschriften 371. Frankfurt am Main: Peter Lang, 1989.

Exum, J. Cheryl. "A Literary and Structural Analysis of the Song of Songs." *Zeitschrift für die alttestamentliche Wissenschaft* 85 (1973): 47–79.

———. *Song of Songs: A Commentary.* Old Testament Library. Louisville: Westminster John Knox, 2005.

Fahraeus, Anna, and AnnKatrin Jonsson (eds.). *Textual Ethos Studies, or Locating Ethics.* Amsterdam: Rodopi, 2005.

Falk, Marcia. *Love Lyrics from the Bible: A Translation and Literary Study of the Song of Songs.* Bible and Literature Series 4. Sheffield: Sheffield Academic Press, 1982.

Farley, Wendy. *Eros for the Other: Retaining Truth in a Pluralistic World.* University Park: Pennsylvania State University Press, 1996.

Feliks, Yehuda. *Song of Songs: Nature Epic and Allegory.* Jerusalem: Israel Society for Biblical Research, 1983.

Felstiner, John. *Can Poetry Save the Earth? A Field Guide to Nature Poems.* New Haven, CT: Yale University Press, 2009.

Field, Fridericus. *Origenis Hexaplorum.* Vol. 2. Oxford: Clarendon, 1875.

Finnegan, Ruth H. *Oral Poetry: Its Nature, Significance, and Social Context.* Cambridge: Cambridge University Press, 1977.

Fisch, Harold. *Poetry with a Purpose: Biblical Poetics and Interpretation.* Bloomington: Indiana University Press, 1988.

Fokkelman, J. P. *Reading Biblical Poetry: An Introductory Guide.* Louisville: Westminster John Knox, 2001.

Fowler, Barbara Hughes. *Love Lyrics of Ancient Egypt.* Chapel Hill: University of North Carolina Press, 1994.

Fox, Michael V. *The Song of Songs and the Ancient Egyptian Love Songs.* Madison: University of Wisconsin Press, 1985.

Frost, Robert. *Robert Frost on Writing.* Edited by Elaine Barry. New Brunswick, NJ: Rutgers University Press, 1973.

Garrett, Duane A. *Song of Songs/Lamentations.* Word Biblical Commentary 23B. Nashville, TN: Thomas Nelson, 2004.

Geller, Stephen A. *Parallelism in Early Biblical Poetry.* Missoula, MT: Scholars Press, 1979.

Gershom, Levi ben (Gersonides). *Commentary on Song of Songs.* Translated from Hebrew with an introduction and annotations by Menachem Marc Kellner. New Haven, CT: Yale University Press, 1998.

Gibson, Andrew. *Postmodernity, Ethics, and the Novel.* London: Routledge, 1999.

Ginsburg, Christian D. *The Song of Songs and Coheleth (Commonly Called the Book of Ecclesiastes).* New York: Ktav, 1970.

Gledhill, Tom. *The Message of the Song of Songs: The Lyrics of Love.* Leicester: Inter-Varsity, 1994.

Goodman, Nelson. *Languages of Art: An Approach to a Theory of Symbols.* Indianapolis: Bobbs-Merrill, 1968.

Gordis, Robert. *The Song of Songs: A Study, Modern Translation, and Commentary.* New York: Jewish Theological Seminary, 1954.
Goulder, M. D. *The Song of Fourteen Songs.* Journal for the Study of the Old Testament Supplement 36. Sheffield: JSOT, 1986.
Grosz, E. A. *Space, Time and Perversion: Essays on the Politics of Bodies.* New York: Routledge, 1995.
Haas, Volkert. *Babylonischer Liebesgarten: Erotik und Sexualität im Alten Orient.* Munich: Beck, 1999.
Halberstam, Judith. *Female Masculinity.* Durham, NC: Duke University Press, 1998.
Hallberg, Robert von. *Lyric Powers.* Chicago: University of Chicago Press, 2008.
Herntrich, Volkmar, Otto Kaiser, James A. Loader, and Hans-Peter Müller. *Das Hohelied, Klagelieder, Das Buch Ester.* Göttingen: Vandenhoeck & Ruprecht, 1992.
Hess, Richard S. *Song of Songs.* Grand Rapids, MI: Baker, 2005.
Hunt, Patrick. *Poetry in the Song of Songs: A Literary Analysis.* New York: Peter Lang, 2008.
Jacobsen, Thorkild. *The Harps That Once—: Sumerian Poetry in Translation.* New Haven, CT: Yale University Press, 1987.
Jenkins, G. Matthew. "Saying Obligation: George Oppen's Poetry and Levinasian Ethics." *Journal of American Studies* 37 (2003): 407–33.
Jenson, Robert W. *Song of Songs.* Interpretation. Louisville: John Knox, 2005.
Jerusalmi, Isaac. *The Song of Songs in the Targumic Tradition: Vocalized Aramaic Text with Facing English Translation and Ladino Versions, Aramaic Concordance, Aramaic-English, Ladino-English Glossaries.* Cincinnati: Ladino, 1993.
Katz, Claire Elise. "'For Love Is as Strong as Death': Taking Another Look at Levinas on Love." *Philosophy Today* 45 (2001): 124–32.
_____. *Levinas, Judaism, and the Feminine: The Silent Footsteps of Rebecca.* Bloomington: Indiana University Press, 2003.
Katz, Dina. *The Image of the Netherworld in the Sumerian Sources.* Bethesda, MD: CDL, 2003.
Kearney, Richard. "Returning to God after God: Levinas, Derrida, Ricoeur." *Research in Phenomenology* 39 (2009): 167–83.
Keel, Othmar. *The Song of Songs: A Continental Commentary.* Minneapolis: Fortress, 1994.
Kimelman, Reuven. "Rabbi Yohanan and Origen on the Song of Songs: A Third-Century Jewish-Christian Disputation." *Harvard Theological Review* 73 (1980): 567–95.
King, Philip J., and Lawrence E. Stager. *Life in Biblical Israel.* Library of Ancient Israel. Louisville: Westminster John Knox, 2001.
Kingsmill, Edmée. *The Song of Songs and the Eros of God: A Study in Biblical Intertextuality.* Oxford: Oxford University Press, 2009.
Kravitz, Leonard S., and Kerry M. Olitzky. *Shir Hashirim: A Modern Commentary on the Song of Songs.* New York: URJ, 2004.
Krinetzki, Leo. *Das Hohe Lied: Kommentar zu Gestalt und Kerygma eines alttestamentlichen Liebesliedes.* Kommentare und Beiträge zum Alten und Neuen Testament. Düsseldorf: Patmos, 1964.
_____. "Die Macht der Liebe." *Münchener theologische Zeitschrift* 13 (1962): 256–79.

Kristeva, Julia. "Le Cantique des cantiques." Pages 65–78 in *La Bible et l'autre: Les dialogues bibliques du Collège des Études Juives de l'Alliance Israélite Universelle tenus de 1998 à 2002 en collaboration avec l'Université de Paris IV–Sorbonne*. Edited by Shmuel Trigano. Paris: Éditions In Press, 2002.

Lacocque, André. *The Feminine Unconventional: Four Subversive Figures in Israel's Tradition*. Minneapolis: Fortress, 1990.

Landy, Francis. *Paradoxes of Paradise: Identity and Difference in the Song of Songs*. Sheffield: Almond, 1983.

Levinas, Emmanuel. *Beyond the Verse: Talmudic Readings and Lectures*. Translated by Gary D. Mole. London: Athlone, 1994.

———. *Collected Philosophical Papers*. Translated by Alphonso Lingis. Pittsburgh: Duquesne University Press, 1998.

———. *Difficult Freedom: Essays on Judaism*. Johns Hopkins Jewish Studies. Baltimore: Johns Hopkins University Press, 1990.

———. *Entre Nous: On Thinking-of-the-Other*. Translated by Michael B. Smith and Barbara Harshave. London: Continuum, 2006.

———. *Existence and Existents*. Translated by Alphonso Lingis. Boston: Kluwer, 1988.

———. *God, Death, and Time*. Translated by Bettina Bergo. Stanford, CA: Stanford University Press, 2000.

———. *Humanism of the Other*. Translated by Nidra Poller. Urbana: University of Illinois Press, 2003.

———. *In the Time of the Nations*. Translated by Michael B. Smith. Bloomington: Indiana University Press, 1994.

———. *New Talmudic Readings*. Translated by Richard A. Cohen. Pittsburgh: Duquesne University Press, 1999.

———. *Nine Talmudic Readings*. Translated with an introduction by Annette Aronowicz. Bloomington: Indiana University Press, 1990.

———. *Of God Who Comes to Mind*. Stanford: Stanford University Press, 1998.

———. *Otherwise Than Being, or, Beyond Essence*. Translated by Alphonso Lingis. Pittsburgh: Duquesne University Press, 1998.

———. *Paul Celan, De l'être à l'autre*. Fontfroide-le-Haut: Fata morgana, 2002.

———. *Proper Names*. Translated by Michael B. Smith. London: Athlone, 1996.

———. "Sensibility." Pages 60–66 in *Ontology and Alterity in Merleau-Ponty*. Translated by Michael B. Smith. Edited by Galen A. Johnson and Michael B. Smith. Evanston, IL: Northwestern University Press, 1990.

———. *Time and the Other and Additional Essays*. Translated by Richard A. Cohen. Pittsburgh: Duquesne University Press, 1987.

———. *Totality and Infinity: An Essay on Exteriority*. Translated by Alphonso Lingis. Pittsburgh: Duquesne University Press, 1969.

———. *Unforeseen History*. Translated by Nidra Poller. Urbana: University of Illinois Press, 2004.

Lingis, Alphonso. "The Sensuality and the Sensitivity." Pages 219–30 in *Face to Face with Lévinas*. SUNY Series in Philosophy. Edited by Richard A. Cohen. Albany: State University of New York Press, 1986.

Livingstone, Alasdair. *Mystical and Mythological Explanatory Works of Assyrian and Babylonian Scholars*. Oxford: Clarendon, 1986.

Longenbach, James. *The Art of the Poetic Lines*. St. Paul, MN: Graywolf, 2008.

Longman, Tremper, III. *The Song of Songs*. NICOT. Grand Rapids, MI: Eerdmans, 2001.
Loretz, Oswald, and Ingo Kottsieper. *Colometry in Ugaritic and Biblical Poetry: Introduction, Illustrations and Topical Bibliography*. Altenberge: CIS, 1987.
Malka, Salomon. *Emmanuel Levinas: His Life and Legacy*. Pittsburgh: Duquesne University Press, 2006.
Marion, Jean-Luc. *The Erotic Phenomenon*. Chicago: University of Chicago Press, 2007.
Matter, E. Ann. *The Voice of My Beloved: The Song of Songs in Western Medieval Christianity*. Philadelphia: University of Pennsylvania Press, 1990.
Meek, Theophile J. "The Song of Songs: Introduction and Exegesis." Pages 91–148 in *The Interpreter's Bible*, vol. 5. Edited by George A Buttrick. New York: Abingdon, 1956.
Meskell, Lynn. *Archaeologies of Social Life: Age, Sex, Class et Cetera in Ancient Egypt*. Oxford: Blackwell, 1999.
Meyers, Carol L. *Discovering Eve: Ancient Israelite Women in Context*. New York: Oxford University Press, 1988.
_____. "Gender Imagery in the Song of Songs." *Hebrew Annual Review* 10 (1986): 209–23.
_____. "Guilds and Gatherings: Women's Groups in Ancient Israel." Pages 154–84 in *Realia Dei: Essays in Archaeology and Biblical Interpretation in Honor of Edward F. Campbell, Jr. at His Retirement*. Edited by Prescott M. Williams Jr. and Theodore Hiebert. Atlanta: Scholars Press, 1999.
_____. "Where the Girls Are: Archaeology and Women's Lives in Ancient Israel." Pages 31–52 in *Between Text and Artifact: Integrating Archaeology in Biblical Studies Teaching*. Edited by Milton C. Moreland. Archaeology and Biblical Studies 8. Atlanta: Society of Biblical Literature, 2003.
Michałowski, Piotr. "Ancient Poetics." Pages 141–53 in *Mesopotamian Poetic Language: Sumerian and Akkadian*. Edited by Marianna E. Vogelzang and H. L. J. Vanstiphout. Groningen: Styx, 1996.
Miles, Margaret R. *Reading for Life: Beauty, Pluralism, and Responsibility*. New York: Continuum, 1997.
Miller, Cynthia, "The Relation of Coordination to Verb Gapping in Biblical Poetry." *Journal for the Study of the Old Testament* 32 (2007): 41–60.
Miller, Patrick. "Theological Significance of Biblical Poetry." Pages 213–30 in *Language, Theology, and the Bible: Essays in Honour of James Barr*. Edited by Samuel E. Balentine and John Barton. Oxford: Clarendon, 1994.
Morgan, Michael L. *Discovering Levinas*. New York: Cambridge University Press, 2007.
Müller, Hans-Peter. "Zur Frage nach dem 'Wesen' früher Lyrik: Am Beispiel des Hohenliedes." Pages 817–32 in *Gott und Mensch im Dialog: Festschrift für Otto Kaiser zum 80. Geburtstag*, vol. 2. Edited by Markus Witte. Berlin: de Gruyter, 2004.
Munro, Jill M. *Spikenard and Saffron: The Imagery of the Song of Songs*. Journal for the Study of the Old Testament Supplement 203. Sheffield: Sheffield Academic Press, 1995.
Murphy, Roland E. *The Song of Songs: A Commentary on the Book of Canticles or the Song of Songs*. Minneapolis: Fortress, 1990.
Neusner, Jacob. *Israel's Love Affair with God: Song of Songs*. Valley Forge, PA: Trinity Press International, 1993.

_____. *Song of Songs Rabbah: An Analytical Translation*. 2 vols. Brown Judaic Studies 197–98. Atlanta: Scholars Press, 1989.
Newton, Adam Zachary. "Versions of Ethics; or, The *SARL* of Criticism: Sonority, Arrogation, Letting-Be." *American Literary History* 13 (2001): 603–37.
Nilus of Ancyra. *Kommentar zum Hohelied*. Edited by Hans-Udo Rosenbaum and Harald Ringshausen. Berlin: de Gruyter, 2004.
Nissinen, Martti. "Is God Mentioned in the Song of Songs? Flame of Yahweh, Love, and Death in Song of Songs 8.6–7A." Pages 273–87 in *A Critical Engagement: Essays on the Hebrew Bible in Honour of J. Cheryl Exum*. Edited by David J. A. Clines and Ellen van Wolde. Sheffield: Phoenix, 2011.
Nissinen, Martti, and Risto Uro (eds.). *Sacred Marriages: The Divine-Human Sexual Metaphor from Sumer to Early Christianity*. Winona Lake, IN: Eisenbrauns, 2008.
Nussbaum, Martha Craven. "'Faint with Secret Knowledge': Love and Vision in Murdoch's 'The Black Prince.'" *Poetics Today* 25 (2004): 689–710.
_____. *Love's Knowledge: Essays on Philosophy and Literature*. New York: Oxford University Press, 1990.
O'Connor, Michael Patrick. *Hebrew Verse Structure*. Winona Lake, IN: Eisenbrauns, 1980.
Origen. *The Song of Songs: Commentary and Homilies*. Translated and annotated by R. P. Lawson. Westminster, MD: Newman, 1957.
Ouaknin, Marc-Alain. *The Burnt Book: Reading the Talmud*. Translated by Llewellyn Brown. Princeton, NJ: Princeton University Press, 1995.
Paul, S. M. "A Lover's Garden of Verse: Literal and Metaphorical Imagery in Ancient Near Easern Love Poetry." Pages 99–110 in *Tehillah le-Moshe: Biblical and Judaic Studies in Honor of Moshe Greenberg*. Edited by Mordechai Cogan, Barry L. Eichler, and Jeffrey H. Tigay. Winona Lake, IN: Eisenbrauns, 1997.
Perdue, Leo G., Joseph Blenkinsopp, John J. Collins, and Carol Meyers (eds.). *Families in Ancient Israel*. The Family, Religion, and Culture Series. Louisville: Westminster John Knox, 1997.
Pinsky, Robert. *The Sound of Poetry: A Brief Guide*. New York: Farrar, Straus & Giroux, 1998.
Platt, Elizabeth E. "Jewelry, Ancient Israelite." Pages 823–34 in vol. 3 of *Anchor Bible Dictionary*. Edited by David Noel Freedman. 6 vols. New York: Doubleday, 1992.
Plotinus. *The Enneads*. Translated by Stephen MacKenna. London: Faber & Faber, 1969.
Pope, Marvin H. *The Song of Songs: A New Translation with Introduction and Commentary*. Anchor Bible 7C. Garden City, NY: Doubleday, 1977.
Porter, B. N. "Beds, Sex, and Politics." Pages 523–35 in *Sex and Gender in the Ancient Near East: Proceedings of the 47th Rencontre Assyriologique Internationale, Helsinki, July 2–6, 2001*. 2 vols. Edited by Simo Parpola and Robert M. Whiting. Helsinki: Neo-Assyrian Text Corpus Project, 2002.
Riera, Gabriel. *Intrigues: From Being to the Other*. New York: Fordham University Press, 2006.
Robert, André, and Raymond Jacques Tournay. *Le Cantique des Cantiques*. Paris: Gabalda, 1963.
Roberts, Donald Phillip. *Let Me See Your Form: Seeking Poetic Structure in the Song of Songs*. Studies in Judaism. Lanham, MD: University Press of America, 2007.

Robins, Jill. *Altered Reading: Levinas and Literature*. Chicago: University of Chicago Press, 1999.
Rudolph, Wilhelm. *Des Buch Ruth, das Hohe Lied, die Klagelieder*. Kommentar zum Alten Testament 17/1–3. Gütersloh: Mohn, 1962.
Rosenblatt, Naomi H. *After the Apple: Women in the Bible—Timeless Stories of Love, Lust, and Longing*. New York: Hyperion, 2005.
Rothenstein, Michael. *The Song of Songs Which Is Solomon's*. Cambridge: Rampant Lions, 1979.
Rozelaar, M. "An Unrecognized Part of the Human Anatomy." *Judaism* 37(1988): 97–101.
Rychter, Ewa. *(Un)Saying the Other: Allegory and Irony in Emmanuel Levinas's Ethical Language*. Frankfurt am Main: Peter Lang, 2004.
Sandford, Stella. *The Metaphysics of Love: Gender and Transcendence in Levinas*. London: Athlone, 2000.
Scarry, Elaine. *On Beauty and Being Just*. Princeton, NJ: Princeton University Press, 1999.
Sefati, Yitschak. *Love Songs in Sumerian Literature: Critical Edition of the Dumuzi-Inanna Songs*. Ramat Gan: Bar-Ilan University Press, 1998.
Sholem, Aleichem. *The Song of Songs*. Translated by Curt Leviant. New York: Simon & Schuster, 1996.
Smith, Barbara Herrnstein. *Poetic Closure: A Study of How Poems End*. Chicago: University of Chicago Press, 1968.
Stauffer, Jill, and Bettina Bergo (eds.). *Nietzsche and Levinas: "After the Death of a Certain God."* New York: Columbia University Press, 2009.
Sudermann, Hermann. *The Song of Songs, 'Das Hohe Lied'*. Translated by Thomas Seltzer. New York: Huebsch, 1923.
Sumi, Akiko Motoyoshi. *Description in Classical Arabic Poetry Waṣf, Ekphrasis, and Interarts Theory*. Leiden: Brill, 2004.
Tamakh, Abraham ben Isaac ha-Levi. *Commentary on the Song of Songs*. Translated by Leon A. Feldman. Studia Semitica Neerlandica 9. Assen: Van Gorcum, 1970.
Tov, Emmanuel. "Introduction to 4QCant[a–c]." Pages 195–219 in *Les 'Petites Grottes' de Qumran (Plates)*. Discoveries in the Judaean Desert 16. Oxford: Clarendon, 2000.
Treat, Jay. "Aquila, Field, and the Song of Songs." Pages 136–76 in *Origen's Hexapla and Fragments: Papers Presented at the Rich Seminar on the Hexapla, Oxford Centre for Hebrew and Jewish Studies, 25th July–3rd August 1994*. Edited by Alison Salveson. Tübingen: Mohr Siebeck, 1998.
————. "A Fiery Dove: The Song of Songs in Codex Venetus 1." Pages 275–301 in *A Multiform Heritage: Studies on Early Judaism and Christianity in Honor of Robert A. Kraft*. Edited by Benjamin G. Wright. Atlanta: Scholars Press, 1999.
————. "Lost Keys: Text and Interpretation in Old Greek Song of Songs and Its Earliest Manuscript Witnesses." Ph.D. diss. University of Pennsylvania, 1996
Trible, Phyllis. *God and the Rhetoric of Sexuality: Overtures to Biblical Theology*. Philadelphia: Fortress, 1978.
Tuell, Steven S. "A Riddle Resolved by an Enigma." *Journal of Biblical Literature* 112 (1993): 99–104.
Turner, Denys. *Eros and Allegory: Medieval Exegesis of the Song of Songs*. Cistercian Studies Series 156. Kalamazoo, MI: Cistercian, 1995.

Uris, Jill, and Leon M. Uris. *Jerusalem, Song of Songs*. Garden City, NY: Doubleday, 1981.
Vendler, Helen Hennessy. *Our Secret Discipline: Yeats and Lyric Form*. Cambridge. MA: Belknap, 2007.
_____. *Poets Thinking: Pope, Whitman, Dickinson, Yeats*. Cambridge: Harvard University Press, 2004.
Walsh, Carey. *Exquisite Desire: Religion, the Erotic and the Song of Songs*. Minneapolis: Augsburg Fortress, 2000.
Walton, Brian (ed.). *Biblia Sacra Polyglotta*. Vol. 6. London: Thomas Roycroft, 1657.
Ward, David, and David Saltz. "Forging at Different Spatial Scales: Dorcas Gazelles Foraging for Lilies in the Negev Desert." *Ecology* 75/1 (1994): 48–58.
Waterman, Leroy. *The Song of Songs*. Ann Arbor: University of Michigan Press, 1948.
Waters, William. *Poetry's Touch: On Lyric Address*. Ithaca, NY: Cornell University Press, 2003.
Webster, Edwin C. "Pattern in the Song of Songs." *Journal for the Study of the Old Testament* 22 (1982): 73–93.
Westenholz, Joan Goodnick. "Symbolic Language in Akkadian Narrative Poetry: The Metaphorical Relationship between Poetical Images and the Real World." Pages 183–206 in *Mesopotamian Poetic Language: Sumerian and Akkadian*. Edited by Marianna E. Vogelzang and H. L. J. Vanstiphout. Groningen: Styx, 1996.
White, John Bradley. *A Study of the Language of Love in the Song of Songs and Ancient Egyptian Poetry*. Missoula, MT: Scholars Press, 1978.
Williams, David-Antoine. "Tête-à-tête, Face-à-face: Brodsky, Levinas, and the Ethics of Poetry." *Poetics Today* 30 (2009): 207–35.
Wolkstein, Diane, and Samuel Noah Kramer. *Inanna, Queen of Heaven and Earth: Her Stories and Hymns from Sumer*. New York: Harper & Row, 1983.
Wright, J. Robert (ed.). *Proverbs, Ecclesiastes, Song of Songs*. Edited by Thomas C. Oden et al. Ancient Christian Commentary on Scripture: Old Testament 9. Downers Grove, IL: InterVarsity, 2005.
Zakovitch, Yair. *Das Hohelied*. Herders theologischer Kommentar zum Alten Testament. Freiburg im Breisgau: Herder, 2004.

Index of Authors

Abram, D. 120
Abu-Lughod, L. 27, 31
Agnon, S. Y. 21
Albright, W. F. 126
Alcoff, L. M. 47
Alter, R. 2, 61, 67, 77
Altieri, C. 5, 13
Anderson, T. 21
Anderson, T. D. 2
Arnold, B. T. 112
Assante, J. 78, 81
Avigad, N. 118
Avishur, Y. 83, 119

Baasten, M. F. J. 34, 84
Bachelard, G. 106
Balthasar, H. U. von 159
Barthes, R. 52, 60, 61, 77, 80, 94
Batnitzkey, L. 59
Bauby, J.-D. 93
Baudelaire, C. 46, 48, 64
Bauer, H. 142, 148, 149
Bergant, D. 31, 36, 71, 119
Berlin, A. 2
Berlyn, P. J. 118
Bernard of Clairvaux 41
Bernasconi, R. 68, 134, 135
Bernat, D. 44
Bevis, K. 22
Beyer, B. 112
Biernoff, S. 54, 55
Black, F. C. 45
Blake, W. 33, 139, 159,
Blanchot, M. 3, 4, 10, 20, 21, 22, 23, 60, 64, 74, 78, 79, 80, 81, 92, 111, 129, 130, 131
Blasing, M. K. 46, 48, 49
Blau, L. 61
Brenner, A. 45
Brodsky, J. 13, 14
Brontë, E. 72, 96
Buckley, C. 66
Budde, K. 120, 145
Butler, J. 132

Caner, D. F. 110
Carson, A. 39, 56, 64, 65, 113
Cazeaux, J. 102
Celan, P. 4, 6, 21, 23, 24, 26, 27, 65, 70, 72, 90, 122
Chapman, C. R. 112
Claudel, P. 20, 160
Clines, D. J. A. 2
Cohen, R. A. 3, 4, 6, 16, 53, 105, 111, 130, 134, 137, 141
Collins, T. 2
Conrad, D. 126
Cooper, J. S. 4, 44
Crignon, P. 55, 67, 68, 151
Critchley, S. 6, 18, 68, 113, 132, 136, 137, 150, 161
Culler, J. 1

Damasio, A. R. 7, 41, 58, 64
Dastur, F. 140
Davies, P. 3, 55
Delitzsch, F. 44
Derrida, J. 25, 92, 103
Deutsch, R. 118
Dobbs-Allsopp, F. W. 2, 34, 37, 81, 83, 143
Dostoyevsky, F. 20, 133
Downing, F. G. 42
Drabinski, J. E. 57, 62
Dudiak, J. 155

Eaglestone, R. 3, 11, 45
Eaton, M. M. 14
Edelglass, W. 20, 21, 22
Empson, W. 110
Exum, J. C. 40, 45, 63, 65, 74, 76, 89, 115, 116, 119, 126, 138, 141, 142, 145, 148

Falk, M. 45, 53, 63, 73, 89
Farley, W. 27
Felsteiner, J. 122
Felstiner, J. 65, 152
Field, F. 122

173

Finnegan, R. H.   29
Fisch, H.   43
Fitzgerald, F. S.   118
Fitzmyer, J. A.   44
Fokkelman, J. P.   63
Foucault, M.   131
Fowler, B. H.   77
Fox, M. V.   44, 45, 63, 73, 76, 119, 120, 121, 142, 147, 148, 149
Frost, R.   15, 122

Garrett, D. A.   63, 73, 76, 81, 89, 119, 148
Garr, W. R.   91
Geller, S. A.   2, 142, 143
George, A. R.   80
Gerleman, G.   48, 147
Gershom, L.   51
Gibbs, R.   59
Gibran, K.   34
Gibson, A.   56, 57
Ginsburg, C. D.   109, 141
Gledhill, T.   53
Gordis, R.   36, 63, 76, 89, 119, 121, 148
Goulder, M. D.   31, 73
Gray, G. B.   2
Grunebaum, G. von   44

Hallberg, R. von   1, 5
Hallo, W. W.   96
Hand, S.   19
Harrington, D. J.   44
Heaney, S.   13
Heidegger, M.   19, 20, 130, 133, 134, 135, 136, 140, 141
Hermann, A.   44
Hess, R. S.   41, 63, 71, 73, 76, 79, 80, 81, 89, 109, 111, 119, 121, 142
Hill, L.   4
Himelfarb, L.   76
Honeyman, A. M.   32
Hrushovski, B.   143
Hume, D.   38

Isserlin, B. S. J.   45

Jabès, E.   21, 23, 26
Jackson, R.   113
Jacobsen, T.   78, 96

James, W.   28, 49, 58
Janzen, J. G.   64
Jenkins, G. M.   4
Jenson, R. W.   36, 87, 88, 97, 109, 159
Johnson, M.   54

Kaiser, O.   145
Kane, P.   4
Kant, I.   7, 140
Katz, D.   96
Kawashima, R. S.   34
Kearney, R.   19, 68, 105, 154, 155
Keats, J.   24
Keel, O.   31, 32, 36, 40, 44, 73, 76, 79, 81, 89, 94, 95
King, P. J.   31, 81
Kosky, J. L.   140, 141
Kramer, S. N.   96
Kravitz, L. S.   63, 89
Krinetzki, L.   109, 119, 121, 141, 142, 152
Kristeva, J.   11, 39
Kugel, J. L.   2, 28, 154
Kuhn, K. G.   142
Kuhn, T. S.   11

Lakoff, G.   54
Lambdin, T. O.   33
Landy, F.   40
Leander, P.   142, 148, 149
Leiris, M.   21
Lemaire, A.   118
Levinas, E.   1, 3, 4, 5, 6, 7, 8, 9, 10, 12, 13, 15, 16, 17, 18, 19, 20, 21, 22, 23, 24, 25, 26, 34, 39, 40, 43, 44, 46, 47, 52, 53, 54, 55, 56, 57, 58, 59, 60, 61, 62, 64, 65, 67, 69, 71, 72, 74, 75, 76, 79, 80, 85, 86, 88, 91, 92, 93, 96, 97, 98, 99, 101, 103, 104, 105, 106, 108, 110, 111, 122, 125, 126, 130, 131, 132, 133, 134, 135, 136, 137, 138, 140, 141, 150, 151, 154, 155, 156, 158, 159, 160, 162
Linafelt, T.   74, 122, 128, 143, 146
Lingis, A.   4, 21, 25, 54, 57, 58
Lipschütz, L.   147
Livingstone, A.   44
Llewelyn, J.   22
Longenbach, J.   28, 49

Longman, T. 32, 45, 66, 73, 76, 89, 109, 120, 126, 137, 142
Loseff, L. 14
Lowth, R. 2

Macfadyen, D. 14
Malka, S. 3, 9, 20, 21, 23, 162
Marcel, G. 136
McCaffery, S. 3, 11
Meek, T. J. 89
Meyers, C. L. 56
Montrose, P. 139
Morgan, M. L. 155
Müller, H.-P. 126, 142
Münnich, M. M. 126
Munro, J. M. 31
Murdoch, I. 38, 39, 46, 47, 68
Murphy, R. E. 73, 76, 89, 119, 121, 141, 142, 145, 148, 149
Murray, L. A. 6, 122

Nancy, J.-L. 109, 130
Newton, A. Z. 3
Nietzsche, F. W. 157, 162
Nissinen, M. 145, 147, 148, 149
Noegel, S. B. 121
Nussbaum, M. C. 1, 13, 17, 38, 39, 44, 46, 47, 65, 66

O'Connor, M. P. 2, 143
O'Hara, J. 128
Olam, B. 119
Olitzky, K. M. 63, 89
Olson, C. 111
Ouaknin, M.-A. 40

Patterson, D. 25
Peirce, C. S. 45
Perry, T. A. 121
Peursen, W. T. van 34, 84
Pinsky, R. 1, 28, 46
Pope, M. H. 5, 32, 76, 83, 86, 89, 141, 143
Proust, M. 21, 38

Ravitch, D. 89
Ravitch, M. 89
Rawls, J. 17
Reifenberg, A. 118
Rendsburg, G. 121

Riera, G. 7, 19, 21, 22, 56, 58, 60, 105, 106
Riffaterre, M. 46
Rilke, R. M. 123, 125, 153
Rivera, M. 152
Robert, A. 118, 119, 142, 145, 148
Roberts, B. J. 76
Roberts, D. P. 120, 143, 147
Robins, J. 3, 19
Rogers, F. 160
Rosenblatt, N. H. 68
Rosenzweig, F. 19
Rousseau, J. J. 59
Rozelaar, M. 32
Rubin, A. D. 88
Rudolph, W. 73, 89, 94, 126, 145, 148
Rumi, I. 55, 127

Sacks, O. W. 56
Saghafi, K. 131
Sandford, S. 68, 102
Sartre, J.-P. 20
Sass, B. 118
Sassoon, S. 12
Sawa, G. D. 48
Scarry, E. 7, 27, 39, 43, 49
Schmiedgen, P. 5, 70
Sefati, Y. 78
Segal, M. H. 45
Segrest, M. 104
Sevcik, M. 20
Shapiro, A. 13
Simmons, J. A. 155
Smith, B. H. 145
Soulen, R. N. 45, 48
Sproxton, J. 55, 56
Stager, L. E. 31, 81
Steinberg, M. 156
Stone, I. F. 133
Sumi, A. M. 44, 45, 47, 48, 52

Taylor, M. L. 150, 154
Terrien, S. 140
Thompson, C. 23
Thoreau, H. D. 150
Tournay, R. J. 118, 119, 142, 145, 148
Tov, E. 28, 32, 50, 63, 76
Townsend, A. 53
Treat, J. 28, 29
Treat, J. C. 144

Tsumura, D. T. 83
Tuell, S. S. 31, 32

Ungar, S. 131

Vendler, H. H. 5, 49, 88, 99, 111, 128
Vries, H. de 20

Walsh, C. 41
Ward, D. 152
Waterman, L. 45
Waters, W. 47, 69, 70
Watson, W. G. E. 2, 137
Weaver, D. 128
Weber, E. 59
Weems, R. J. 73
Wetzstein, J. G. 44

Whitman, W. 27, 70, 85
Wickes, W. 76
Williams, D.-A. 3, 4, 14, 77, 151
Williams, R. 161
Winnicott, D. W. 97
Wittgenstein, L. 46
Wolkstein, D. 96
Wordsworth, B. 100
Wylie, E. 90

Yeats, W. B. 4, 10
Younger, K. L. 96

Zakovitch, Y. 63, 71, 76, 81, 84, 89, 94, 119, 121, 143, 148
Zhang, S. 144, 145

Index of Scripture

Genesis
  1:1–2:4 37
  1:27 158
  2:24 117
  4:9 135
  12:11 34
  12:13 88
  12:14 34
  14:23 35
  15:10 66
  19:20 88
  23:6 148
  24:65 31
  25:23 82
  27:4 88
  32:13 77
  33:3 37
  34:13 89
  35:18 88
  38:14 31
  38:18 118
  38:19 31

Exodus
  3:2 147
  4:25 81
  13:21 147
  14:21 147
  14:24 147
  19:18 147
  24:17 147
  33:20 155
  40:38 147

Leviticus
  23:3–8 37

Deuteronomy
  6:4 18
  6:8 120
  7:1 37
  7:8 109

Deuteronomy (cont.)
  8:12 17
  11:18 119
  32:24 126

Joshua
  2:10 147
  3:13 147
  4:23 147
  5:1 147
  6:4 37

Judges
  2:11 17
  5:7 63
  16:12 35
  19:22 77, 78

Ruth
  3:4 81

1 Samuel
  14:15 148

2 Samuel
  1:10 120
  11:11 81
  13:15 109
  14:25 34
  22:6 126

1 Kings
  18:38 147
  20:37 96
  21:8 118

2 Kings
  2:14 147
  12:10 81

Esther
  8:6 81

Job
  3:13 75
  5:7 126
  14:2 63
  14:7–9 7
  15:26 36
  15:30 142
  15:33 123
  19:18 89
  27:16 123
  27:18 123
  40–41 44
  41:7 119
  41:23 123

Psalms
  3:6 75
  4:9 75
  18:10–16 155
  18:16 147
  21:10 123
  22:16 123
  22:17 123
  22:17b 123
  33:7 123
  36:7 148
  37:6 123
  43:5 82
  45:2 10
  48:12–13 36
  56:6 89
  66:12 127
  71:6 82
  72:6 123
  75:5–6 36
  75:6 89
  76:4 126
  78:15 123
  78:19 89
  78:27 123
  78:48 126
  78:52 123

Psalms (cont.)
  79:3 139
  89:48 126
  90:9 123
  93:4 147
  94:9–10 145
  94:10 145, 146
  102:12 63
  105:45 143
  106:1 143
  106:48 143
  109:4 109
  111:1 143
  112:1 143
  113:1 143
  115:18 143
  116:3 126
  116:19 143
  117:2 143
  123:2 63
  133 34
  135:21 143
  144:1 83
  146:1 143
  147:1 143
  148:1 143
  149:1 143
  150:1 143

Proverbs
  1:8 18
  1:28 92
  3:3 119
  5:19 109
  6:5 123
  6:21 119
  7:3 119
  7:11 94
  21:13 92
  31:10–31 44

Qoheleth
  1:15 160
  1:16 83
  3:1 143
  4:12 35

Song of Songs
  1:1 53, 113, 117, 120
  1:1–4 37

Song of Songs (cont.)
  1:2 35, 53, 61, 121, 129
  1:3 102, 116, 144
  1:4 102
  1:5 37, 71
  1:6 31, 71
  1:7 64, 102, 113, 125
  1:8 116
  1:10 32
  1:10–11 36
  1:12 63
  1:13 67
  1:15 39, 60, 61, 62
  1:16–17 145
  1:17 84
  2:1 71, 83
  2:3 9, 116
  2:5 71, 101, 102, 118, 121
  2:6 34, 53, 113
  2:7 63, 100, 101, 113, 114, 115
  2:8 61, 76
  2:8–9 113
  2:9 34, 81, 113
  2:10–13 113, 116
  2:11 83, 86, 121
  2:14 121
  2:15 116
  2:16 71, 101, 128
  2:17 66, 67
  3:1 64, 75, 92, 93, 95, 113, 117, 125, 129
  3:1–4 102
  3:1–5 30, 95, 101
  3:1–8 87
  3:2 64, 91, 95, 112, 113, 125
  3:3 64, 95, 100, 113, 125
  3:4 63, 64, 95, 113, 125, 133
  3:5 63, 100, 113, 115
  3:6 115
  3:6–11 115
  3:7 17
  3:8 9

Song of Songs (cont.)
  3:10 102, 116
  3:11 115
  4:1 53, 54, 60, 61
  4:1–5 63
  4:1–7 8, 27, 28, 31, 33, 39, 42, 44, 47, 49, 63, 67, 68, 69
  4:1a 30, 36
  4:1ab 62
  4:1b 35
  4:1c 34, 35, 39, 50, 62, 63
  4:1c–2a 50
  4:1c–2b 51
  4:1c–2d 34, 53
  4:1c–3a 35
  4:1cd 62
  4:1d 50
  4:1e 34, 39
  4:2 36
  4:2a 35, 39
  4:2b 35
  4:2c 50, 51
  4:2d 50
  4:3 9, 28, 29, 30, 32, 50
  4:3–4 49
  4:3a 35, 36, 39
  4:3a–4a 36
  4:3a–4d 34, 35
  4:3a–b 32
  4:3ab 50
  4:3b 36
  4:3c 35, 39, 62
  4:3d 50
  4:4a 35, 39
  4:4b 36
  4:4d 51
  4:5 37, 53, 56, 66, 67
  4:5a 39
  4:5a–6c 34
  4:5a–b 30
  4:6 30, 31, 33, 35, 37, 63, 65
  4:6c 50
  4:7 34, 38, 51, 53, 63, 66
  4:7a 37

Index of Scripture

Song of Songs (cont.)
4:8   67
4:12–5:1   67
4:16   75, 100
4:16–5:1   100
4:21–22   32
5:1–4   113
5:2   9, 71, 73, 75, 76, 78, 80, 85, 100, 113, 114, 129
5:2–3   78
5:2–6   71, 113
5:2–6:3   103
5:2–6b   95
5:2–7   98, 100
5:2–8   8, 71, 73, 74, 87, 90, 99, 106, 107, 117
5:2a   78
5:2ab   78, 101
5:2c–3d   78, 101
5:2c–f   78
5:2e   78
5:2f   78
5:3   81, 82, 100
5:3a   79
5:3a–b   79
5:3b   79
5:3c   79
5:3c–d   79
5:3d   78, 79
5:4   77, 82, 113, 114
5:4–5   120
5:4a   85
5:4a–6b   101
5:4a–b   82, 83, 84
5:4b   82, 86, 97, 113
5:4b–c   95
5:5   71, 77, 83, 85
5:5–6   83, 89
5:5a   83
5:5b   83
5:5b–c   83, 84
5:5c   83, 84
5:5c–d   85
5:5d   84
5:6   9, 12, 71, 85, 86, 102, 112, 113, 114, 129, 131, 133

Song of Songs (cont.)
5:6–7   101
5:6–8   102
5:6a   83, 85
5:6b   85, 86
5:6c–7   88
5:6c–7e   101
5:6c–e   94
5:6d   90, 91, 92
5:6d–e   91
5:6e   91
5:7   73, 77, 94, 95, 96, 99, 102, 113
5:7a–b   95
5:7b   95
5:7d–e   95
5:7e   95
5:8   71, 100, 101, 102, 114
5:8ab   100
5:8c   101, 102
5:8d   102
5:8e   101
5:9   102
5:9–16   44, 71, 102, 116
5:10   102
5:10–16   102
5:13   32, 53
5:14   82
5.26   32
6:1   102, 113, 116
6:1–3   71
6:2   102
6:2–3   102, 116
6:3   71, 101, 102, 128, 142
6:4   34
6:4–10   44
6:5b–7   35
6:7   32
6:8–9   116
6:10   38
6:12   7, 160
7:2   86
7:2–6   44
7:3   9
7:4   31
7:9   67
7:11   71, 101

Song of Songs (cont.)
8:1   53, 79, 102, 113, 117
8:1–2   36, 113, 115
8:1–3   115, 116, 129
8:1–4   101, 111, 117
8:1–7   8, 127
8:1b   115
8:1d   112
8:2   32, 36, 115
8:3   34, 53, 113, 121
8:3a   121
8:4   63, 100, 113, 114, 115
8:5   115, 116, 117
8:5–6   129
8:5–7   114
8:5a   115
8:5c–7   138
8:5d   115
8:6   8, 9, 108, 109, 110, 113, 114, 116, 117, 118, 119, 121, 122, 123, 126, 127, 128, 129, 131, 133, 134, 136, 137, 138, 139, 141, 142, 146, 147, 148, 151, 152, 158, 159
8:6–7   111, 117, 142, 147, 148
8:6a   121, 128, 152
8:6ab   115, 128, 136, 158
8:6a–d   123, 133, 145
8:6a–f   144
8:6b   120
8:6c–d   122
8:6cd   121, 143
8:6c–e   147
8:6c–f   144
8:6d   120
8:6e   124, 143
8:6ef   143, 144
8:6f   142, 143, 144, 152
8:7   127, 128, 144, 147

Song of Songs (cont.)
  8:7a   127
  8:7a–c   127, 142, 144
  8:7d–f   142
  8:8   38, 114
  8:9   78
  8:10   38, 71, 94, 102, 117
  8:12   144

Isaiah
  1:25   123
  2:8   83
  5:24d   123
  5:25d   123
  16:3   63
  16:11   82
  17:8   83
  23:16   94
  28:15   126
  31:13   123
  44:24   147
  47:2   31

Isaiah (cont.)
  49:1   82
  49:23   112
  51:3   148
  59:3   83
  59:17a   123
  60:16   112
  65:12   92

Jeremiah
  2:31   149
  4:19   82
  5:21   67, 68
  6:4   63
  7:27   92
  15:9   88
  22:24   120
  31:20   82, 89
  31:22   86
  34:18–19   66
  51:55   147

Ezekiel
  8:7   81
  21:3   142
  31:15   147

Hosea
  13:14   126

Amos
  5:24   123

Jonah
  3:3   148

Habakkuk
  2:5   126
  3:5   126

Zephaniah
  1:18   128

Haggai
  2:23   120

New Testament

Matthew
  19:12   110

1 John
  4:8   109

Deuterocanonical Literature

Sirach
  22:27   119
  42:6   119
  49:11   120
  51:4   142